Emerging Technologies in Healthcare 4.0

AI and IoT Solutions

Dr. Alok Kumar Srivastav
Dr. Priyanka Das

Emerging Technologies in Healthcare 4.0: AI and IoT Solutions

Dr. Alok Kumar Srivastav
Department of Health Science, University of
the People, Pasadena, California, USA

Dr. Priyanka Das
Department of Health Science, University of
the People, Pasadena, California, USA

ISBN-13 (pbk): 979-8-8688-1013-8
https://doi.org/10.1007/979-8-8688-1014-5

ISBN-13 (electronic): 979-8-8688-1014-5

Copyright © 2024 by Dr. Alok Kumar Srivastav, Dr. Priyanka Das

Managing Director, Apress Media LLC: Welmoed Spahr
Acquisitions Editor: Spandana Chatterjee
Coordinating Editor: Kripa Joseph
Copy Editor: William McManus

Cover designed by eStudioCalamar

Cover image designed by Freepik (www.freepik.com)

Distributed to the book trade worldwide by Springer Science+Business Media New York, 233 Spring Street, 6th Floor, New York, NY 10013. Phone 1-800-SPRINGER, fax (201) 348-4505, e-mail orders-ny@springer-sbm.com, or visit www.springeronline.com. Apress Media, LLC is a California LLC and the sole member (owner) is Springer Science + Business Media Finance Inc (SSBM Finance Inc). SSBM Finance Inc is a **Delaware** corporation.

For information on translations, please e-mail booktranslations@springernature.com; for reprint, paperback, or audio rights, please e-mail bookpermissions@springernature.com.

Apress titles may be purchased in bulk for academic, corporate, or promotional use. eBook versions and licenses are also available for most titles. For more information, reference our Print and eBook Bulk Sales web page at https://www.apress.com/bulk-sales.

Any source code or other supplementary material referenced by the author in this book can be found here: https://www.apress.com/gp/services/source-code.

If disposing of this product, please recycle the paper

To my family and friends, whose unwavering support and encouragement have been my guiding light throughout this journey. Your belief in me has been the foundation upon which this work stands.

To my students, whose curiosity and enthusiasm inspire every page I write.

And to those who seek to understand the world through both science and faith, may this book contribute to your journey of discovery and wonder.

—Dr. Alok Kumar Srivastav

Table of Contents

About the Authors

Dr. Alok Kumar Srivastav is an accomplished Assistant Professor in the Department of Health Science at the University of the People, Pasadena, California, USA. His academic background includes a Ph.D., M.Tech, and M.Sc. in Bio-Technology, a Post-Doctoral Fellowship (Research) in Bio-Technology from Lincoln University College, Malaysia, and an MBA in Human Resource Management. He is a distinguished figure in Academia and Research, honored with the "International Pride of Educationist Award" at AIT, Thailand, in 2022 for pioneering contributions to advancing education in the digital era, and recipient of a prestigious "Innovative Academic Researcher Award" at HULT, France, UK, in 2024 for his exceptional creativity, innovation, and impact in academic research.

Dr. Priyanka Das serves as an Assistant Professor in the Department of Health Science at the University of the People in Pasadena, California, USA. She holds a Ph.D., M.Tech, and M.Sc. in Biotechnology along with an MBA in Human Resource Management. Prior to her current position, she was a Post-Doctoral Fellow (Research) in Biotechnology at Lincoln University College, Malaysia. Dr. Priyanka Das is a dedicated scholar, contributing significantly to the field of Biotechnology.

About the Technical Reviewer

 **Atonu Ghosh** is a Ph.D. research scholar in the Department of Computer Science & Engineering at the Indian Institute of Technology Kharagpur, West Bengal, India. He also has an M.Tech. and a B.Tech. in computer science and engineering. Atonu's research domain includes the Internet of Things (IoT), edge computing, low-power networks, and Industry 4.0. Atonu has built IoT solutions for over eight years and has executed several projects. He is also an active reviewer of research journals and books. Find out more about Atonu or reach him through his personal website, https://www.atonughosh.com/.

Acknowledgments

Writing a book is a journey that often involves the support, encouragement, and contributions of many individuals and organizations. As we present this work, *Emerging Technologies in Healthcare 4.0: AI and IoT Solutions*, we would like to express our heartfelt gratitude to those who have made this endeavor possible.

First and foremost, we extend our sincere appreciation to our families for their unwavering support, patience, and understanding throughout the writing process. Your encouragement has been a constant source of motivation. We are deeply thankful to our colleagues and mentors whose guidance and expertise have enriched this book. Your insights have shaped our understanding of the emerging technologies in Healthcare 4.0, particularly AI and IoT. We would like to acknowledge the contributions of the research institutions and libraries that provided access to valuable resources, making our research more comprehensive and thorough. Our gratitude goes to the reviewers and experts in the field who provided valuable feedback and constructive criticism, helping us refine the content and ensure its accuracy.

We extend our thanks to the publishing team, editors, and designers who have worked diligently to transform our manuscript into a published book. Last but not least, we are grateful to our readers, students, and fellow researchers who find value in this book. Your interest and engagement in the subject of emerging technologies in Healthcare 4.0 drive our commitment to promoting sustainable practices and environmental stewardship.

This book would not have been possible without the collective effort and support of these individuals and institutions. We humbly acknowledge your contributions and express our deepest appreciation.

Introduction

Welcome to the transformative world of Healthcare 4.0, where cutting-edge technologies like artificial intelligence (AI), the Internet of Things (IoT), and real-time data analytics converge to revolutionize patient care, disease management, and healthcare operations. This book is a comprehensive guide designed to help you navigate through the intricate landscape of Healthcare 4.0, offering insights into its evolution, applications, challenges, and future trends. It delves into the evolution of healthcare technologies, exploring their impact on patient care and management. This book provides a comprehensive exploration of the "industrial revolution" in healthcare.

In this book, you'll explore the fundamentals of artificial intelligence (AI) in healthcare, including an overview of AI and machine learning, applications in healthcare domains, and challenges and opportunities in AI implementation. This books progresses to explore the integration of AI and the Internet of Things (IoT) in Healthcare 4.0, discussing synergies, real-time data analysis, and future trends in telemedicine. The book also addresses critical aspects like data security and privacy, focusing on regulations, standards, and strategies for ensuring data protection. Practical applications of AI and IoT in remote patient monitoring, disease diagnosis, and healthcare operations management are thoroughly examined, alongside ethical and legal considerations in Healthcare 4.0. The final chapters offer insights into emerging trends, potential challenges, and recommendations for successfully adopting AI and IoT in Healthcare 4.0.

You will gain a comprehensive understanding of how AI and IoT are transforming healthcare by improving outcomes, enhancing efficiency, and addressing ethical and legal challenges in data privacy. This book equips healthcare professionals, policymakers, and technology enthusiasts with the knowledge to navigate and leverage the transformative potential of Healthcare 4.0 technologies effectively.

You will benefit most from this book if you have a foundational understanding of healthcare systems and technologies. Specifically, a basic knowledge of healthcare operations, medical terminology, and information technology would be advantageous. Familiarity with concepts related to AI and IoT in healthcare, though not mandatory, would also enhance comprehension of the advanced topics covered in the book.

This book is composed of the following eight chapters:

- Chapter 1, "Introduction to Healthcare 4.0": In this chapter, we will explore the transformative impact of the Fourth Industrial Revolution on the healthcare sector. We will examine how evolving technologies are shaping patient care and management, setting the stage for a comprehensive understanding of Healthcare 4.0.

- Chapter 2, "Fundamentals of Artificial Intelligence (AI) in Healthcare": This chapter provides a foundational overview of artificial intelligence and machine learning, focusing on their applications within the healthcare industry. We will also address the challenges and opportunities associated with implementing AI technologies.

- Chapter 3, "Internet of Things (IoT) in Healthcare": Here, we delve into the Internet of Things, its components, and its various applications in healthcare. We will also discuss the benefits and challenges of integrating IoT technologies into healthcare systems.

- Chapter 4, "Integration of AI and IoT in Healthcare 4.0": This chapter explores the synergy between AI and IoT, emphasizing their combined potential in real-time data analysis and decision-making. We will also look ahead to future trends in the integration of these technologies in telemedicine.

- Chapter 5, "Data Security and Privacy in Healthcare 4.0": In this chapter, we will highlight the critical importance of data security and privacy in Healthcare 4.0. We will review regulations, standards, and strategies essential for protecting sensitive healthcare data.

- Chapter 6, "AI and IoT in Remote Patient Monitoring": This chapter focuses on the role of AI and IoT in remote patient monitoring, including wearable devices and sensors. We will discuss how these technologies contribute to improved patient outcomes.

- Chapter 7, "AI and IoT in Disease Diagnosis and Management": This chapter explores how AI-based diagnostic tools and IoT-enabled devices are revolutionizing disease diagnosis and management. We will also discuss the impact of these technologies on precision medicine.

- Chapter 8, "AI and IoT in Healthcare Operations Management": This chapter examines how AI and IoT technologies streamline hospital operations, from supply chain management to optimizing resource allocation, enhancing overall efficiency in healthcare operations.

- Chapter 9, "Ethical and Legal Considerations in Healthcare 4.0": This chapter covers the ethical issues and legal frameworks essential for ensuring responsible practices in Healthcare 4.0. We will address the ethical and legal implications of implementing AI and IoT in healthcare.

- Chapter 10, "Future Perspectives and Challenges": This final chapter provides insights into emerging trends, potential challenges, and solutions for the future of Healthcare 4.0. We will offer recommendations for successfully adopting AI and IoT technologies in the healthcare sector.

Let the journey into Healthcare 4.0 begin.

CHAPTER 1

Introduction to Healthcare 4.0

This chapter delves into the transformative era brought about by the Fourth Industrial Revolution in healthcare, known as Healthcare 4.0. This chapter provides an overview of the technological evolution that has revolutionized patient care and management. You will gain insights into how advanced technologies are reshaping healthcare delivery, improving patient outcomes, and streamlining healthcare operations.

Healthcare 4.0, also known as Health 4.0 or Medicine 4.0, is characterized by the integration of digital technologies, data-driven approaches, and personalized medicine to transform the delivery of healthcare services. Building upon previous industrial revolutions, Healthcare 4.0 leverages advanced technologies such as artificial intelligence (AI), the Internet of Things (IoT), big data analytics, cloud computing, and genomics to drive innovation, improve patient outcomes, enhance operational efficiency, and empower individuals to take control of their health.

At its core, Healthcare 4.0 represents a paradigm shift from traditional reactive, one-size-fits-all healthcare models to proactive, personalized, and data-driven approaches that focus on prevention, prediction, and precision medicine. By harnessing the power of digital technologies and data-driven insights, Healthcare 4.0 aims to revolutionize healthcare

Dr. A. K. Srivastav and Dr. P. Das, *Emerging Technologies in Healthcare 4.0*, https://doi.org/10.1007/979-8-8688-1014-5_1

delivery across the entire continuum of care, from diagnosis and treatment to disease management and wellness promotion (Figure 1-1).

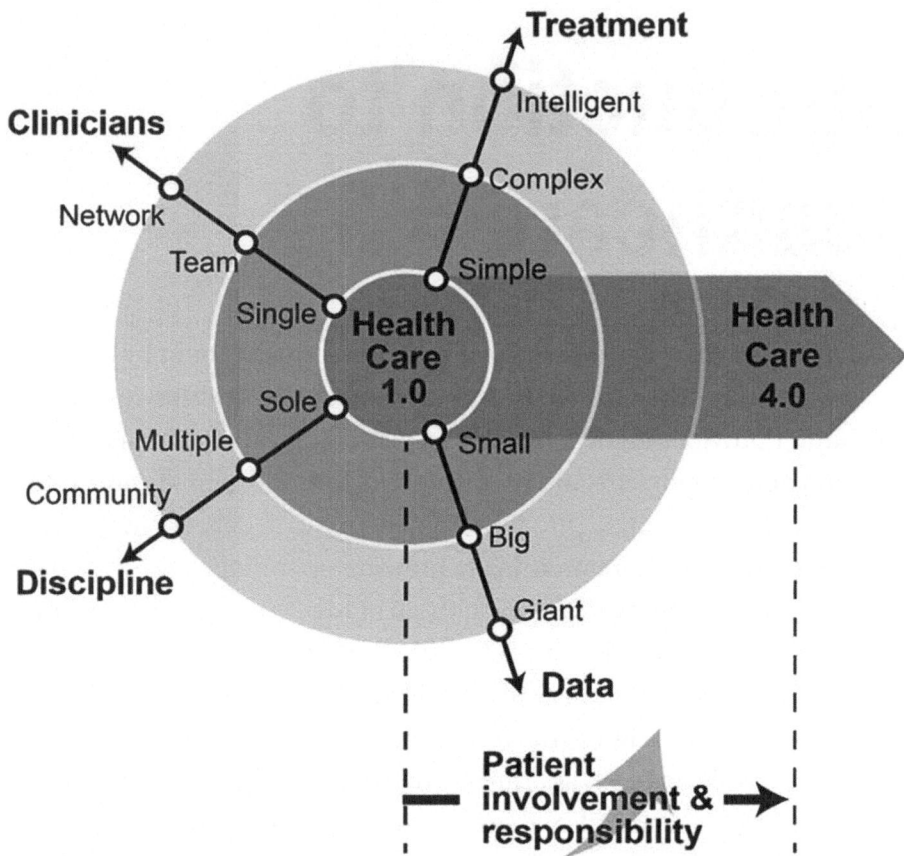

Figure 1-1. *Evolution of Healthcare 1.0 to Healthcare 4.0*

Understanding the Fourth Industrial Revolution in Healthcare

The Fourth Industrial Revolution (4IR) has ushered in an era of unprecedented technological advancement across various sectors, and healthcare stands at the forefront of this transformative wave. Marked by the convergence of digital, biological, and physical innovations, the 4IR is reshaping healthcare delivery, diagnosis, treatment, and patient outcomes (see Figure 1-2). The 4IR is characterized by the integration of advanced digital technologies, data analytics, and AI into various sectors, including healthcare delivery systems, thereby revolutionizing the way medical services are provided.

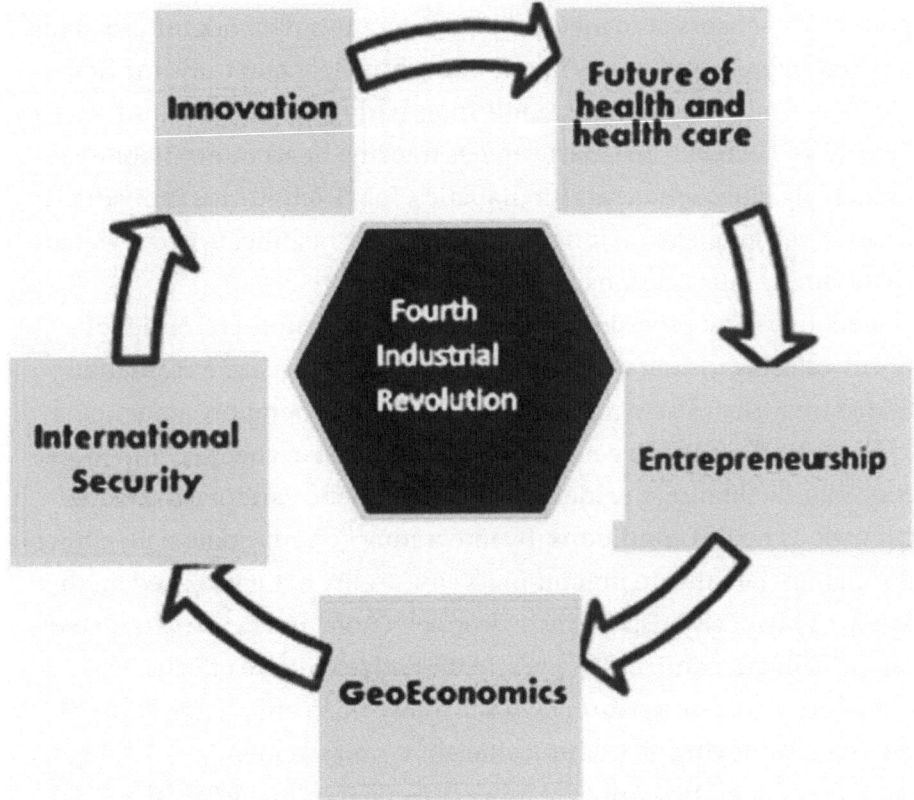

Figure 1-2. *Fourth Industrial Revolution in healthcare*

Technological Innovations Driving the 4IR in Healthcare

Artificial intelligence emerges as a cornerstone of the 4IR in healthcare, empowering clinicians with tools for data analysis, predictive modeling, and personalized medicine. Machine learning (ML) algorithms analyze vast datasets to identify patterns, predict disease progression, and optimize treatment regimens. Moreover, AI-powered virtual assistants enhance patient engagement, provide real-time medical advice, and streamline administrative tasks, thereby improving overall healthcare delivery.

The Internet of Medical Things (IoMT) revolutionizes patient monitoring and disease management by connecting wearable devices, implantable sensors, and medical equipment to a network infrastructure. These interconnected devices continuously collect and transmit vital health data, enabling remote monitoring, early intervention, and personalized care. From smartwatches tracking heart rate variability to implantable glucose sensors for diabetics, IoMT empowers individuals to proactively manage their health and enables healthcare providers to deliver timely interventions.

Genomics and precision medicine represent another frontier of the 4IR, offering insights into the genetic basis of disease and enabling tailored treatment strategies. Advances in next-generation sequencing technologies have made genome sequencing faster, cheaper, and more accessible, facilitating the identification of genetic variants associated with various health conditions. By integrating genomic data with clinical information, healthcare practitioners can stratify patients based on their genetic predispositions, optimize drug selection, and develop targeted therapies that maximize efficacy and minimize adverse effects.

Robotics and automation play a pivotal role in enhancing surgical precision, improving procedural efficiency, and augmenting healthcare workforce capabilities. Surgical robots enable minimally invasive procedures with greater accuracy and dexterity, reducing patient recovery times and postoperative complications. Furthermore, robots assist in repetitive tasks such as medication dispensing, inventory management, and patient transportation, freeing up human resources to focus on complex care delivery and patient interaction.

Virtual reality (VR) and augmented reality (AR) technologies are transforming medical education, training, and therapeutic interventions. Immersive simulations provide healthcare professionals with realistic training scenarios, allowing them to refine their skills in a safe and controlled environment. Additionally, virtual reality therapy offers novel approaches for pain management, rehabilitation, and mental health treatment, harnessing the therapeutic potential of immersive experiences to alleviate symptoms and improve patient outcomes.

Challenges and Opportunities in the 4IR Healthcare Landscape

Despite its immense potential, the 4IR in healthcare presents numerous challenges that warrant careful consideration. Data privacy and security concerns loom large as healthcare systems amass vast amounts of sensitive patient information, raising questions about data ownership, consent, and protection against cyber threats. Moreover, the digital divide exacerbates healthcare disparities, as underserved populations may lack access to advanced technologies or struggle to navigate digital interfaces, widening the gap in healthcare access and outcomes.

Interoperability remains a significant barrier to realizing the full benefits of 4IR technologies, as disparate systems often fail to communicate and share data seamlessly. Standardization efforts are underway to establish common data exchange protocols and interoperability frameworks, facilitating the integration of electronic health records, medical devices, and diagnostic platforms. By fostering interoperability, healthcare organizations can unlock valuable insights from aggregated data sources, drive innovation, and deliver coordinated care across diverse settings.

Ethical considerations loom large in the era of 4IR healthcare, raising questions about data governance, algorithmic bias, and the equitable distribution of technological benefits. Algorithmic decision-making algorithms may perpetuate disparities if trained on biased datasets or fail to account for diverse patient populations, exacerbating existing healthcare inequities. Furthermore, the commodification of health data raises ethical dilemmas regarding consent, transparency, and the commercialization of patient information. As healthcare becomes increasingly data-driven, stakeholders must uphold ethical principles and safeguard patient rights while harnessing the transformative power of technology.

Regulatory frameworks must evolve to keep pace with the rapid innovation occurring in the 4IR healthcare landscape, balancing the need for patient safety, data privacy, and technological advancement. Regulatory agencies face the challenge of adapting existing frameworks to accommodate novel technologies such as AI, IoMT, and genomic medicine, ensuring that innovations meet rigorous standards of safety, efficacy, and quality. Moreover, international collaboration is essential to harmonize regulatory approaches, streamline market access, and facilitate the global adoption of transformative healthcare technologies.

The Future of 4IR Healthcare: Emerging Trends and Implications

Looking ahead, several emerging trends are poised to shape the future of 4IR healthcare and redefine the delivery of care. Telemedicine and remote monitoring solutions are poised to gain prominence, enabling virtual consultations, home-based care, and chronic disease management. Telehealth platforms leverage video conferencing, mobile apps, and remote monitoring devices to connect patients with healthcare providers, offering convenience, accessibility, and continuity of care.

Blockchain technology holds promise for enhancing data security, integrity, and interoperability in healthcare ecosystems. By leveraging decentralized ledger technology, blockchain platforms enable secure and transparent sharing of health information, facilitating data exchange among disparate stakeholders while preserving patient privacy and confidentiality. Moreover, blockchain-based smart contracts automate administrative processes such as claims processing, billing, and credentialing, reducing administrative overhead and improving operational efficiency.

Bioinformatics and computational biology are driving breakthroughs in drug discovery, biomarker identification, and disease modeling, accelerating the pace of medical innovation. Machine learning algorithms analyze genomic, proteomic, and metabolomic data to identify disease signatures, predict drug responses, and uncover novel therapeutic targets. Furthermore, computational models simulate biological processes at the molecular level, enabling researchers to design drugs with greater precision and efficacy.

The democratization of healthcare through open-access platforms, community-driven initiatives, and decentralized networks empowers individuals to take control of their health and participate in medical research. Open source software, collaborative research platforms, and citizen science projects facilitate knowledge sharing, data sharing, and collaborative problem-solving, fostering innovation and inclusivity in healthcare. Moreover, decentralized networks such as health cooperatives and peer-to-peer healthcare platforms empower communities to collectively address health challenges, pool resources, and advocate for equitable access to care.

In conclusion, the Fourth Industrial Revolution is reshaping the landscape of healthcare, catalyzing innovation, and driving paradigm shifts in diagnosis, treatment, and patient care. From artificial intelligence and genomics to robotics and telemedicine, transformative technologies are revolutionizing healthcare delivery, empowering patients, and improving outcomes. However, realizing the full potential of the 4IR in healthcare requires addressing challenges such as data privacy, interoperability, and ethical considerations while embracing emerging trends and opportunities. By leveraging technology responsibly, fostering collaboration, and prioritizing patient-centric care, we can navigate the complexities of the 4IR healthcare landscape and usher in a future where healthcare is accessible, equitable, and empowered by innovation.

The Fourth Industrial Revolution has reshaped numerous sectors, including healthcare, through advancements in digital technologies and artificial intelligence. As healthcare embraces these transformative technologies, it's crucial to trace their evolution and understand their impact on modern medical practices.

Evolution of Healthcare Technologies

The evolution of healthcare technologies spans millennia, reflecting humanity's enduring quest to alleviate suffering, cure ailments, and prolong life. From ancient remedies and traditional healing practices to modern medical marvels powered by cutting-edge science and technology, the journey of healthcare innovation is a testament to human ingenuity, perseverance, and the relentless pursuit of better health outcomes (Figure 1-3).

The National Health Service (NHS) is the publicly funded healthcare system in the United Kingdom, established in 1948. It provides comprehensive healthcare services free at the point of use for UK residents, funded through taxation. The NHS has embraced digital transformation to enhance patient care, streamline operations, and modernize healthcare delivery.

Brother UK, a technology solutions provider, specializes in supporting industries, including healthcare, with innovative tools like managed print services (MPS) and other digital solutions. Their expertise aids the NHS in integrating technologies that improve both operational efficiency and patient outcomes. Brother UK's involvement underscores their commitment to advancing healthcare technology for better service delivery.

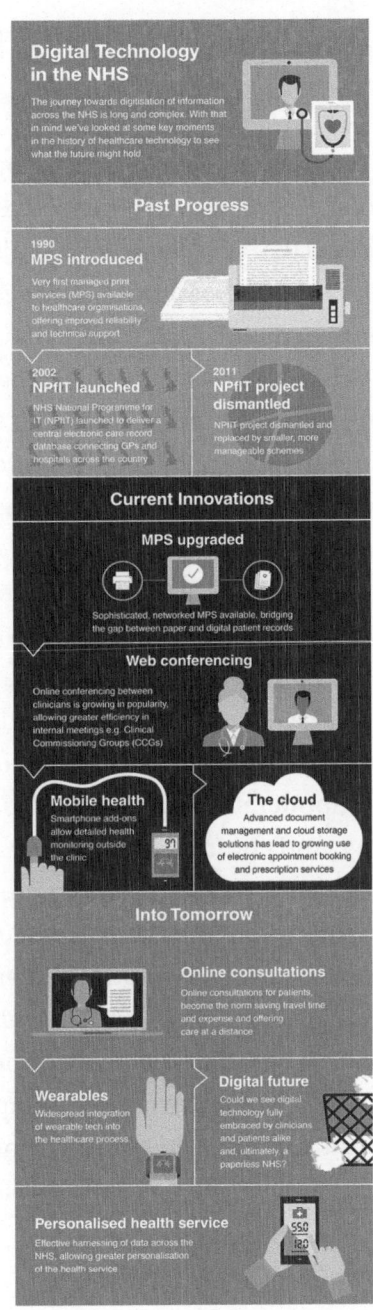

Figure 1-3. *Charting the progress of healthcare technology in the NHS*

Ancient Remedies and Traditional Healing Practices

The roots of healthcare technologies can be traced back to ancient civilizations, where early humans relied on natural remedies, plant extracts, and spiritual rituals to treat illnesses and injuries. Ancient medical systems such as Ayurveda in India, traditional Chinese medicine (TCM) in China, and Hippocratic medicine in ancient Greece laid the foundation for holistic approaches to health and wellness. Herbal medicines, acupuncture, and therapeutic massage were among the cornerstones of these ancient healing traditions, informed by observations of the natural world and the interconnectedness of mind, body, and spirit.

In ancient Egypt, the Ebers Papyrus, dating back to around 1550 BCE, documented hundreds of medicinal plants and remedies used to treat various ailments ranging from digestive disorders to infectious diseases. Similarly, the Edwin Smith Papyrus provided insights into surgical techniques and wound management practices practiced in ancient Egypt. The ancient Greeks made significant contributions to medical knowledge, with luminaries such as Hippocrates and Galen advancing theories of disease etiology, anatomy, and clinical observation.

Medical innovations in ancient civilizations were often intertwined with religious beliefs, mythological narratives, and cultural practices. Healing temples dedicated to gods and goddesses served as centers of medical care and spiritual healing, where priests and healers administered treatments, performed rituals, and offered prayers for divine intervention. The concept of holistic health, emphasizing the balance of bodily humors and the harmony of the mind, body, and spirit, permeated ancient healing traditions and continues to influence modern approaches to healthcare.

The Renaissance and the Birth of Modern Medicine

The Renaissance marked a pivotal period in the evolution of healthcare technologies, heralding a resurgence of scientific inquiry, anatomical dissection, and empirical observation. The invention of the printing press facilitated the dissemination of medical knowledge, enabling the publication of seminal works such as Andreas Vesalius's *De Humani Corporis Fabrica Libri Septem* (*Seven Books on the Fabric of the Human Body*), which revolutionized the study of anatomy and laid the groundwork for modern anatomical illustration.

Advancements in medical instrumentation and surgical techniques paved the way for the emergence of modern medicine during the Renaissance period. Innovations such as the microscope, developed by Antonie van Leeuwenhoek in the 17th century, revealed previously unseen worlds of microorganisms and cellular structures, transforming scientific understanding of disease causation and pathophysiology. William Harvey's discovery of the circulatory system and the pumping action of the heart furthered scientific knowledge of human physiology and laid the foundation for evidence-based medicine.

The 19th century witnessed unprecedented progress in medical science and technology, fueled by rapid industrialization, scientific discovery, and medical reform. The development of anesthesia, pioneered by William Morton and others, revolutionized surgical practice by enabling painless procedures and reducing patient mortality rates. The discovery of germ theory by Louis Pasteur and Robert Koch provided a scientific basis for understanding infectious diseases and revolutionized public health practices such as sanitation, vaccination, and disease surveillance.

The advent of modern medical imaging techniques, beginning with Wilhelm Roentgen's discovery of X-rays in 1895, enabled noninvasive visualization of internal structures and revolutionized diagnostic radiology. Subsequent innovations such as computed tomography (CT), magnetic resonance imaging (MRI), and positron emission tomography (PET) have further expanded the capabilities of medical imaging, allowing clinicians to detect and diagnose a wide range of diseases with unprecedented precision and accuracy.

The 20th Century: The Era of Biomedical Innovation

The 20th century witnessed a proliferation of biomedical innovations, driven by advances in genetics, pharmacology, and medical technology. The discovery of DNA's structure by James Watson and Francis Crick in 1953 heralded a new era of molecular biology, paving the way for breakthroughs in genomics, personalized medicine, and gene therapy. The Human Genome Project, completed in 2003, mapped the entire human genome, providing invaluable insights into the genetic basis of health and disease.

The development of antibiotics, beginning with Alexander Fleming's discovery of penicillin in 1928, revolutionized the treatment of infectious diseases and saved countless lives. However, the widespread use and misuse of antibiotics have led to the emergence of antibiotic-resistant bacteria, posing a growing threat to global public health. The search for new antimicrobial agents and alternative treatment modalities remains a pressing challenge in contemporary medicine.

The rise of medical technology in the 20th century gave birth to a myriad of lifesaving devices and therapeutic interventions. From cardiac pacemakers and implantable defibrillators to insulin pumps and artificial organs, medical devices have transformed the management of chronic conditions and extended the lives of patients with complex medical needs.

Moreover, advancements in minimally invasive surgery, robotic-assisted procedures, and telemedicine have expanded access to specialized care and improved surgical outcomes for patients around the world.

The Digital Revolution and the Era of Precision Medicine

The 21st century has witnessed the convergence of digital technologies, data science, and biomedicine, giving rise to the era of precision medicine and personalized healthcare. The proliferation of electronic health records (EHRs), wearable sensors, and mobile health apps has generated vast amounts of health data, enabling real-time monitoring, personalized risk assessment, and data-driven decision-making. Artificial intelligence and machine learning algorithms analyze these data streams to identify patterns, predict disease trajectories, and optimize treatment strategies, ushering in a new era of predictive, preventive, and personalized medicine.

Genomics and precision medicine hold the promise of tailoring medical interventions to individual genetic profiles, enabling targeted therapies that maximize efficacy and minimize adverse effects. The integration of genomic data with clinical information allows healthcare practitioners to stratify patients based on their genetic predispositions, identify at-risk populations, and develop personalized treatment regimens. Furthermore, advances in gene editing technologies such as CRISPR-Cas9 offer unprecedented opportunities for correcting genetic mutations, curing genetic diseases, and engineering designer cells for therapeutic purposes.

Telemedicine and digital health platforms have emerged as indispensable tools for remote patient monitoring, virtual consultations, and telehealth interventions, particularly in the wake of the COVID-19 pandemic. Telemedicine enables patients to access healthcare services from the comfort of their homes, overcoming geographical barriers, reducing healthcare costs, and improving patient satisfaction. Moreover, telemedicine platforms leverage AI-driven triage algorithms, chatbots, and remote monitoring devices to deliver timely interventions, optimize care pathways, and enhance the efficiency of healthcare delivery.

The Future of Healthcare Technologies: Emerging Trends and Challenges

Looking ahead, several emerging trends are poised to shape the future of healthcare technologies and redefine the delivery of care. Augmented reality (AR) and virtual reality (VR) technologies hold promise for enhancing medical education, surgical training, and patient engagement. Immersive simulations provide healthcare professionals with realistic training scenarios, allowing them to refine their skills in a safe and controlled environment. Furthermore, AR and VR applications offer novel approaches for pain management, rehabilitation, and mental health treatment, harnessing the therapeutic potential of immersive experiences to improve patient outcomes.

Nanotechnology and bioengineering are driving breakthroughs in drug delivery, tissue engineering, and regenerative medicine, opening new frontiers in the treatment of chronic diseases and traumatic injuries. Nanomaterials such as liposomes, nanoparticles, and nanofibers enable targeted drug delivery, controlled release, and enhanced bioavailability, minimizing systemic toxicity and improving therapeutic efficacy. Moreover, 3D bioprinting technologies allow researchers to fabricate complex tissue constructs and organoids for drug screening, disease modeling, and transplantation, offering new solutions for organ shortage and personalized regenerative therapies.

However, the rapid pace of technological innovation brings its own set of challenges and ethical considerations. Data privacy and security concerns loom large as healthcare systems amass vast amounts of sensitive patient information, raising questions about data ownership, consent, and protection against cyber threats. Moreover, the digital divide exacerbates healthcare disparities, as underserved populations may lack access to advanced technologies or struggle to navigate digital interfaces, widening the gap in healthcare access and outcomes.

From the early stages of medical imaging to the current era of AI-driven diagnostics, healthcare technologies have evolved significantly to enhance diagnostic accuracy and treatment efficacy. This evolution sets the stage for exploring how Healthcare 4.0 is revolutionizing patient care and management, marking a pivotal shift toward personalized and integrated healthcare solutions.

Impact of Healthcare 4.0 on Patient Care and Management

As previously mentioned, Healthcare 4.0 is characterized by the integration of digital technologies, data analytics, AI, robotics, and IoT into healthcare systems. Figure 1-4 visually illustrates the progression of healthcare from Healthcare 1.0 to Healthcare 4.0 as a continuous cycle rather than a linear evolution. This cyclical representation emphasizes how advancements in healthcare build upon one another, creating an iterative and interconnected process rather than a single endpoint. Below is a breakdown of each phase:

Healthcare 1.0: Internal efficiency through automation and reduced paperwork.

Healthcare 2.0: Inter-organization connectivity with data sharing.

Healthcare 3.0: National-level systems using big data and patient interaction.

Healthcare 4.0: Global integration with AI, real-time monitoring, and analytics.

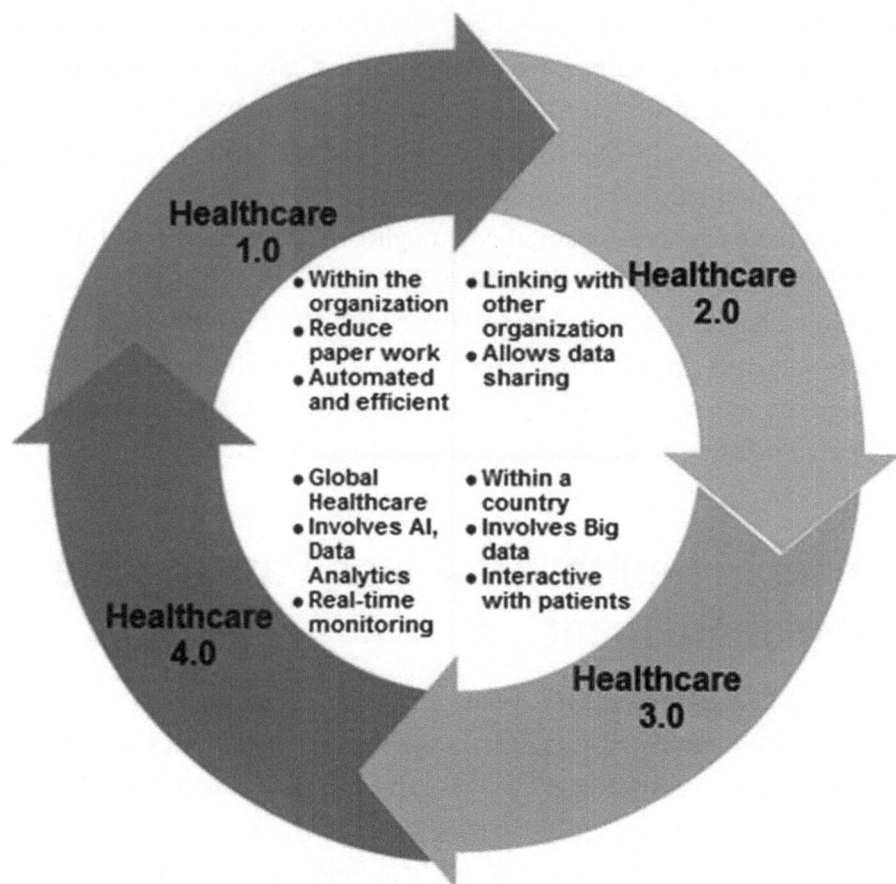

Figure 1-4. *From Healthcare 1.0 to Healthcare 4.0*

This integration has significant implications for patient care and management:

- **Personalized medicine:** Healthcare 4.0 facilitates the collection and analysis of vast amounts of patient data, including genetic information, medical history, lifestyle factors, and real-time health metrics. This wealth of data enables healthcare providers to tailor treatments and interventions to individual patients, leading to more precise and effective care.

- **Predictive analytics:** Advanced analytics and AI algorithms can analyze patient data to identify patterns and trends, allowing healthcare providers to predict and prevent adverse health events. For example, predictive analytics can help identify patients at risk of developing chronic conditions or experiencing complications, enabling early interventions to mitigate risks and improve outcomes.

- **Remote monitoring:** IoT devices and wearable sensors enable continuous monitoring of patients outside traditional healthcare settings. Remote monitoring technologies allow healthcare providers to track vital signs, medication adherence, and other health metrics in real time, facilitating proactive interventions and reducing the need for frequent in-person visits.

- **Telemedicine:** Healthcare 4.0 has accelerated the adoption of telemedicine, enabling patients to access healthcare services remotely through video consultations, remote monitoring, and digital communication tools. Telemedicine improves access to care, particularly for patients in remote or underserved areas, and reduces the burden on healthcare facilities (see Figure 1-5).

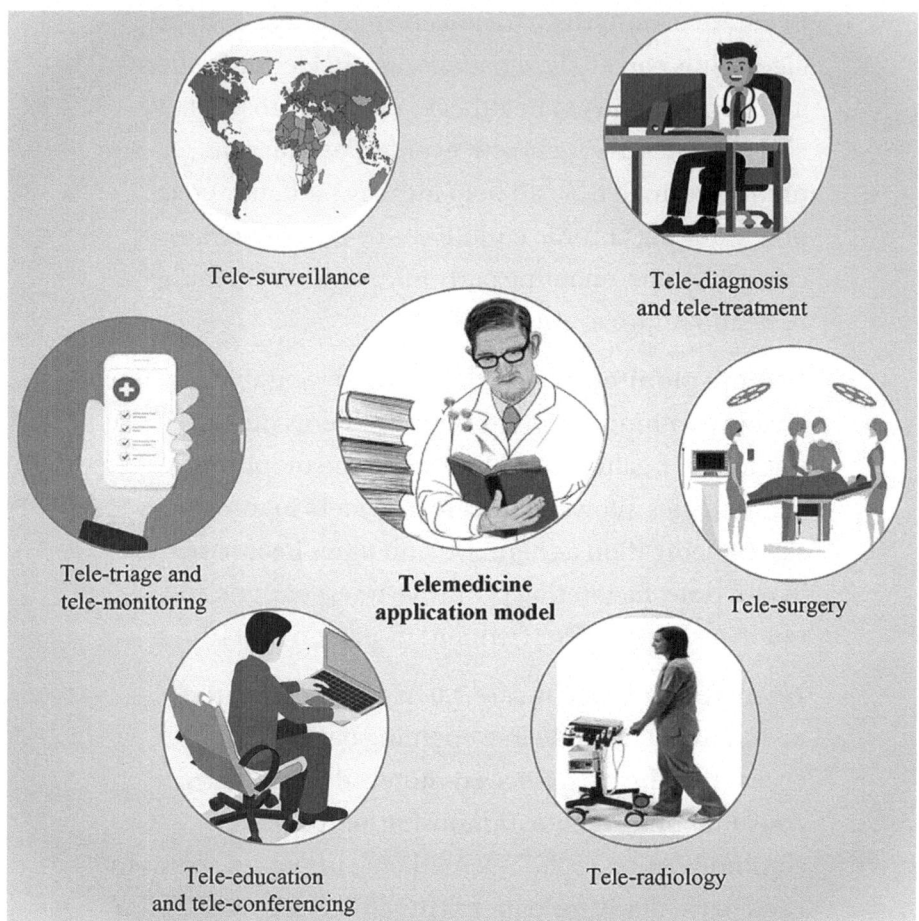

Tele-surveillance

Tele-diagnosis
and tele-treatment

Tele-triage and
tele-monitoring

**Telemedicine
application model**

Tele-surgery

Tele-education
and tele-conferencing

Tele-radiology

Figure 1-5. *Telemedicine application model*

- **Efficient resource allocation:** Data analytics and AI
  algorithms can optimize resource allocation within
  healthcare systems by predicting patient demand,
  identifying inefficiencies, and streamlining workflows.
  By improving operational efficiency, healthcare
  providers can deliver timely and cost-effective care
  while reducing wait times and enhancing patient
  satisfaction.

- **Enhanced patient engagement:** Digital health tools, such as mobile apps, patient portals, and wearable devices, empower patients to actively participate in their care by accessing health information, monitoring their progress, and communicating with healthcare providers. Increased patient engagement promotes adherence to treatment plans, fosters collaboration between patients and providers, and ultimately improves health outcomes.

- **Healthcare delivery transformation:** Healthcare 4.0 is driving a shift toward value-based care models that prioritize outcomes and patient satisfaction over volume of services. This transformation requires healthcare providers to focus on preventive care, care coordination, and patient-centered approaches to achieve better results at lower costs.

- **Data security and privacy:** As healthcare becomes increasingly digitized, ensuring the security and privacy of patient data is paramount. Healthcare organizations must implement robust cybersecurity measures and adhere to strict regulatory requirements to protect sensitive health information from unauthorized access, breaches, and misuse.

Overall, Healthcare 4.0 has the potential to revolutionize patient care and management by leveraging technology to deliver more personalized, efficient, and accessible healthcare services while improving outcomes and reducing costs. However, realizing these benefits requires careful integration of digital technologies, investment in infrastructure and workforce training, and a commitment to addressing challenges related to data privacy, interoperability, and equity of access. Figure 1-6 illustrates a comprehensive concept of healthcare that integrates physical healthcare systems, communication networks, and cyber healthcare systems to provide seamless and efficient medical care. Physical healthcare systems encompass a wide range of environments, including hospitals, offices, homes, rehab centers, and industries such as healthcare logistics and insurance. These systems employ advanced monitoring devices like ECG patches, blood pressure sensors, motion sensors, SpO2 sensors, body temperature sensors, and robotic braces to collect patient data in real-time. Communication networks, including Wide Area Networks (WAN), Personal Area Networks (PAN), and Body Area Networks (BAN), connect these devices and enable real-time sensing and actuation. Cyber healthcare systems leverage this data to create digital human models that support diagnostic and prognostic functions. Diagnostic capabilities include heart rate, sleep, nutrition, and mental stress analysis, while prognostic functions focus on chronic disease management, motion analysis, respiration analysis, and stress and sleep management. Together, these interconnected systems illustrate a holistic approach to modern healthcare, bridging the gap between physical and digital domains to improve patient outcomes.

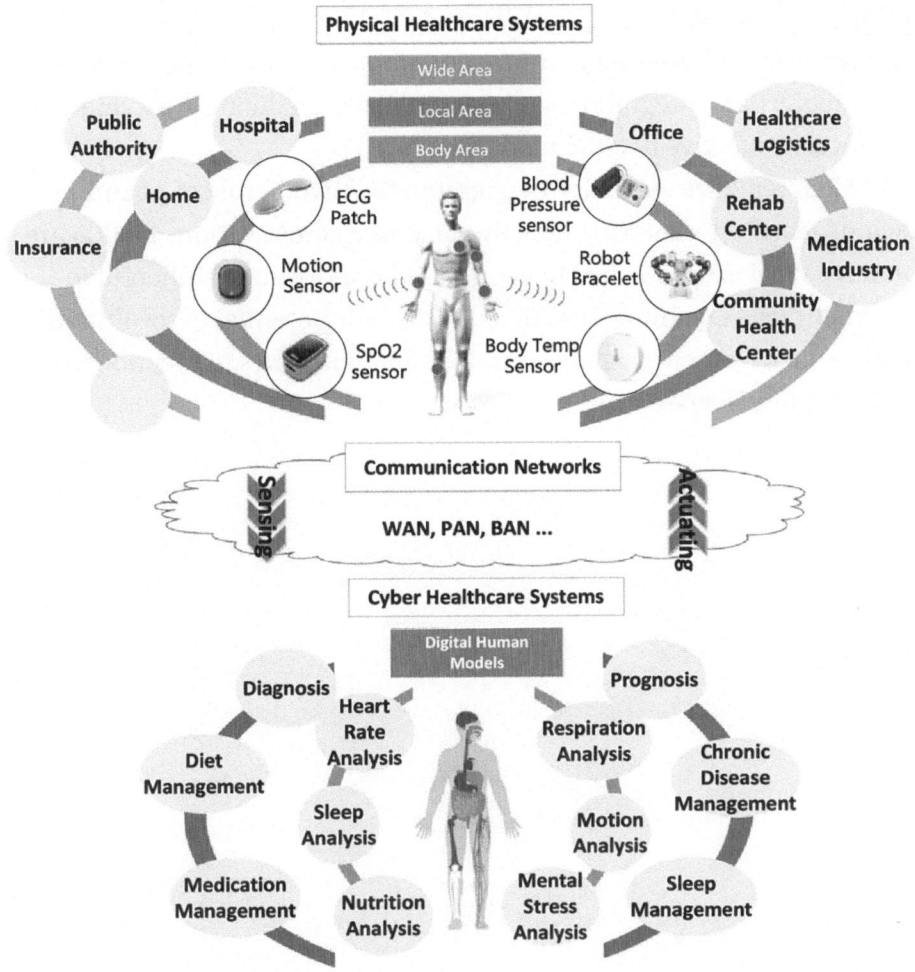

Figure 1-6.   *Concept of healthcare*

Summary

This chapter described the transformative era of the Fourth Industrial Revolution in healthcare. It explored the historical evolution of healthcare technologies, tracing advancements from traditional methods to the cutting-edge innovations of Healthcare 4.0. This chapter underscored how Healthcare 4.0 reshapes patient care and management through enhanced connectivity, data integration, and personalized medicine, fostering more efficient and effective healthcare delivery systems.

In Chapter 2, we will delve deeper into the pivotal role of AI and machine learning, exploring their applications across various healthcare domains. We'll examine the challenges and opportunities inherent in implementing AI technologies, illustrating their potential to revolutionize diagnostics, treatment strategies, and patient outcomes in the modern healthcare landscape.

CHAPTER 2

Fundamentals of Artificial Intelligence in Healthcare

In Chapter 1, we explored the transformative impact of the Fourth Industrial Revolution on healthcare, highlighting the technological advancements reshaping patient care and management. This chapter focuses on the fundamentals of artificial intelligence (AI) in healthcare, providing an in-depth understanding of AI and machine learning (ML), their applications in various healthcare domains, and the challenges and opportunities associated with AI implementation.

The integration of advanced digital technologies, data analytics, and AI into healthcare delivery systems is revolutionizing the way medical services are provided, improving efficiency, accuracy, and patient outcomes. Building upon the foundation of previous healthcare paradigms, Healthcare 4.0 leverages emerging technologies to transform the way healthcare is accessed, delivered, and managed, with a focus on enhancing patient outcomes, improving operational efficiency, and driving innovation across the healthcare ecosystem.

In Healthcare 4.0, interconnected digital systems, smart devices, and intelligent algorithms converge to create a connected healthcare environment that enables seamless data exchange, personalized

care delivery, and proactive health management. Key components of
Healthcare 4.0 include AI-driven diagnostic tools, Internet of Things (IoT)
enabled medical devices, telemedicine platforms, predictive analytics, and
precision medicine approaches, among others.

The overarching goal of Healthcare 4.0 is to harness the power
of digital transformation to address the complex challenges facing
modern healthcare systems, such as rising healthcare costs, aging
populations, chronic disease burden, and disparities in access to care.
By leveraging AI, IoT, and other advanced technologies, Healthcare 4.0
aims to improve healthcare quality, increase patient satisfaction, reduce
medical errors, optimize resource utilization, and promote population
health management. Figure 2-1 depicts the diverse applications of
Artificial Intelligence (AI) in healthcare, categorized into various sectors
such as virtual nursing assistants, AI-assisted robotic surgery, medical
image analysis, drug discovery, medical data security, and more. These
applications aim to enhance patient care, improve diagnostic accuracy,
streamline workflows, and ensure data security.

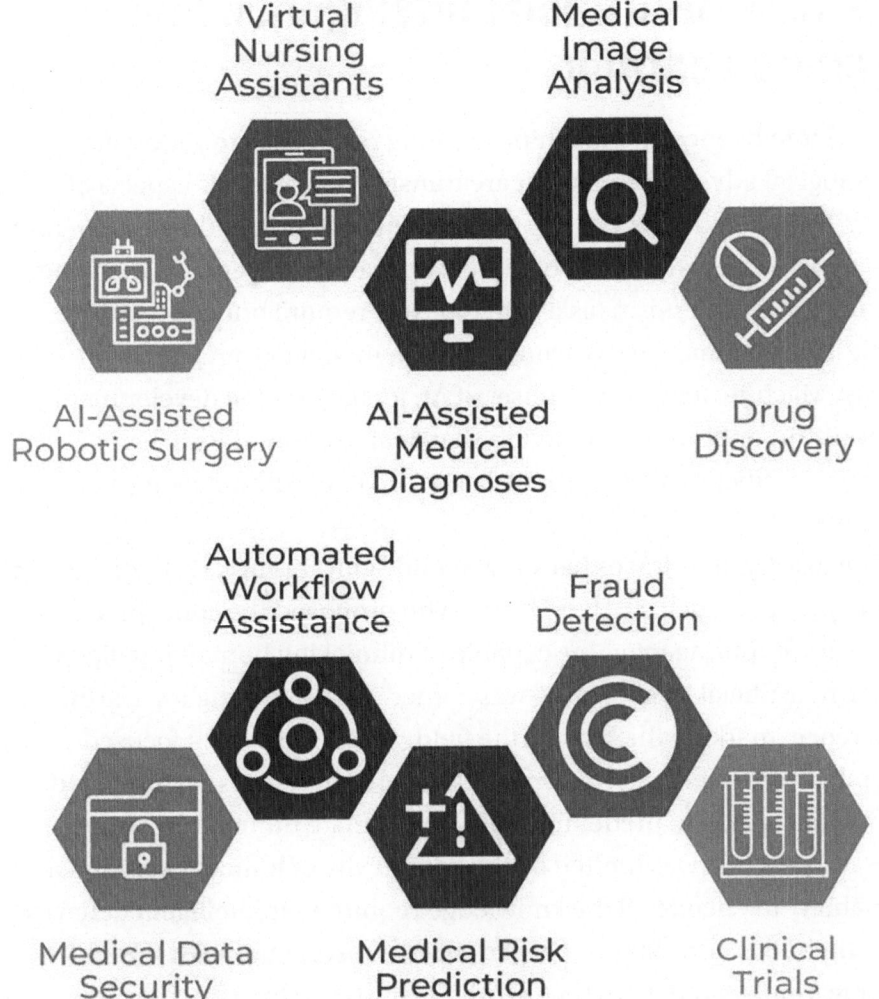

Figure 2-1. *Application of Artificial Intelligence (AI) in Healthcare*

Healthcare 4.0 represents a paradigm shift in healthcare delivery toward a data-driven, interconnected, and patient-centric model enabled by cutting-edge technologies. It holds the promise of revolutionizing healthcare delivery, driving innovation, and ultimately improving health outcomes for individuals and communities worldwide.

Overview of Artificial Intelligence and Machine Learning

Artificial intelligence and machine learning represent groundbreaking technological advancements that are transforming various aspects of society, from healthcare and finance to transportation and entertainment. At its core, AI refers to the simulation of human intelligence in machines, allowing them to perform tasks that typically require human cognitive abilities, such as learning, reasoning, problem-solving, and decision-making. Machine learning, a subset of AI, focuses on the development of algorithms and statistical models that enable computers to learn from and make predictions or decisions based on data, without being explicitly programmed.

The history of AI traces back to the mid-20th century, with the seminal work of pioneers such as Alan Turing, who proposed the concept of a universal computing machine capable of mimicking human intelligence. The term "artificial intelligence" was coined in 1956 during the Dartmouth Conference, marking the birth of the field. Early AI research focused on symbolic or rule-based approaches, where computers manipulated symbols according to predefined rules to simulate human reasoning. However, progress was limited by the complexity of human cognition and the inability to encode all the knowledge required for intelligent behavior.

In the 1980s and 1990s, AI experienced a resurgence with the advent of connectionism and neural networks, inspired by the structure and function of the human brain. Neural networks consist of interconnected nodes or neurons that process information through layers of computation, enabling them to recognize patterns and learn from data. Despite initial excitement, progress was hindered by computational limitations and insufficient amounts of data for training complex models.

The early 21st century witnessed a paradigm shift in AI and ML fueled by the exponential growth of data, advances in computing power, and breakthroughs in algorithms. This era of "big data" provided the fuel needed to train sophisticated machine learning models capable of handling vast amounts of information. Additionally, the emergence of deep learning, a subfield of ML based on neural networks with multiple layers, revolutionized AI by enabling unprecedented levels of accuracy in tasks such as image recognition, natural language processing, and speech recognition.

Fundamental concepts underpinning AI and ML include supervised learning, unsupervised learning, and reinforcement learning. In supervised learning, algorithms learn from labeled data, where each input is associated with a corresponding output or target variable. The goal is to learn a mapping function that can accurately predict outputs for new, unseen inputs. Common supervised learning algorithms include linear regression, logistic regression, decision trees, support vector machines, and neural networks.

Unsupervised learning, on the other hand, involves training algorithms on unlabeled data to discover hidden patterns or structures. Unlike supervised learning, there are no predefined output variables, and the algorithm must infer the underlying relationships within the data. Clustering algorithms, such as k-means clustering and hierarchical clustering, are commonly used in unsupervised learning to group similar data points together based on their features.

Reinforcement learning is a third paradigm of machine learning where agents learn to make sequential decisions by interacting with an environment to maximize cumulative rewards. The agent receives feedback from the environment in the form of rewards or penalties based on its actions, allowing it to learn optimal strategies through trial and error. Reinforcement learning has been successfully applied to various domains, including robotics, gaming, and autonomous vehicles.

Real-world applications of AI and ML span a wide range of industries and domains, revolutionizing processes, enhancing efficiency, and unlocking new opportunities. In healthcare, AI-powered systems are transforming diagnosis, treatment, and drug discovery by analyzing medical images, predicting patient outcomes, and identifying potential drug candidates. In finance, ML algorithms are used for fraud detection, algorithmic trading, credit scoring, and risk management, improving decision-making and reducing financial losses.

Transportation is another area where AI and ML are making significant strides, particularly with the development of autonomous vehicles and intelligent transportation systems. Companies like Tesla, Waymo, and Uber are leveraging ML algorithms to enable self-driving cars that can navigate roads, interpret traffic signals, and respond to dynamic environments. Intelligent transportation systems utilize AI to optimize traffic flow, reduce congestion, and improve safety through predictive analytics and real-time decision-making.

In the realm of natural language processing (NLP), AI is powering virtual assistants, language translation tools, sentiment analysis, and chatbots that can understand, generate, and interact with human language. Companies like Google, Amazon, and Microsoft are investing heavily in NLP technologies to enhance user experiences and streamline communication processes.

Ethical considerations and societal implications are integral to the development and deployment of AI and ML systems. Concerns regarding bias, fairness, transparency, accountability, and privacy have prompted calls for responsible AI practices and regulatory oversight. Addressing these ethical challenges requires interdisciplinary collaboration, ethical frameworks, algorithmic transparency, and ongoing dialogue between stakeholders.

Looking ahead, the future of AI and ML holds immense promise, with continued advancements expected in areas such as explainable AI, federated learning, quantum computing, and neuromorphic computing. Explainable AI aims to enhance the interpretability and transparency of ML models, enabling humans to understand and trust the decisions made by AI systems. Federated learning extends ML to decentralized environments, allowing models to be trained across distributed devices while preserving data privacy and security.

Quantum computing, with its potential to perform complex calculations at unprecedented speeds, could revolutionize AI by enabling more efficient optimization algorithms and solving problems that are currently intractable for classical computers. Neuromorphic computing, inspired by the architecture of the human brain, seeks to build artificial neural networks that mimic the parallelism, plasticity, and energy efficiency of biological systems.

Figure 2-2 illustrates the various approaches that AI encompasses. Symbolic AI, also referred to as "good old-fashioned AI" (GOFAI), uses explicitly defined rules and symbolic representations for problem-solving. It's similar to traditional programming in the sense that predefined guidelines drive the process, but it's more advanced because it permits inference and adaptation to new situations. Machine learning allows algorithms to learn from data. Deep learning (DL) is a subset of ML that uses multilayered, artificial neural networks. Figure 2-3 shows how symbolic AI and ML differ.

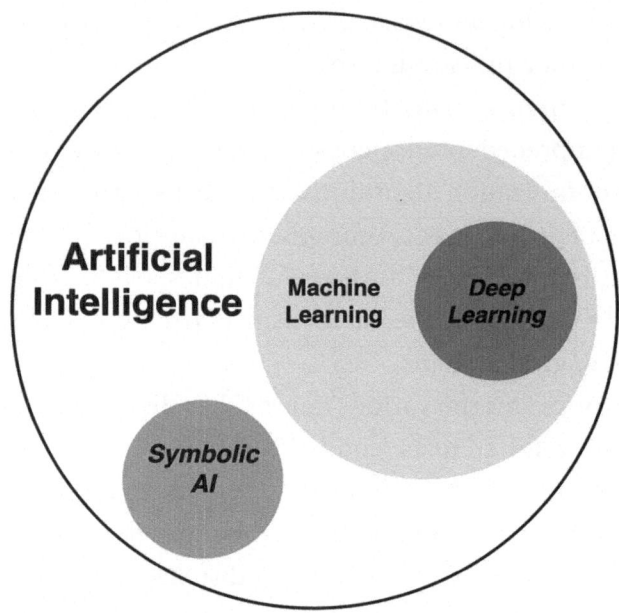

Figure 2-2. *AI encompasses various approaches*

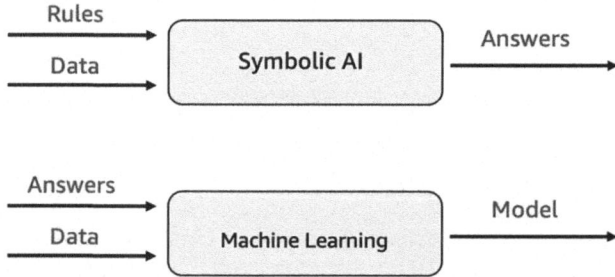

Figure 2-3. *Comparison of symbolic AI and ML workflows*

In conclusion, AI and ML represent transformative technologies with profound implications for society, economy, and human well-being. From healthcare and finance to transportation and beyond, AI is reshaping industries, driving innovation, and unlocking new possibilities. However, realizing the full potential of AI requires addressing ethical concerns, ensuring transparency and accountability, and fostering collaboration between stakeholders. With ongoing research, investment, and responsible deployment, AI and ML have the power to create a future where intelligent machines augment human capabilities, improve decision-making, and enrich lives.

How Does a Machine Learning Model Learn?

Machine learning, a subset of AI, empowers computers to learn and improve from experience without being explicitly programmed. At the heart of this capability lies a complex process that allows machine learning models to absorb data, extract patterns, and make predictions or decisions. Understanding how an ML model learns involves delving into its fundamental components, including data representation, model architecture, optimization algorithms, and training process.

At the outset, an ML model learns through data. Data serves as the raw material from which patterns and relationships are extracted. This data can come in various forms, such as text, images, audio, or numerical values, depending on the nature of the problem being addressed. However, raw data often needs to be preprocessed and transformed into a suitable format for the model to effectively learn from it. Preprocessing steps may include cleaning data to remove noise or inconsistencies, scaling numerical features to a similar range, encoding categorical variables, and splitting the data into training, validation, and testing sets.

Once the data is prepared, it is fed into the ML model for learning. At the core of an ML model lies its architecture, which determines its structure and behavior. There are various types of ML models, each with its own unique architecture suited for specific types of tasks. For instance, in supervised learning, where the model learns to map input data to corresponding output labels, common architectures Feedforward neural networks (FNNs) are used for tasks like classification, regression, and pattern recognition, where the input data is mapped directly to output labels without sequential or spatial dependencies. They consist of input, hidden, and output layers, with data flowing in one direction. Convolutional neural networks (CNNs) for image data, recurrent neural networks (RNNs) for sequential data, and transformers for natural language processing tasks.

Regardless of the specific architecture, a machine learning model comprises interconnected layers of neurons or nodes. These layers transform input data through a series of mathematical operations, with each layer extracting increasingly abstract features from the data. In a neural network, for example, the initial layers might capture low-level features like edges or textures in an image, while deeper layers learn to combine these features to recognize more complex patterns or objects.

During the learning process, the ML model's parameters are adjusted iteratively to minimize the disparity between its predictions and the actual ground-truth labels in the training data. This adjustment is accomplished through an optimization algorithm, such as stochastic gradient descent (SGD) or one of its variants. The goal of optimization is to find the set of parameters that minimizes a predefined loss function, which quantifies the disparity between predicted and actual values. By computing the gradient of the loss function with respect to each parameter, the optimization algorithm determines how to update the parameters to reduce the loss incrementally.

The training process involves feeding batches of data into the ML model, computing predictions, comparing them with the true labels, and using the resulting error to update the model's parameters. This process is repeated for multiple epochs, with each epoch representing a complete pass through the entire training dataset. As the model iterates over the data, it gradually learns to generalize patterns beyond the training examples, thereby improving its performance on unseen data.

However, the learning process is not without challenges. One common issue is overfitting, where the ML model learns to memorize the training data rather than capturing underlying patterns. Overfitting occurs when the model is too complex relative to the amount of training data available, leading it to fit noise rather than true relationships. To mitigate overfitting, techniques such as regularization, dropout, and early stopping are employed. Regularization penalizes overly complex models by adding a term to the loss function that discourages large parameter values, while dropout randomly deactivates neurons during training to prevent them from co-adapting excessively. Early stopping halts training when the model's performance on a separate validation set begins to degrade, thus preventing it from overoptimizing on the training data.

Conversely, underfitting arises when the ML model is too simplistic to capture the underlying structure of the data. This often occurs when the model architecture is not expressive enough or when insufficient training data is available. To address underfitting, one can consider using more complex models, collecting more data, or engineering better features to enhance the model's representational power.

Moreover, the performance of a machine learning model depends not only on its architecture and training process but also on the quality and quantity of the data it learns from. High-quality, diverse, and representative datasets are essential for training robust and generalizable models. Biases present in the data can propagate to the model's predictions, leading to unfair or inaccurate outcomes, particularly in sensitive applications like healthcare or criminal justice. Therefore, data collection, annotation, and curation require careful attention to ensure equitable and reliable model performance.

In addition to supervised learning, where the ML model learns from labeled data, other paradigms such as unsupervised learning, semi-supervised learning, and reinforcement learning offer alternative approaches to learning from data. Unsupervised learning tasks involve discovering hidden patterns or structures in unlabeled data, such as clustering similar data points together or dimensionality reduction for visualization or compression purposes. Semi-supervised learning leverages both labeled and unlabeled data to improve model performance, useful in scenarios where labeling data is costly or time-consuming. Reinforcement learning, inspired by behavioral psychology, entails training agents to make sequential decisions through trial and error, guided by a reward signal indicating the desirability of actions taken.

In conclusion, a machine learning model learns through a multifaceted process that involves ingesting data, extracting patterns, adjusting parameters, and iteratively refining its predictions. The interplay between data representation, model architecture, optimization algorithms, and training procedures determines the model's ability to generalize from past experience to unseen situations. By understanding the mechanisms underlying machine learning, researchers and practitioners can develop more effective models that address real-world challenges across diverse domains.

Example of ML Model Learning

The ML model described in this section represents the relationship between centimeters and inches through a mathematical formula. However, the specific formula is not provided in the example. To fully understand the relationship between centimeters and inches as described in the example, we would need the exact formula.

Typically, the relationship between centimeters and inches can be expressed using a linear equation of the following form, where A and B are constants representing the slope and the y-intercept of the linear equation, respectively:

$$\text{Inches} = \text{Centimeters} + \text{Inches} = A \times \text{Centimeters} + B$$

This equation suggests a linear relationship between centimeters and inches, where the number of inches is equal to the number of centimeters multiplied by a conversion factor (slope) plus an offset (y-intercept).

However, without the specific formula mentioned in the example, it's challenging to provide further insight into the nature of the relationship between centimeters and inches as described in the context.

What Is Deep Learning?

Deep learning, a subset of machine learning, is a powerful computational approach inspired by the structure and function of the human brain, particularly the interconnected network of neurons. At its core, deep learning focuses on the development of artificial neural networks (ANNs) that can learn and make intelligent decisions from vast amounts of data. What sets deep learning apart from traditional machine learning algorithms is its ability to automatically discover and learn intricate patterns and representations within the data without relying on explicit programming.

At the heart of deep learning are neural networks, which are composed of layers of interconnected nodes, or artificial neurons, arranged in a hierarchical fashion. Each neuron receives inputs, processes them using weighted connections, and produces an output signal that is passed on to the next layer. Through a process called *back propagation*, neural networks adjust these weights based on the error between predicted and actual outputs, gradually improving their performance over time.

One of the key strengths of deep learning lies in its capacity to handle and extract features from high-dimensional data, such as images, videos, audio recordings, and text. Convolutional neural networks (CNNs), a type of deep neural network particularly well-suited for image analysis, employ convolutional layers to automatically detect hierarchical patterns and spatial dependencies within images. Recurrent neural networks (RNNs), on the other hand, are designed to process sequential data by preserving information across time steps, making them effective for tasks such as natural language processing and time series prediction.

The success of deep learning can largely be attributed to the availability of massive datasets and advancements in computational power, particularly the utilization of graphics processing units (GPUs) and distributed computing frameworks. These technological developments have enabled researchers and practitioners to train increasingly complex neural network architectures on vast amounts of data, leading to breakthroughs in various domains, including computer vision, speech recognition, natural language understanding, healthcare, finance, and autonomous driving.

In computer vision, deep learning has revolutionized the field by achieving unprecedented accuracy in tasks such as object detection, image classification, and semantic segmentation. Models like AlexNet, VGGNet, and ResNet have set new benchmarks on widely recognized datasets such as ImageNet, showcasing the effectiveness of deep neural networks in extracting meaningful features from visual data.

Similarly, in the realm of natural language processing (NLP), deep learning techniques have led to remarkable advancements in tasks such as machine translation, sentiment analysis, and text generation. Models like Transformer, Bidirectional Encoder Representations from Transformers (BERT), and Generative Pre-trained Transformer (GPT) have demonstrated state-of-the-art performance on a range of NLP benchmarks, pushing the boundaries of language understanding and generation.

Beyond computer vision and NLP, deep learning has also found applications in speech recognition, drug discovery, genomics, recommender systems, and many other domains. For instance, in healthcare, deep learning models have been developed for medical image analysis, disease diagnosis, and personalized treatment planning, offering invaluable support to healthcare professionals in decision-making processes.

Despite its numerous successes, deep learning still faces several challenges and limitations. One significant challenge is the need for large amounts of labeled data to train accurate models, which can be both time-consuming and costly to acquire. Additionally, deep neural networks are often perceived as "black-box" models, meaning that it can be challenging to interpret the inner workings of these complex systems and understand the reasoning behind their predictions.

To address these challenges, researchers are actively exploring techniques such as transfer learning, semi-supervised learning, and explainable AI, aiming to improve the efficiency, interpretability, and robustness of deep learning models. Transfer learning, for instance, involves leveraging pretrained models on large datasets and fine-tuning them on smaller, domain-specific datasets, thus reducing the need for extensive labeled data.

Moreover, ongoing research in areas such as neural architecture search, attention mechanisms, and adversarial training continues to push the boundaries of deep learning, paving the way for more robust and versatile AI systems. Neural architecture search (NAS), for example, automates the process of designing optimal neural network architectures, leading to more efficient and effective models tailored to specific tasks and constraints (see Figure 2-4).

Looking ahead, the future of deep learning holds immense promise, with potential applications ranging from autonomous vehicles and robotics to personalized medicine and climate modeling. As advancements in hardware, algorithms, and data availability continue to accelerate, deep learning is poised to play an increasingly pivotal role in shaping the future of AI and driving innovation across diverse industries and societal domains. However, it is essential to remain mindful of ethical considerations, such as data privacy, bias mitigation, and the societal impact of AI technologies, to ensure that deep learning is deployed responsibly and equitably for the benefit of all.

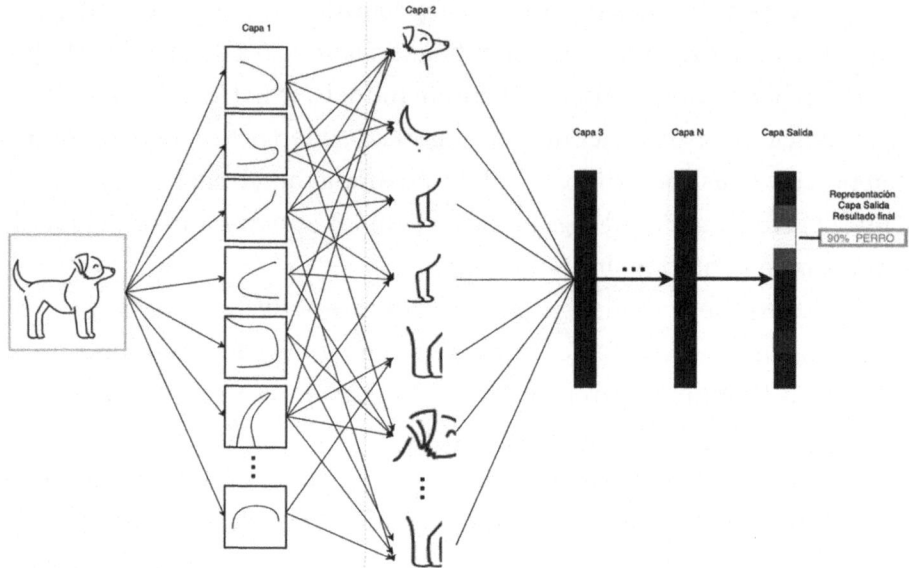

Figure 2-4. *Neural network architecture for image recognition*

Phases of the Life Cycle of a Machine Learning Project

The life cycle of a machine learning project encompasses a series of interconnected phases, each crucial for the successful development, deployment, and maintenance of machine learning models. These phases provide a structured framework for practitioners to follow, guiding them through the various stages of problem formulation, data preparation, model building, evaluation, deployment, and iteration. Understanding and effectively navigating through these phases are essential for delivering robust and scalable machine learning solutions that meet the desired objectives and requirements of stakeholders.

The first phase of the machine learning project life cycle is problem definition and formulation. In this phase, the project team collaborates with stakeholders to identify and define the problem that machine learning can help solve. It involves understanding the business context, defining clear objectives and success criteria, and determining the feasibility and impact of applying ML techniques to the problem at hand. This phase also entails scoping the project, defining project milestones, and establishing communication channels with stakeholders to ensure alignment throughout the project life cycle.

Once the problem is clearly defined, the next phase of the ML project life cycle involves data collection and preparation. This phase is often the most time-consuming and resource-intensive part of the ML process, as it requires gathering, cleaning, and preprocessing the relevant data required to train and evaluate ML models. Data sources may vary widely depending on the problem domain, ranging from structured databases to unstructured text, images, or sensor data. Data preprocessing tasks typically include handling missing values, removing outliers, standardizing or normalizing features, and encoding categorical variables to prepare the data for analysis.

Following data collection and preparation, the next phase of the ML project life cycle is exploratory data analysis (EDA), where the project team examines and analyzes the dataset to gain insights into its underlying structure, patterns, and relationships. EDA techniques may involve statistical analysis, data visualization, and dimensionality reduction to uncover meaningful trends and correlations within the data. This phase helps inform feature selection, model design, and hypothesis generation, guiding subsequent steps in the ML pipeline.

With a solid understanding of the problem and the data, the project enters the model development phase, where ML algorithms are selected, trained, and evaluated on the prepared dataset. Model selection depends on various factors, including the nature of the problem, the size and complexity of the dataset, and computational constraints. Common ML algorithms include linear regression, logistic regression, decision trees, support vector machines (SVM), k-nearest neighbors (KNN), and neural networks.

During the next phase, model training, the dataset is split into training, validation, and test sets to assess the performance of the trained models accurately. Training involves fitting the selected algorithm to the training data, optimizing model parameters through techniques like cross-validation, regularization, and hyperparameter tuning to minimize prediction errors and improve generalization. The validation set is used to fine-tune model hyperparameters and compare different algorithms' performance, while the test set provides an unbiased estimate of the model's performance on unseen data.

Following model training and evaluation, the next phase is model deployment, where the trained model is integrated into production systems or applications to make predictions on new, unseen data. Model deployment involves building scalable, robust, and efficient pipelines for data ingestion, preprocessing, feature extraction, and inference, ensuring seamless integration with existing infrastructure and workflows. Depending on the application requirements, models can be deployed locally on edge devices, in the cloud, or as web services accessible via application programming interfaces (APIs).

Once deployed, the final phase of the ML project life cycle is monitoring and maintenance, where the performance of deployed models is continuously monitored, evaluated, and updated to adapt to changing data distributions and evolving business requirements. Monitoring metrics such as accuracy, precision, recall, and F1 score are tracked over time to detect performance degradation or drift, triggering retraining or recalibration of models as needed. Additionally, ongoing maintenance involves addressing issues such as software updates, security patches, and model retraining to ensure the reliability, scalability, and security of deployed ML systems.

Throughout the entire machine learning project life cycle, effective communication, collaboration, and documentation are essential for fostering transparency, reproducibility, and accountability. Project teams should maintain clear documentation of all project-related activities, including data sources, preprocessing steps, model architectures, hyperparameters, evaluation metrics, and deployment procedures, enabling seamless knowledge transfer and collaboration across team members. Moreover, interdisciplinary collaboration between domain experts, data scientists, engineers, and business stakeholders is critical for aligning technical solutions with business objectives and ensuring the successful delivery of ML projects. By following a systematic approach to the ML project life cycle and leveraging best practices and methodologies, organizations can maximize the value and impact of ML technologies, driving innovation, efficiency, and competitive advantage in today's data-driven world.

The phases in the machine learning life cycle (e.g., problem definition, data collection, EDA, model development) are a general framework that applies to various projects, including healthcare. However, the phases in Table 2-1 are tailored specifically for fraud detection in banking, with a focus on business objectives, data processing, and real-time deployment. While both sets follow similar steps, the banking example is used here due to its concrete application in fraud detection, which allows for clearer demonstration of model deployment, performance metrics, and real-time inference. The same framework can be adapted to healthcare, but banking provides a more tangible example in this context.

Table 2-1. *Phases of Implementing a Machine Learning Solution for Fraud Detection*

Phase	Description
Commercial objective	The primary focus of this phase is to identify the business objective, which in this case is to reduce fraud in bank transactions. It involves defining measurable values for the business, such as a decrease in fraud rate by a certain percentage point, resulting in improvements in refund costs and customer satisfaction. This phase also assesses the necessity of utilizing machine learning to solve the problem, considering data availability, organizational capabilities, and alignment with leadership.
Define ML solution	Once the business objective is established, this phase involves defining the ML solution, including performance metrics and success criteria. For instance, a supervised classifier model must correctly identify at least 85% of fraudulent transactions with an error rate of no more than 10%. The strategy for data collection, labeling, and processing is also formulated, focusing on historical transaction data with labeled fraud and legitimate transactions, along with anonymized customer information.
Data processing	In this phase, the available data sources are defined, which may include events, time series, IoT devices, and social media interactions. Data ingestion and aggregation processes are established to prepare and label the data for training and testing the ML model. This involves defining data ingestion pipelines and preprocessing techniques to ensure the data is suitable for input into the learning model.

(continued)

Table 2-1. (*continued*)

Phase	Description
Model development: deployment	The trained and evaluated ML model is taken to production in this phase to make real-time inferences. The deployment strategy, infrastructure requirements, and inference latency patterns (real-time, asynchronous, or batch) are defined. For the bank fraud detection system, the focus is on deploying the model on an infrastructure capable of supporting real-time inferences, such as a web service invoked at the time of transaction processing.
Monitoring	This phase involves defining rules for detecting problems and sending alerts, such as data and model quality issues or deviations in bias. It includes monitoring whether incoming data is statistically similar to the training data and ensuring that the project is meeting its objectives. Additionally, experts may review suspicious transactions to provide feedback for model retraining, and reports or visualization panels are generated to present the final results of transactions and fraud detection performance.

Artificial intelligence and machine learning are revolutionizing healthcare by enabling computers to learn from data and perform tasks that traditionally require human intelligence. Understanding the breadth of AI's capabilities lays the foundation for exploring its diverse applications in modern healthcare settings.

Applications of AI in Healthcare

Artificial intelligence has swiftly become a cornerstone in modern healthcare, offering a plethora of applications that revolutionize medical practice, diagnosis, treatment, and management. The integration of AI into various facets of healthcare has opened up new possibilities for improving patient care, optimizing processes, and advancing medical research. The following list details numerous applications of AI in healthcare, spanning from medical imaging analysis to clinical decision support systems, and from drug discovery to healthcare operations and management (see Figure 2-5).

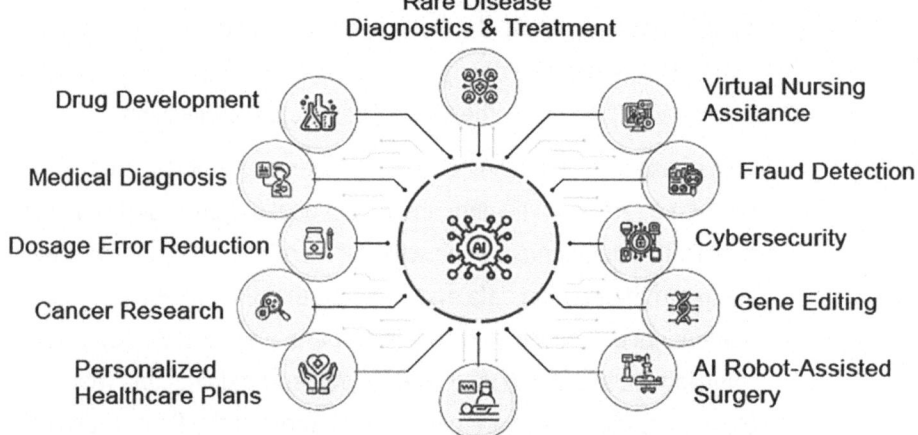

Applications of AI in Healthcare

Figure 2-5. *Applications of AI in healthcare and related fields*

- **Medical imaging analysis:** Among the most prominent applications of AI in healthcare is its role in medical imaging analysis. AI algorithms are adept at interpreting and analyzing medical images such as X-rays, MRIs, CT scans, and mammograms. These algorithms can detect subtle abnormalities, lesions, or anomalies in the images, assisting radiologists in making accurate diagnoses. By leveraging deep learning techniques, AI can identify patterns and features indicative of various conditions, including cancer, fractures, neurological disorders, and cardiovascular diseases. This capability significantly enhances the efficiency and accuracy of diagnostic processes, leading to faster identification of diseases and improved patient outcomes.

- **Predictive analytics and early disease detection:** AI excels in predictive analytics, leveraging machine learning algorithms to analyze vast amounts of patient data and identify patterns or trends indicative of certain diseases or medical events. By analyzing electronic health records (EHRs), genetic information, lifestyle factors, and other patient data, AI models can predict the likelihood of developing specific diseases or experiencing adverse health events. This capability enables early detection and intervention, allowing healthcare providers to initiate timely treatments, prevent disease progression, and improve patient outcomes. Moreover, predictive analytics can facilitate population health management initiatives by identifying high-risk patient populations and implementing targeted interventions to mitigate health risks.

- **Personalized treatment plans:** AI-driven personalized medicine is revolutionizing healthcare by tailoring treatment plans to individual patients based on their unique characteristics and medical histories. By analyzing patient data, including genetic information, biomarkers, treatment responses, and disease progression, AI can identify optimal treatment strategies customized to each patient's needs. This personalized approach improves treatment outcomes, minimizes adverse reactions to medications, and enhances patient satisfaction. Moreover, AI enables clinicians to continuously monitor patients' responses to treatment and adjust interventions accordingly, ensuring optimal therapeutic efficacy and patient safety.

- **Virtual health assistants and chatbots:** AI-powered virtual health assistants and chatbots are transforming patient engagement and healthcare delivery by providing personalized medical advice, answering questions about symptoms or medications, scheduling appointments, and delivering follow-up care instructions. These virtual assistants leverage NLP algorithms to understand and respond to patient inquiries, enhancing access to healthcare services and improving patient satisfaction. Additionally, virtual health assistants can triage patients, identify urgent medical concerns, and escalate issues to healthcare providers, facilitating timely interventions and reducing unnecessary healthcare utilization.

- **Drug discovery and development:** AI has revolutionized the drug discovery and development process by accelerating the identification of potential drug candidates, predicting their efficacy, and optimizing drug design. Traditional drug discovery approaches are time-consuming and expensive, and often yield low success rates. However, AI algorithms can analyze large-scale biological data, including genomic, proteomic, and chemical datasets, to identify novel drug targets, predict molecular interactions, and optimize drug properties. Furthermore, AI-driven drug repurposing algorithms can identify existing drugs with therapeutic potential for new indications, offering a faster and more cost-effective approach to drug development. By expediting the drug discovery process, AI contributes to the development of innovative therapies, addressing unmet medical needs and improving patient outcomes across various disease areas.

- **Remote monitoring and telemedicine:** AI-enabled remote monitoring devices and telemedicine platforms are revolutionizing healthcare delivery by enabling remote patient monitoring, virtual consultations, and remote diagnosis. These technologies leverage AI algorithms to analyze patient-generated health data, such as vital signs, symptoms, and medication adherence, allowing healthcare providers to monitor patients' health status in real time and intervene promptly when necessary. Remote monitoring devices, including wearable sensors, smart devices, and mobile health applications, empower patients to actively participate in their care and manage chronic conditions from the comfort of their homes. Additionally, telemedicine platforms powered by AI facilitate virtual consultations between patients and healthcare providers, improving access to healthcare services, particularly in underserved or remote areas. By reducing geographical barriers, increasing healthcare access, and minimizing healthcare disparities, remote monitoring and telemedicine contribute to improved patient outcomes and enhanced healthcare efficiency.

- **Robotic surgery:** AI-driven robotic surgery systems have transformed the field of minimally invasive surgery, offering enhanced precision, dexterity, and

47

visualization capabilities. These robotic systems, controlled by surgeons, utilize AI algorithms to assist in surgical procedures, such as laparoscopic surgeries, cardiac surgeries, and orthopedic procedures. By providing surgeons with augmented visualization, motion scaling, and tremor reduction capabilities, robotic surgery systems improve surgical accuracy, reduce tissue trauma, and shorten recovery times. Moreover, AI-powered surgical robots can perform complex tasks autonomously under the supervision of surgeons, further enhancing surgical outcomes and patient safety. Robotic surgery represents a paradigm shift in surgical practice, enabling less invasive procedures, shorter hospital stays, and faster patient recovery, ultimately improving overall patient care and satisfaction.

- **Healthcare operations and management:** AI plays a vital role in optimizing healthcare operations and management processes, including hospital resource allocation, patient flow management, staffing optimization, and inventory management. By leveraging machine learning algorithms and predictive analytics, healthcare organizations can forecast patient admission rates, predict resource needs, and optimize bed allocation, staffing schedules, and inventory levels. These AI-driven solutions enable healthcare providers to streamline operations, reduce costs, and enhance patient experiences. Furthermore, AI-powered revenue cycle management tools automate billing processes, identify billing discrepancies, and optimize reimbursement strategies, improving financial performance and revenue capture for healthcare organizations. By enhancing operational efficiency and resource utilization, AI contributes to the overall sustainability and effectiveness of healthcare delivery systems.

- **Clinical decision support systems:** AI-based clinical decision support systems (CDSSs) empower healthcare providers with real-time, evidence-based recommendations for diagnosis, treatment planning, and medication prescribing. These systems analyze patient data, medical literature, clinical guidelines, and best practices to assist clinicians in making informed decisions at the point of care. AI-driven CDSSs can alert clinicians to potential drug interactions, recommend appropriate diagnostic tests, and provide treatment guidelines tailored to individual patient profiles. By integrating CDSSs into EHR systems and clinical workflows, healthcare providers can access timely and relevant information, reduce medical errors, and improve patient outcomes. Moreover, CDSSs can support care coordination efforts, facilitate multidisciplinary collaboration, and promote adherence to clinical protocols, enhancing the quality and safety of patient care delivery.

- **Medical research and data analysis:** AI facilitates medical research and data analysis by analyzing large-scale healthcare datasets to identify patterns, correlations, and insights that may not be apparent to human researchers. By applying machine learning algorithms to diverse sources of healthcare data, including clinical records, imaging studies, genomic

49

data, and population health data, AI enables researchers to uncover new insights into disease mechanisms, treatment effectiveness, and public health trends. Moreover, AI-driven predictive models can forecast disease outbreaks, identify emerging health threats, and inform public health interventions, contributing to the prevention and control of infectious diseases and chronic conditions. Additionally, AI accelerates biomedical research by facilitating data-driven discovery, drug repurposing, and biomarker identification, driving innovation and advancing scientific knowledge in various medical disciplines.

In conclusion, the applications of AI in healthcare are diverse and multifaceted, spanning from medical imaging analysis and predictive analytics to personalized medicine and robotic surgery. AI-driven solutions have the potential to transform healthcare delivery by improving diagnostic accuracy, enhancing treatment outcomes, and optimizing operational efficiency. Moreover, AI facilitates patient engagement, empowers healthcare providers with decision support tools, and accelerates medical research and innovation. However, realizing the full potential of AI in healthcare requires addressing challenges related to data privacy, security, regulatory compliance, and ethical considerations. By harnessing the power of AI responsibly and ethically, healthcare stakeholders can leverage its transformative capabilities to deliver high-quality, patient-centered care and improve health outcomes for individuals and populations alike.

AI applications in healthcare range from diagnostic support systems to personalized treatment recommendations, enhancing both clinical decision-making and patient outcomes. With AI making significant strides, it's vital to address the challenges and opportunities associated with its widespread implementation in healthcare systems.

Challenges and Opportunities in AI Implementation

The implementation of AI in various industries, including healthcare, presents a myriad of challenges and opportunities. This section delves into the key challenges and opportunities associated with AI implementation in healthcare, exploring the implications for patient care, operational efficiency, regulatory compliance, ethical considerations, and more.

The following are the primary challenges of implementing AI in healthcare:

- **Data privacy and security:** One of the foremost challenges in AI implementation in healthcare is ensuring the privacy and security of sensitive patient data. Healthcare organizations are entrusted with vast amounts of personal health information (PHI), and AI systems require access to this data for training and decision-making purposes. However, safeguarding patient privacy and protecting against data breaches, unauthorized access, and cyber threats is paramount. Regulations such as the EU General Data Protection Regulation (GDPR) and the US Health Insurance Portability and Accountability Act (HIPAA) impose strict requirements on the handling of patient data, adding complexity to AI implementation efforts.

- **Data quality and bias:** The quality and reliability of data used to train AI algorithms are critical determinants of their performance and accuracy. However, healthcare data is often heterogeneous, noisy, and subject to bias, stemming from factors such as demographic disparities, sampling biases, and data

51

collection methods. Biased data can lead to skewed outcomes and exacerbate healthcare disparities, posing ethical and equity concerns. Addressing data quality issues and mitigating bias in AI models require careful data curation, algorithmic transparency, and ongoing monitoring and validation processes.

- **Regulatory compliance:** Healthcare is a highly regulated industry, governed by a complex framework of regulations, standards, and guidelines aimed at protecting patient safety, privacy, and rights. AI applications in healthcare must navigate regulatory requirements imposed by agencies such as the US Food and Drug Administration (FDA), the European Medicines Agency (EMA), and other regulatory bodies worldwide. Achieving regulatory compliance involves conducting rigorous testing, obtaining necessary approvals, and adhering to standards for safety, efficacy, and quality assurance. Moreover, the rapid pace of technological innovation in AI poses challenges for regulatory agencies in keeping pace with emerging AI applications and ensuring appropriate oversight.

- **Ethical considerations:** The use of AI in healthcare raises profound ethical considerations related to patient autonomy, consent, transparency, and accountability. AI systems have the potential to impact patients' lives in significant ways, influencing decisions about diagnosis, treatment, and care. Ensuring that AI algorithms operate ethically and responsibly requires attention to principles such as fairness, transparency, interpretability, and accountability. Moreover, addressing ethical concerns surrounding AI requires interdisciplinary collaboration, stakeholder engagement, and the development of ethical guidelines and frameworks that prioritize patient welfare and uphold ethical standards.

- **Integration with existing systems:** Healthcare organizations often have complex IT infrastructures comprising disparate systems, platforms, and data sources. Integrating new AI technologies with existing systems poses challenges in terms of interoperability, compatibility, and data exchange. AI implementation efforts must account for legacy systems, data formats, and workflow integration to ensure seamless interoperability and minimize disruptions to clinical workflows. Moreover, interoperability standards and data exchange protocols are essential for facilitating data sharing and collaboration across healthcare systems and stakeholders.

- **Skills gap and training:** AI implementation in healthcare requires specialized skills and expertise in areas such as data science, machine learning, statistics, and computer programming. However, there is a shortage of professionals with these skills, creating a skills gap that impedes AI adoption and implementation. Healthcare organizations must invest in workforce training, education, and professional development initiatives to build internal capacity and expertise in AI technologies. Moreover, fostering collaboration between data scientists, clinicians, and domain experts is essential for developing AI solutions that address real-world healthcare challenges and deliver meaningful clinical insights.

- **Cost and resource constraints:** Implementing AI technologies in healthcare can be costly and resource-intensive, requiring investments in infrastructure, software, hardware, and personnel. Small and medium-sized healthcare organizations, in particular, may face budgetary constraints and resource limitations that hinder AI adoption. Finding ways to overcome cost barriers, secure funding, and allocate resources effectively is a significant challenge for healthcare leaders and decision-makers. Moreover, demonstrating the return on investment (ROI) and cost-effectiveness of AI initiatives is essential for gaining buy-in from stakeholders and securing support for ongoing implementation efforts.

Despite the previously listed challenges, implementing AI in healthcare offers tremendous opportunities, including the following:

- **Improved patient outcomes:** AI has the potential to revolutionize healthcare delivery by enabling more accurate diagnoses, personalized treatment plans, and better patient outcomes. By leveraging AI technologies such as machine learning, natural language processing, and predictive analytics, healthcare providers can analyze vast amounts of data to identify patterns, trends, and insights that inform clinical decision-making and improve patient care. From early disease detection to treatment optimization, AI-driven solutions empower healthcare professionals to deliver timely, evidence-based interventions that enhance patient outcomes and quality of life.

- **Efficiency and productivity:** AI technologies can automate routine tasks, streamline processes, and enhance workflow efficiency in healthcare settings. By reducing manual labor, administrative burdens, and cognitive overload, AI enables healthcare professionals to focus their time and expertise on higher-value activities that require human judgment, empathy, and critical thinking. From automating documentation and billing tasks to optimizing patient scheduling and resource allocation, AI-driven solutions improve operational efficiency, increase productivity, and enhance the overall quality of care delivery.

- **Cost savings:** AI implementation in healthcare can lead to cost savings by reducing errors, minimizing waste, and optimizing resource utilization. By improving operational efficiency, streamlining workflows, and preventing adverse events, AI-driven solutions help healthcare organizations achieve cost savings across various domains, including labor costs, administrative expenses, and healthcare utilization. Moreover, AI-enabled predictive analytics can identify opportunities for cost containment, risk mitigation, and revenue enhancement, contributing to the financial sustainability and long-term viability of healthcare organizations.

- **Enhanced decision-making:** AI-based decision support systems empower healthcare providers with real-time insights, evidence-based recommendations, and predictive analytics that inform clinical decision-making and improve patient care. By synthesizing vast amounts of clinical data, scientific evidence, and patient preferences, AI-driven decision support tools help clinicians make informed decisions at the point of care, leading to better outcomes, reduced variability, and enhanced patient safety. From diagnostic assistance to treatment planning and medication management, AI augments clinical expertise, facilitates shared decision-making, and optimizes care delivery across diverse clinical settings.

- **Remote monitoring and telemedicine:** AI-enabled remote monitoring devices and telemedicine platforms expand access to healthcare services, especially in underserved or remote areas where traditional healthcare delivery models may be limited or inaccessible. By leveraging AI technologies such as wearable sensors, remote monitoring devices, and virtual health platforms, healthcare providers can remotely monitor patients' health status, deliver virtual consultations, and coordinate care across care settings. This enables proactive interventions, early detection of health problems, and timely access to medical care, improving health outcomes and patient satisfaction while reducing healthcare disparities.

- **Innovation and research:** AI accelerates innovation in healthcare by enabling new approaches to medical research, drug discovery, precision medicine, and population health management. By analyzing large-scale healthcare datasets, AI facilitates data-driven discovery, hypothesis generation, and knowledge extraction that drive scientific discovery and innovation. From identifying novel drug targets to predicting disease trajectories and optimizing treatment responses, AI-driven research initiatives hold the promise of unlocking new insights into disease mechanisms, improving therapeutic outcomes, and advancing precision medicine approaches. Moreover, AI enables collaborative research efforts, data sharing initiatives, and interdisciplinary collaborations that foster innovation and accelerate the translation of research findings into clinical practice.

- **Population health management:** AI-powered population health management tools enable healthcare organizations to analyze population health trends, predict disease outbreaks, and target interventions more effectively. By leveraging AI algorithms such as machine learning, predictive modeling, and risk stratification, healthcare providers can identify high-risk patient populations, implement preventive interventions, and allocate resources strategically to improve health outcomes and reduce healthcare disparities. Moreover, AI facilitates proactive care management, care coordination, and community-based interventions that address social determinants of health and promote holistic approaches to population health management.

In conclusion, the challenges and opportunities associated with AI implementation in healthcare underscore the transformative potential of AI technologies to revolutionize healthcare delivery, improve patient outcomes, and drive innovation. By addressing challenges related to data privacy, bias, regulatory compliance, and ethical considerations, healthcare organizations can harness the power of AI to enhance clinical decision-making, optimize operational efficiency, and deliver high-quality, patient-centered care. Moreover, seizing opportunities for innovation, collaboration, and research in AI enables healthcare providers to unlock new insights, develop novel therapies, and advance population health initiatives that benefit individuals and communities alike. As AI continues to evolve and mature, its integration into healthcare ecosystems holds the promise of transforming the future of healthcare delivery and shaping a more sustainable, equitable, and effective healthcare system for generations to come.

Summary

This chapter provided a comprehensive overview of artificial intelligence and machine learning, illustrating their critical roles in transforming healthcare delivery. It explored how AI applications enhance diagnostics, personalized medicine, and operational efficiency in healthcare settings. The chapter also examined the challenges of implementing AI in healthcare, such as data privacy and integration hurdles, alongside the vast opportunities for AI implementation in improving patient care and clinical outcomes.

In Chapter 3, we will explore the integration of IoT technologies within healthcare systems. Chapter 3 discusses the components of IoT, its specific applications in monitoring, diagnosis, and patient care, and the benefits and challenges associated with leveraging IoT to enhance healthcare delivery and patient outcomes.

CHAPTER 3

Internet of Things in Healthcare

In Chapter 2, we delved into the fundamentals of artificial intelligence (AI) in healthcare, exploring its applications, challenges, and opportunities. This chapter shifts focus to the Internet of Things (IoT) in healthcare, introducing the concept of IoT, its components, and how it is revolutionizing healthcare delivery.

Introduction to IoT and Its Components

Internet of Things (IoT) refers to the network of interconnected physical objects, or "things," embedded with sensors, software, and other technologies to collect and exchange data over the Internet. These objects can range from everyday devices such as smartphones, wearable fitness trackers, and home appliances to industrial machines and infrastructure components.

The primary goal of IoT is to enable these objects to communicate, analyze data, and make intelligent decisions autonomously, thereby creating opportunities for increased efficiency, productivity, and convenience in various domains. IoT systems typically involve the integration of hardware (sensors, actuators), software (applications, analytics), and connectivity protocols (Wi-Fi, Bluetooth, RFID) to enable seamless data exchange and control (see Figure 3-1).

© Dr. Alok Kumar Srivastav, Dr. Priyanka Das 2024
Dr. A. K. Srivastav and Dr. P. Das, *Emerging Technologies in Healthcare 4.0*,
https://doi.org/10.1007/979-8-8688-1014-5_3

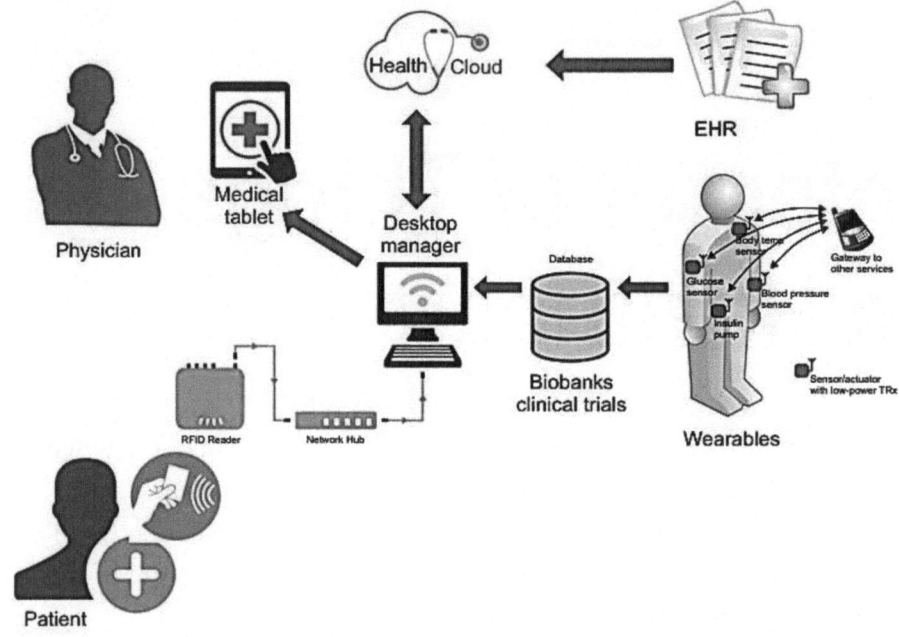

Figure 3-1. *Use case scenario of IoT in healthcare*

IoT has emerged as a transformative technology paradigm, revolutionizing various industries by connecting physical objects and devices to the Internet, enabling them to collect, transmit, and exchange data. The following are the key components of IoT, their functionalities, and their implications for different sectors:

- **Devices or things:** At the heart of IoT are physical objects or devices embedded with sensors, actuators, and communication modules. These devices come in various forms, ranging from consumer electronics like smart thermostats and wearable fitness trackers to industrial sensors and autonomous vehicles. Each device is equipped with sensors to detect changes in its environment and actuators to initiate physical actions based on the data collected.

- **Sensors and actuators:** Sensors play a crucial role in IoT by detecting changes in the environment and converting them into electrical signals. These changes can include temperature, humidity, light, motion, pressure, and more. Actuators, on the other hand, receive signals from the IoT system and initiate physical actions in response. For example, a smart thermostat may use temperature sensors to detect changes in room temperature and actuators to adjust the heating or cooling system accordingly.

- **Connectivity:** Connectivity is a fundamental aspect of IoT, enabling devices to connect to the Internet and transmit data. IoT devices rely on various communication technologies, including Wi-Fi, Bluetooth, Zigbee, Z-Wave, cellular networks (3G/4G/5G), and low-power wide-area networks (LPWANs) like LoRaWAN and Narrowband IoT (NB-IoT). The choice of connectivity depends on factors such as range, bandwidth, power consumption, and deployment environment.

- **Data processing and analytics:** IoT generates vast amounts of data from connected devices, which needs to be processed, analyzed, and transformed into actionable insights. Edge computing, cloud computing, and fog computing are utilized to handle data processing tasks efficiently. Machine learning and artificial intelligence algorithms are often employed to derive meaningful patterns, predictions, and optimizations from IoT data, enabling intelligent decision-making and automation.

Fog computing extends edge computing by processing data at an intermediate layer between edge devices and the cloud. It enables faster, localized processing, reduces latency, and eases the load on cloud infrastructure. By offloading tasks to nearby nodes, fog computing supports real-time insights and intelligent decision-making in large-scale IoT networks, complementing edge and cloud computing.

- **Gateways:** Gateways act as intermediaries between IoT devices and the cloud or central server. They aggregate data from multiple devices, perform preprocessing tasks, filter redundant information, and securely transmit data to the cloud. Gateways also facilitate communication between devices that use different protocols or standards, ensuring seamless interoperability within IoT ecosystems.

- **Cloud infrastructure:** Cloud platforms provide scalable storage, computing resources, and analytics tools for managing and processing IoT data. They enable real-time data streaming, historical data storage, remote device management, and application development. Cloud services also ensure data security, reliability, and accessibility for IoT deployments, empowering organizations to leverage the full potential of IoT technologies.

- **Security:** Security is a critical aspect of IoT to protect sensitive data, prevent unauthorized access, and safeguard devices from cyber threats. Encryption, authentication mechanisms, secure bootstrapping, firmware updates, and access control measures are

implemented to mitigate security risks in IoT systems.
Additionally, IoT security standards and best practices
are continuously evolving to address emerging
threats and vulnerabilities, ensuring the integrity and
confidentiality of IoT deployments.

- **Applications and services:** IoT applications
  encompass a wide range of use cases across
  industries, including smart home automation,
  industrial automation, healthcare monitoring, smart
  cities, agriculture, transportation, and more. These
  applications leverage IoT technologies to enhance
  operational efficiency, improve decision-making,
  optimize resource utilization, and enhance the overall
  quality of life. From remote monitoring and predictive
  maintenance to asset tracking and environmental
  monitoring, IoT offers innovative solutions to address
  diverse challenges and opportunities in today's
  interconnected world.

In conclusion, the key components of IoT form the foundation of a
connected ecosystem that enables seamless interaction between physical
objects, devices, and digital systems. By harnessing the power of sensors,
actuators, connectivity, data processing, and analytics, organizations
can unlock new opportunities for innovation, automation, and efficiency
across various industries. However, addressing challenges such as security,
interoperability, and scalability is essential to realizing the full potential
of IoT and ensuring its successful adoption and integration into existing
infrastructure and workflows. With continued advancements in technology
and collaboration across sectors, IoT promises to reshape industries,
transform business models, and improve quality of life for individuals and
communities worldwide.

Architecture of IoT

The architecture of the Internet of Things encompasses the underlying framework, components, and technologies that enable the seamless integration and communication of devices, sensors, and systems in interconnected ecosystems. This architecture is designed to facilitate the collection, processing, and exchange of data between IoT devices and applications, enabling diverse use cases across industries such as healthcare, manufacturing, transportation, agriculture, and smart cities. At its core, the IoT architecture comprises several layers that work together to enable the creation of scalable, secure, and interoperable IoT solutions (see Figure 3-2).

In the IoT architecture shown, the perception layer consists of three sublayers:

1. Perception Node Layer: Includes IoT devices like sensors and actuators.

2. Short-Range Communication Layer: Handles data transmission using protocols like Zigbee and Bluetooth.

3. Edge Computing Layer: Processes data locally before sending it to higher layers.

The communication protocols are part of the short-range communication layer, and the edge computing layer is separate but closely linked to the perception layer for local data processing.

The foundational layer of the IoT architecture is the perception layer, which consists of physical devices embedded with sensors, actuators, and communication modules. These IoT devices can range from simple sensors and actuators to complex smart devices such as wearables, industrial machines, environmental sensors, and connected appliances. Each IoT device is equipped with sensors to collect data from the surrounding environment, actuators to perform physical actions based on commands, and communication modules to transmit data over wired or wireless networks.

Above the perception layer is the network (or Internet) layer, which encompasses the communication infrastructure that connects IoT devices to each other, to edge gateways, and to cloud platforms. This layer includes various communication protocols and technologies such as Wi-Fi, Bluetooth, Zigbee, Z-Wave, cellular networks (3G/4G/5G), and LPWANs like LoRaWAN and NB-IoT. The choice of communication technology depends on factors such as range, bandwidth, power consumption, and deployment environment.

The next layer in the IoT architecture is the middleware layer, which serves as an intermediary between IoT devices and applications, providing essential functionalities such as data processing, protocol translation, device management, and security. Middleware platforms enable data aggregation, normalization, and transformation, allowing IoT data to be ingested, processed, and routed to the appropriate destination. These platforms also provide application programming interfaces (APIs) and software development kits (SDKs) for application development, device provisioning, and integration with third-party services.

The two middleware sublayers shown on the right in Figure 3-2 are:

1. Data Abstraction Layer: Responsible for abstracting the data, enabling easier access and integration across different systems.

2. Data Storage or Analytics Layer: This layer handles the storage of data and provides analytics services for data processing and insights generation.

The IoT Service and Application Layer comprises the software applications and services that utilize IoT data to deliver value-added services, insights, and functionalities to end users. These applications can range from consumer-facing applications for smart homes, wearables, and personal health monitoring to enterprise applications for industrial automation, asset tracking, predictive maintenance, and supply chain management. The IoT Service and Application Layer leverages IoT data to enable real-time monitoring, analytics, visualization, and decision-making, driving business outcomes and enhancing user experiences.

Another critical component of the IoT architecture is the edge computing layer, which extends cloud computing capabilities to the network edge, closer to IoT devices and data sources. Edge computing platforms enable data processing, analytics, and decision-making to be performed locally on IoT devices or edge gateways, reducing latency, bandwidth usage, and dependency on centralized cloud infrastructure. Edge computing is particularly useful for applications that require real-time responsiveness, offline operation, or compliance with privacy regulations.

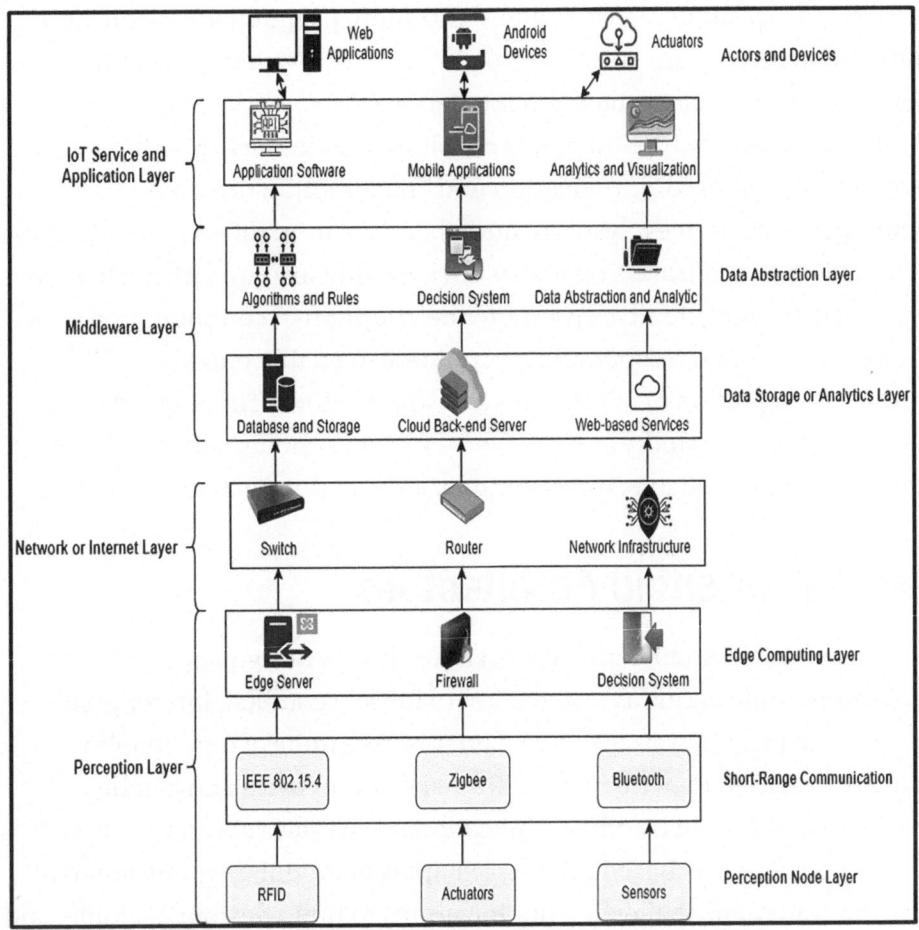

Figure 3-2. *IoT architecture diagram showcasing layers from perception to application, including devices, networking, edge computing, middleware, and data analytics*

Security is an essential aspect of the IoT architecture, spanning multiple layers to protect IoT devices, networks, data, and applications from cyber threats, unauthorized access, and data breaches. Security measures include encryption of data in transit and at rest, authentication and access control mechanisms, secure bootstrapping of devices, secure firmware updates, and intrusion detection systems. Additionally, privacy-preserving techniques such as anonymization, pseudonymization, and differential privacy are employed to protect sensitive user data and ensure compliance with data protection regulations.

Interoperability is another key consideration in the IoT architecture, enabling seamless communication and collaboration between heterogeneous devices, systems, and platforms from different vendors and ecosystems. Standardization efforts such as industry consortia, alliances, and open-source initiatives promote the adoption of common protocols, data models, and interoperability standards to enable plug-and-play integration of IoT devices and applications. These standards facilitate interoperability across diverse IoT ecosystems and enable the development of scalable, interoperable, and vendor-agnostic solutions.

Service-Oriented Architecture

Service-oriented architecture (SOA) is a software design approach that structures applications as a collection of loosely coupled, interoperable services. In an SOA, services represent discrete units of functionality that are designed to perform specific tasks or processes and can be accessed and reused by other applications or services over a network. This architectural style is based on the principles of modularity, reusability, and interoperability, allowing organizations to build flexible, scalable, and distributed systems that can adapt to changing business requirements and integrate with diverse technologies and platforms (Figure 3-3).

The image depicts an IoT architecture with four layers:

1. Sensing Layer: This layer consists of sensors that collect data from the environment, such as cameras, GPS, microphones, and heart rate sensors.

2. Network Layer: This layer is responsible for communication between devices and systems using protocols like Bluetooth, Wi-Fi, and cellular networks. It includes gateways that facilitate the transfer of data to higher layers.

3. Data Processing Layer: This layer involves processing units such as CPUs and GPUs, which handle data analysis, computation, and decision-making based on the collected data.

4. Application Layer: The top layer where applications utilize the processed data to provide user-facing services and insights, such as health monitoring apps, smart home systems, and vehicle tracking.

At the heart of SOA is the concept of a service, which encapsulates a unit of functionality and exposes it through a well-defined interface. Services in an SOA are typically implemented as self-contained components that can be deployed, invoked, and managed independently of other services. Each service performs a specific task or operation, such as processing a customer order, retrieving data from a database, or performing a calculation, and communicates with other services using standardized protocols and message formats.

One of the key benefits of SOA is its emphasis on modularity, which enables organizations to break down complex systems into smaller, more manageable components or services. By decomposing applications into modular services, developers can focus on building and maintaining discrete units of functionality, which can be developed, tested, and deployed independently. This modular approach simplifies development, maintenance, and scalability, as changes to one service do not necessarily require modifications to other parts of the system.

Another important aspect of SOA is reusability, which allows organizations to leverage existing services to build new applications or enhance existing ones. By designing services with well-defined interfaces and functionality, organizations can create reusable building blocks that can be easily integrated into different applications or business processes. This reusability promotes efficiency and consistency across the organization, as developers can leverage existing services rather than reinventing the wheel for each new project.

Interoperability is a fundamental principle of SOA, enabling services to communicate and collaborate with each other regardless of the underlying technology or platform. Services in an SOA are designed to be platform-independent and communicate using standardized protocols and data formats, such as Hypertext Transfer Protocol (HTTP), Simple Object Access Protocol (SOAP), Extensible Markup Language (XML), and JavaScript Object Notation (JSON). This interoperability allows organizations to integrate disparate systems, applications, and data sources, enabling seamless communication and data exchange across the enterprise.

Service composition is another key concept in SOA, which involves combining multiple services to create higher-level business processes or workflows. Service composition allows organizations to orchestrate and automate complex business processes by chaining together individual services in a coordinated manner. This approach enables organizations to streamline operations, improve efficiency, and respond quickly to changing business requirements by reconfiguring and adapting service compositions as needed.

Service discovery and registry are essential components of SOA, providing mechanisms for locating and accessing available services within an enterprise or across distributed networks. Service discovery allows clients to dynamically locate and invoke services based on their capabilities and interfaces, while service registries provide centralized repositories for publishing, cataloging, and managing service metadata and endpoints. These mechanisms enable organizations to discover, invoke, and reuse services effectively, facilitating the creation of dynamic and flexible service-based architectures.

Service governance is a critical aspect of SOA, involving the establishment of policies, standards, and processes for designing, deploying, and managing services within an organization. Service governance encompasses various activities such as service design, versioning, life-cycle management, security, monitoring, and performance management. By implementing robust service governance practices, organizations can ensure the quality, reliability, and security of their services and promote consistency, compliance, and alignment with business goals.

Security is another important consideration in SOA, as services often need to access and manipulate sensitive data or resources. SOA security mechanisms include authentication, authorization, encryption, and message integrity mechanisms to protect services and data from unauthorized access, tampering, and disclosure. Additionally, organizations may implement security policies, access controls, and audit trails to enforce security requirements and compliance with regulatory standards.

Scalability and resilience are inherent characteristics of SOA, allowing organizations to scale services horizontally or vertically to handle increasing workloads and ensure high availability and fault tolerance. By designing services with scalability and resilience in mind, organizations can deploy redundant instances of services, implement load balancing and failover mechanisms, and leverage distributed computing technologies to achieve robustness and performance.

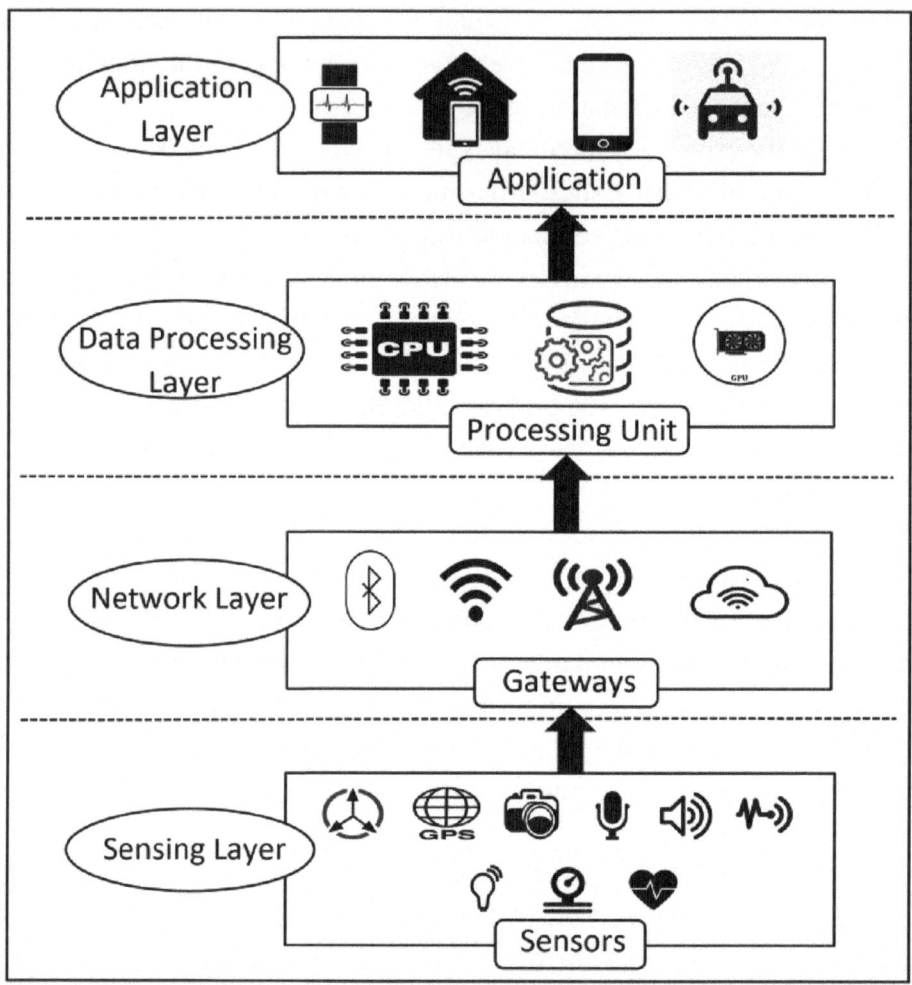

Figure 3-3. *IoT Architecture with Four Layers: Sensing, Network, Data Processing, and Application Layers*

In summary, SOA is a software design approach that emphasizes modularity, reusability, interoperability, and service composition to build flexible, scalable, and distributed systems. By decomposing applications into modular services, leveraging existing services, promoting interoperability, orchestrating service compositions, and implementing robust governance and security practices, organizations can realize the benefits of SOA and create agile, adaptive, and resilient architectures that can evolve and grow with changing business needs and technological advancements.

Table 3-1 provides a comprehensive overview of the advantages and disadvantages associated with implementing a microservices architecture.

Table 3-1. *Advantages and Disadvantages of Microservices Architecture*

Aspect	Advantages	Disadvantages
Scalability	Enables scalability by breaking down complex systems into smaller, manageable services that can be independently scaled based on demand. Allows for horizontal scaling, where additional instances of services can be deployed to handle increased load, providing flexibility in resource allocation.	Requires careful design and planning to ensure proper service decomposition and inter-service communication, as poorly designed services can lead to performance bottlenecks and scalability issues.

(*continued*)

Table 3-1. (*continued*)

Aspect	Advantages	Disadvantages
Flexibility	Offers flexibility in technology selection, as services can be developed using different programming languages, frameworks, and technologies based on individual requirements. Facilitates easier integration of new functionalities or updates without disrupting the entire system, as changes can be made to specific services independently.	Complexity can increase with a large number of services, making it challenging to manage and maintain the architecture effectively. Dependency on external services and APIs may introduce risks related to service availability, reliability, and versioning.
Reusability	Promotes reusability of services across multiple applications or business processes, reducing development time and effort. Allows for the creation of standardized interfaces and protocols, enabling interoperability between heterogeneous systems and facilitating integration with third-party services.	Overreliance on shared services may lead to dependencies and tight coupling between components, making it difficult to modify or replace services without affecting other parts of the system.

(*continued*)

Table 3-1. (*continued*)

Aspect	Advantages	Disadvantages
Agility	Enhances agility and responsiveness by enabling rapid development, deployment, and updates of services independently. Facilitates the adoption of DevOps practices and continuous integration/continuous deployment (CI/CD) pipelines, streamlining the software development life cycle and promoting collaboration between development and operations teams.	Managing service versioning and backward compatibility can become complex, especially when dealing with a large number of interconnected services. Testing and ensuring the overall system's stability may require additional effort due to the distributed nature of the architecture.
Maintainability	Simplifies maintenance and troubleshooting by encapsulating business logic within individual services, making it easier to identify and isolate issues. Allows for granular monitoring and logging of services, enabling proactive maintenance and efficient debugging of problems.	Over time, service sprawl and dependency management may become challenging, requiring robust governance and version control processes to ensure the stability and reliability of the architecture.

(*continued*)

Table 3-1. (*continued*)

Aspect	Advantages	Disadvantages
Interoperability	Facilitates interoperability between disparate systems and applications through standardized communication protocols such as RESTful APIs, SOAP, or message queues. Supports the integration of legacy systems and new technologies, enabling organizations to leverage existing investments while modernizing their IT infrastructure.	Ensuring seamless integration and data consistency across heterogeneous systems may require additional effort in designing and implementing robust data synchronization mechanisms. Differences in service interfaces and protocols can lead to compatibility issues and integration complexities.

Sensing Layer

The sensing layer, also known as the sensing tier or sensing network, is a fundamental component of IoT architecture. It refers to the bottommost layer in the IoT stack, responsible for capturing data from the physical world through sensors. The sensing layer serves as the interface between the physical environment and the digital realm, enabling the collection of real-world data for further processing, analysis, and decision-making in higher layers of the IoT architecture.

At the core of the sensing layer are various types of sensors and actuators that detect, measure, and interact with physical phenomena, such as temperature, humidity, pressure, light, motion, sound, and chemical composition, among others. Sensors convert physical signals or stimuli into electrical or digital signals, while actuators initiate physical actions or responses based on input received from the IoT system.

The sensing layer encompasses a wide range of sensor devices, including but not limited to

- **Environmental sensors:** These sensors monitor environmental conditions such as temperature, humidity, air quality, pollution levels, and radiation levels.

- **Motion sensors:** Motion sensors detect movement or changes in position, velocity, or acceleration and are commonly used for security, occupancy detection, and activity tracking applications.

- **Proximity sensors:** Proximity sensors detect the presence or absence of nearby objects or obstacles and are often used in robotics, automation, and smart devices for object detection and avoidance.

- **Biometric sensors:** Biometric sensors measure physiological characteristics such as fingerprints, facial features, iris patterns, and heart rate for authentication, identification, and health monitoring purposes.

- **Chemical sensors:** Chemical sensors detect and measure chemical compounds or gases in the environment and are used in environmental monitoring, industrial safety, and medical diagnostics.

- **Imaging sensors:** Imaging sensors capture visual or thermal images and videos using technologies such as cameras, infrared sensors, and Light Detection and Ranging (LiDAR) for surveillance, navigation, and remote sensing applications.

- **Positioning sensors:** Positioning sensors determine
  the location, orientation, or movement of objects
  in space using technologies like Global Positioning
  System (GPS), Radio Frequency Identification (RFID),
  and inertial measurement units (IMUs).

The data collected by sensors in the sensing layer is typically
transmitted to higher layers of the IoT architecture, such as the network
layer, for processing, analysis, and decision-making. This data may be
transmitted wirelessly or wired using communication protocols such
as Wi-Fi, Bluetooth, Zigbee, LoRaWAN, cellular networks, or Ethernet,
depending on factors such as range, bandwidth, power consumption, and
deployment requirements.

Overall, the sensing layer plays a critical role in enabling IoT
systems to perceive and interact with the physical world, facilitating the
capture of real-time data for various applications in industries such as
healthcare, agriculture, transportation, manufacturing, smart cities, and
environmental monitoring. By integrating sensors and actuators into IoT
solutions, organizations can gain valuable insights, automate processes,
optimize resource utilization, and enhance decision-making capabilities to
drive innovation and efficiency in diverse domains.

Table 3-2 provides an analysis of the benefits and potential challenges
associated with the implementation of real-time data sensing layers.

Table 3-2. *Advantages and Disadvantages of Real-Time Data Sensing Layers*

Aspect	Advantages	Disadvantages
Real-time data	Provides real-time data acquisition and processing, enabling timely decision-making and response to events or changes in the environment. Enables continuous monitoring of physical or digital systems, facilitating proactive maintenance and optimization.	Requires high-speed data processing capabilities to handle large volumes of data in real time, which may increase infrastructure and operational costs. Real-time data processing can introduce complexities in data management and synchronization, especially in distributed systems.
Improved accuracy	Enhances data accuracy by capturing information directly from the source, reducing errors and latency associated with manual data entry or batch processing. Minimizes data staleness and ensures the freshness of information, leading to more reliable insights and predictions.	Dependency on sensor reliability and accuracy can impact the quality of data collected, requiring regular calibration and maintenance of sensing equipment. Environmental factors such as noise, interference, and sensor drift may introduce inaccuracies and biases in the data, affecting the overall reliability of the sensing layer.

(continued)

Table 3-2. (*continued*)

Aspect	Advantages	Disadvantages
Cost efficiency	Reduces operational costs by automating data collection and eliminating the need for manual intervention or human resources. Enables resource optimization by focusing on relevant data acquisition, storage, and processing, minimizing unnecessary overhead.	Initial setup costs for deploying sensing infrastructure, including sensors, networks, and data storage, can be significant, particularly for large-scale deployments. Maintenance costs associated with sensor calibration, battery replacement, and network maintenance may accumulate over time, impacting the overall cost-effectiveness of the sensing layer.
Scalability	Offers scalability to accommodate growth in data volume and diversity, allowing for the seamless expansion of sensing capabilities as needed. Supports modular design and deployment, enabling the addition or replacement of sensors and components without disrupting the entire system.	Scaling the sensing layer may require careful planning and coordination to maintain system reliability and performance, especially in distributed environments with interconnected sensors. Achieving seamless integration and interoperability between heterogeneous sensors and networks can be challenging, potentially limiting scalability and hindering the adoption of new technologies.

(*continued*)

Table 3-2. (*continued*)

Aspect	Advantages	Disadvantages
Enhanced automation	Facilitates automation of data collection, processing, and analysis tasks, reducing manual effort and increasing operational efficiency. Enables the implementation of autonomous systems and IoT applications that can adapt to changing conditions and requirements in real time.	Overreliance on automation may lead to a loss of human oversight and control, increasing the risk of errors or misinterpretation of data. Security and privacy concerns related to automated data collection and transmission require robust safeguards to protect sensitive information and prevent unauthorized access or manipulation.
Environmental monitoring	Supports environmental monitoring and surveillance across various domains, including agriculture, healthcare, and industrial operations, enabling early detection of anomalies or environmental hazards. Facilitates data-driven decision-making in resource management, pollution control, and disaster response, leading to improved environmental sustainability and resilience.	Complexities in sensor deployment and calibration may arise in harsh or remote environments, posing challenges in ensuring sensor reliability and data accuracy. Limited coverage or accessibility in certain geographic areas may constrain the effectiveness of environmental monitoring initiatives, requiring strategic placement of sensors and network infrastructure.

(*continued*)

Network Layer

The network layer, also known as the communication layer or networking tier, is a pivotal component within the architecture of various systems, including the Internet of Things, where it facilitates the seamless exchange of data between devices, gateways, and cloud services. Positioned above the sensing layer and below the service layer, the network layer plays a crucial role in enabling connectivity, communication, and interoperability across distributed IoT ecosystems.

At its core, the network layer is responsible for managing the transmission of data packets between interconnected devices and systems within an IoT deployment. This layer encompasses a diverse array of networking technologies, protocols, and standards designed to address the unique requirements and challenges of IoT deployments, such as scalability, reliability, security, and resource efficiency.

One of the primary functions of the network layer is to establish and maintain communication pathways or network topologies that enable devices to exchange data reliably and efficiently. Depending on the specific requirements of the IoT application, various network topologies may be employed, including star, mesh, tree, and hybrid topologies, each offering distinct advantages in terms of coverage, scalability, and fault tolerance.

In addition to managing network topologies, the network layer is responsible for addressing, routing, and forwarding data packets between source and destination devices within the IoT network. This involves the assignment of unique identifiers, such as IP addresses or MAC addresses, to individual devices to facilitate end-to-end communication and data transmission. Routing algorithms and protocols, such as IPv4, IPv6, Routing Protocol for Low-Power and Lossy Networks (RPL), and Message Queuing Telemetry Transport (MQTT), are utilized to determine the most efficient paths for data delivery based on network conditions, traffic patterns, and quality of service (QoS) requirements.

Furthermore, the network layer encompasses a wide range of communication protocols and technologies that enable devices to transmit data over various wired and wireless communication channels. These include

- **Wireless protocols:** Wireless communication protocols, such as Wi-Fi, Bluetooth, Zigbee, Z-Wave, LoRaWAN, NB-IoT, and LTE for Machines (LTE-M), enable devices to communicate over short-range, medium-range, and long-range wireless networks, catering to different use cases and deployment scenarios.

- **Cellular networks:** Cellular networks, including 3G, 4G LTE, and emerging 5G technologies, provide ubiquitous connectivity and high-speed data transmission capabilities, making them ideal for IoT applications requiring wide-area coverage, mobility support, and reliable connectivity in remote or outdoor environments.

- **Wired networks:** Wired communication technologies, such as Ethernet and Power over Ethernet (PoE), and industrial protocols, like Modbus and PROFIBUS, offer reliable, high-bandwidth connectivity for IoT deployments in industrial automation, smart buildings, and infrastructure monitoring applications.

- **Satellite communication:** Satellite communication technologies enable IoT devices to transmit data over satellite networks, extending connectivity to remote or isolated locations where terrestrial networks may be unavailable or impractical, such as maritime, aviation, and rural areas.

- **Protocol gateways:** Protocol gateways or edge devices serve as intermediaries between devices using different communication protocols or standards, facilitating protocol translation, data aggregation, and interoperability within heterogeneous IoT environments.

In addition to enabling device-to-device communication, the network layer also facilitates communication between IoT devices and cloud-based services or edge computing resources. Cloud connectivity protocols, such as HTTP, MQTT, Constrained Application Protocol (CoAP), and Advanced Message Queuing Protocol (AMQP), enable devices to securely transmit data to cloud platforms for storage, processing, analysis, and visualization, enabling real-time insights, predictive analytics, and actionable intelligence.

Moreover, the network layer encompasses security mechanisms and protocols to safeguard data privacy, integrity, and confidentiality in IoT deployments. Encryption, authentication, access control, and secure communication protocols, such as Transport Layer Security (TLS), Datagram Transport Layer Security (DTLS), and Open Authorization (OAuth), are employed to mitigate security risks, prevent unauthorized access, and protect sensitive information transmitted over IoT networks.

In summary, the network layer forms the backbone of IoT architecture, providing the infrastructure and protocols necessary to establish and maintain connectivity, facilitate data exchange, and enable seamless communication between IoT devices, gateways, and cloud services. By leveraging a diverse array of networking technologies and protocols, organizations can build scalable, interoperable, and secure IoT solutions that unlock new opportunities for innovation, efficiency, and value creation across industries and domains.

Table 3-3 outlines the advantages and disadvantages of various aspects related to network connectivity and management at the network layer.

Table 3-3. *Advantages and Disadvantages of Network Connectivity and Management*

Aspect	Advantages	Disadvantages
Connectivity	Facilitates communication and data exchange between devices and systems within a network, enabling seamless interaction and collaboration. Supports various networking protocols and technologies, such as TCP/IP, Ethernet, Wi-Fi, and Bluetooth, ensuring compatibility and interoperability across heterogeneous devices and platforms.	Network congestion and bandwidth limitations can impact data transfer speeds and reliability, leading to delays or packet loss in data transmission. Vulnerabilities in network protocols and security breaches may expose sensitive information to unauthorized access or cyberattacks, compromising the confidentiality, integrity, and availability of network resources.
Scalability	Offers scalability to accommodate growth in network size and traffic volume, allowing for the expansion of network infrastructure and resources as needed. Supports dynamic allocation of network resources and load balancing techniques to optimize performance and resource utilization across distributed systems.	Scaling network infrastructure may require additional investments in hardware, software, and maintenance, increasing upfront costs and operational expenses. Managing network scalability can be complex, particularly in large-scale deployments with diverse devices, services, and geographic locations, requiring careful planning and coordination to ensure seamless operation and performance.

(continued)

Table 3-3. (*continued*)

Aspect	Advantages	Disadvantages
Reliability	Enhances reliability and fault tolerance through redundancy and failover mechanisms, ensuring continuous operation and availability of network services. Provides fault detection and recovery features to mitigate disruptions and minimize downtime caused by network failures or hardware/software issues.	Implementing redundant network components and failover systems can increase infrastructure complexity and cost, requiring ongoing maintenance and management to ensure effectiveness. Network reliability may be affected by external factors such as environmental conditions, power outages, and natural disasters, necessitating contingency plans and disaster recovery strategies.
Performance	Optimizes network performance through bandwidth management, QoS controls, and traffic prioritization mechanisms, ensuring efficient data transfer and response times for critical applications and services. Supports caching, compression, and acceleration techniques to improve data delivery speed and reduce latency in network communication.	Network performance may degrade under heavy loads or network congestion, affecting the responsiveness and throughput of applications and services. Ensuring consistent performance across distributed networks and diverse devices can be challenging, requiring ongoing monitoring and optimization efforts to maintain satisfactory levels of service quality.

(*continued*)

Table 3-3. (*continued*)

Aspect	Advantages	Disadvantages
Security	Enhances network security through encryption, authentication, and access control mechanisms, protecting data integrity and confidentiality against unauthorized access and cyber threats. Implements intrusion detection and prevention systems (IDPSs) to detect and respond to suspicious network activities and attacks in real-time, minimizing the risk of data breaches and network intrusions.	Maintaining network security requires continuous monitoring, patching, and updates to address emerging threats and vulnerabilities, increasing operational overhead and complexity. Security measures such as encryption and authentication may introduce performance overhead and latency in network communication, impacting the responsiveness and efficiency of data transfer.

(*continued*)

Table 3-3. (*continued*)

Aspect	Advantages	Disadvantages
Manageability	Simplifies network management and administration through centralized control and configuration tools, enabling efficient provisioning, monitoring, and troubleshooting of network devices and services. Provides network visibility and analytics capabilities to monitor traffic patterns, identify performance bottlenecks, and optimize resource allocation for improved operational efficiency.	Complex network configurations and heterogeneous environments may complicate management tasks, requiring specialized skills and expertise to maintain and troubleshoot network infrastructure effectively. Inadequate documentation and lack of standardized procedures can hinder collaboration and knowledge sharing among network administrators and stakeholders, leading to inefficiencies and potential errors in network management.

Service Layer

The service layer, also referred to as the application layer or service-oriented architecture (SOA) layer, constitutes a pivotal component within complex software systems, including enterprise applications, cloud platforms, and distributed systems. Positioned atop the underlying infrastructure and network layers, the service layer encompasses a suite of services, functionalities, and APIs that enable the implementation of business logic, data processing, and user interactions within the system.

In essence, the service layer acts as the interface between the underlying infrastructure and the end users or external systems, providing a set of well-defined services and endpoints for accessing and manipulating data, executing business processes, and delivering value-added functionalities.

At its core, the service layer is characterized by its modular, service-oriented architecture, where system functionalities are encapsulated into discrete, reusable services or microservices. These services are designed to perform specific tasks or operations, such as data retrieval, computation, transaction processing, authentication, authorization, and notification, independently of each other, fostering modularity, flexibility, and scalability within the system. By decomposing complex applications into smaller, manageable services, the service layer enables easier development, maintenance, and evolution of software systems, facilitating agility, innovation, and rapid response to changing business requirements.

One of the key principles underlying the service layer is service abstraction, which entails hiding the implementation details of individual services behind well-defined interfaces or APIs. This abstraction layer shields service consumers from the complexities of underlying systems, allowing them to interact with services in a standardized, uniform manner, regardless of the underlying implementation or technology stack. Service abstraction promotes loose coupling between services, enabling independent development, versioning, and deployment of services without impacting other parts of the system, thus fostering agility, interoperability, and resilience.

Furthermore, the service layer is characterized by its emphasis on service composition and orchestration, where multiple services are combined or orchestrated to fulfill complex business processes or use cases. Service composition involves chaining together multiple services to achieve a specific business goal or workflow, while service orchestration entails coordinating the execution of these services in a predefined sequence or workflow, often guided by business rules, policies, or workflows. Service composition and orchestration enable the

89

creation of flexible, adaptive, and customizable business processes that can be tailored to meet diverse user needs, regulatory requirements, or operational constraints.

In addition to service composition and orchestration, the service layer encompasses service discovery, registration, and invocation mechanisms that enable service consumers to dynamically locate, access, and invoke services at runtime. Service discovery involves the automatic detection and registration of available services within the system, typically facilitated by service registries, directories, or discovery protocols. Once services are discovered and registered, service consumers can invoke them using well-defined APIs or communication protocols, such as RESTful APIs, SOAP, gRPC (an open source framework that implements Remote Procedure Call), or messaging protocols like AMQP or MQTT, enabling seamless interaction and interoperability between services.

Moreover, the service layer encompasses a range of cross-cutting concerns and functionalities, including security, reliability, scalability, and performance optimization, that are essential for building robust, enterprise-grade software systems. Security mechanisms, such as authentication, authorization, encryption, and access control, are integrated into the service layer to protect sensitive data, prevent unauthorized access, and mitigate security threats. Reliability features, such as fault tolerance, retry strategies, and circuit breakers, ensure the resilience and availability of services in the face of failures or disruptions. Scalability techniques, such as load balancing, horizontal scaling, and auto-scaling, enable services to handle varying workloads and accommodate growing user demands efficiently. Performance optimization techniques, such as caching, data indexing, and query optimization, enhance the responsiveness and efficiency of services, enabling faster data retrieval and processing.

Furthermore, the service layer facilitates integration with external systems, applications, and data sources through well-defined integration interfaces and protocols. Integration adapters, connectors, and APIs enable services to interact with external systems, such as databases, legacy applications, third-party services, and cloud platforms, seamlessly exchanging data and invoking functionalities across heterogeneous environments. This interoperability enables organizations to leverage existing investments, integrate with external ecosystems, and extend the capabilities of their systems, fostering innovation, collaboration, and value creation.

In summary, the service layer serves as the backbone of modern software systems, providing a modular, scalable, and interoperable framework for implementing business logic, data processing, and user interactions. By encapsulating functionality into reusable services, promoting service abstraction, composition, and orchestration, and addressing cross-cutting concerns such as security, reliability, and scalability, the service layer enables organizations to build flexible, resilient, and adaptive software systems that meet the evolving needs of users, stakeholders, and markets.

Table 3-4 outlines the advantages and disadvantages of various characteristics of the service layer in software architecture.

Table 3-4. *Advantages and Disadvantages of Service Layer Characteristics*

Aspect	Advantages	Disadvantages
Abstraction	Provides a high level of abstraction, allowing users to interact with services without needing to understand the underlying complexities of implementation. Abstracts away technical details such as infrastructure management, protocol handling, and data storage, enabling simpler and more intuitive service consumption.	Overreliance on abstraction may lead to a lack of transparency, making it challenging to diagnose and troubleshoot issues that arise within the service layer. Complex service interactions and dependencies can obscure the flow of data and control, potentially introducing performance bottlenecks or vulnerabilities that are difficult to identify.
Encapsulation	Promotes encapsulation of functionality within individual services, enhancing modularity, and reusability. Allows for the isolation of services, reducing dependencies and promoting loose coupling between components, which facilitates easier maintenance and updates.	Excessive encapsulation may lead to service fragmentation and redundancy, making it difficult to manage and coordinate interdependent services effectively. Tight coupling between services can hinder flexibility and agility, as changes to one service may require modifications to multiple interconnected services.

(*continued*)

Table 3-4. (*continued*)

Aspect	Advantages	Disadvantages
Scalability	Facilitates scalability by distributing service functionalities across multiple instances or nodes, allowing for horizontal scaling to handle increased load and user demand. Supports elastic scaling, where resources can be dynamically allocated or deallocated based on workload fluctuations, ensuring optimal resource utilization and performance.	Achieving seamless scalability may require careful design and architecture to address challenges such as state management, session persistence, and load balancing across distributed service instances. Scaling individual services independently may result in resource imbalances or bottlenecks, impacting overall system performance.
Interoperability	Promotes interoperability between heterogeneous systems and technologies through standardized communication protocols and interfaces. Enables seamless integration with external services, APIs, and third-party platforms, fostering collaboration and ecosystem expansion.	Ensuring compatibility and compliance with diverse standards and protocols can be complex and time-consuming, requiring thorough testing and validation. Differences in service interfaces and data formats may introduce interoperability challenges, necessitating mediation layers or transformation mechanisms.

(*continued*)

Table 3-4. (*continued*)

Aspect	Advantages	Disadvantages
Fault tolerance	Enhances fault tolerance and resilience through redundancy, failover mechanisms, and error handling strategies. Supports fault isolation, where failures in one service do not propagate to other components, ensuring system reliability and availability.	Implementing robust fault tolerance mechanisms can introduce overhead and complexity, potentially impacting performance and resource utilization. Overreliance on redundancy and failover may lead to increased infrastructure costs and management overhead, requiring careful balancing of fault tolerance measures.
Security	Strengthens security by enforcing access controls, authentication, and encryption mechanisms at the service layer. Enables the implementation of security policies and enforcement points, protecting sensitive data and resources from unauthorized access or tampering.	Designing and implementing comprehensive security measures can introduce additional complexity and overhead, affecting system performance and usability. Overlooking security considerations may expose vulnerabilities and risks, leading to data breaches, privacy violations, or regulatory noncompliance.

(*continued*)

Interface Layer

The interface layer, also known as the presentation layer or user interface (UI) layer, constitutes a critical component of software systems, serving as the bridge between users or external systems and the underlying application logic and data. Positioned at the top of the software stack, the interface layer encompasses the user-facing components, functionalities, and interactions that enable users to interact with and manipulate data, access system features, and perform tasks within the application. In essence, the interface layer plays a pivotal role in facilitating communication, collaboration, and engagement between users and the underlying software system, providing intuitive, responsive, and accessible interfaces tailored to user needs and preferences. The interface layer typically is a separate layer from the application layer, though they are closely related and often interact with each other. The interface layer is responsible for communication and interaction, while the application layer focuses on the business logic and operations.

The interface layer is characterized by its focus on usability, accessibility, and user experience (UX), aiming to design interfaces that are intuitive, visually appealing, and easy to navigate for users across diverse demographics, skill levels, and devices. User interfaces may take various forms, including graphical user interfaces (GUIs), command-line interfaces (CLIs), voice interfaces, and conversational interfaces, each tailored to different use cases, user contexts, and interaction modalities. Regardless of the interface type, the interface layer prioritizes simplicity, consistency, and clarity in design, minimizing cognitive load and user friction while maximizing efficiency, effectiveness, and satisfaction.

One of the key functions of the interface layer is to present information and data to users in a meaningful and comprehensible manner, transforming raw data into actionable insights, visualizations, or representations that facilitate decision-making and problem-solving. Through data visualization techniques, such as charts, graphs, dashboards, and maps, the interface layer enables users to explore, analyze, and interpret complex datasets, trends, and patterns, gaining valuable insights into their data and making informed decisions. By presenting information in a clear, concise, and contextualized format, the interface layer enhances user understanding and engagement, empowering users to derive value from data and drive business outcomes.

Moreover, the interface layer facilitates user interaction and input through a variety of input mechanisms, including keyboards, mice, touchscreens, gestures, voice commands, and stylus inputs, accommodating diverse user preferences and accessibility needs. Interaction design principles, such as affordances, feedback, and error prevention, guide the design of user interfaces to ensure intuitive, responsive, and error-tolerant interactions that align with user expectations and mental models. Through thoughtful interface design, the interface layer enables users to navigate through application features, perform actions, input data, and receive feedback in a seamless, natural, and frictionless manner, enhancing user satisfaction and productivity.

In addition to presenting information and facilitating user interaction, the interface layer encompasses a range of user-facing features and functionalities that enhance the overall user experience and usability of the application. These may include navigation menus, search bars, filters, sorting options, bookmarks, notifications, alerts, and help documentation, among others, designed to streamline user workflows, assist users in finding relevant content, and provide guidance or assistance when needed. By incorporating these features into the interface layer, software applications can cater to diverse user needs, preferences, and usage scenarios, enhancing user engagement, retention, and loyalty.

Furthermore, the interface layer is responsible for adapting the user interface to different devices, screen sizes, resolutions, and form factors, ensuring a consistent and responsive user experience across desktops, laptops, tablets, smartphones, and other devices. Responsive design techniques, such as fluid layouts, flexible grids, and media queries, enable user interfaces to adapt dynamically to varying viewport sizes and orientations, optimizing content layout and presentation for different screen sizes and resolutions. Through responsive design, the interface layer maximizes accessibility and usability, enabling users to access and interact with the application seamlessly across a wide range of devices and contexts.

Additionally, the interface layer plays a crucial role in facilitating integration with external systems, services, and APIs, enabling interoperability and data exchange between the application and external ecosystems. Integration interfaces, such as RESTful APIs, GraphQL endpoints, or WebSockets, provide standardized communication channels for interacting with external systems, fetching data, submitting requests, and receiving responses. Through these integration interfaces, the interface layer enables seamless integration with third-party services, data sources, and platforms, enriching the functionality and capabilities of the application and extending its reach and impact.

In summary, the interface layer serves as the gateway for users to interact with and experience software applications, providing intuitive, engaging, and accessible interfaces that empower users to accomplish tasks, access information, and achieve goals effectively and efficiently. By focusing on usability, accessibility, and user experience, the interface layer enhances user engagement, satisfaction, and productivity, driving adoption and success of software applications in diverse domains and contexts.

Table 3-5 outlines the advantages and disadvantages of various characteristics of the interface layer in software architecture.

Table 3-5. *Advantages and Disadvantages of Interface Layer*
Characteristics

Aspect	Advantages	Disadvantages
Abstraction	Provides a simplified and standardized interface for interacting with underlying systems, services, or components, shielding users from complexity and technical details. Abstracts away implementation specifics, enabling users to focus on functionality rather than implementation details.	Overreliance on abstraction may lead to a lack of transparency and control, making it challenging to understand and debug issues that arise within the interface layer. Complex or opaque interfaces can hinder usability and adoption, requiring additional training or support for users to effectively navigate and utilize the interface.
Standardization	Facilitates interoperability and integration by enforcing standardized protocols, formats, and communication mechanisms. Enables seamless communication and data exchange between disparate systems, platforms, and technologies.	Enforcing strict standards may limit flexibility and innovation, constraining the ability to adapt to evolving requirements or emerging technologies. Differences in interface standards and compatibility issues may arise when integrating with external systems or legacy platforms, requiring mediation or translation layers.

(continued)

Table 3-5. (*continued*)

Aspect	Advantages	Disadvantages
Flexibility	Promotes flexibility and extensibility by decoupling the interface from underlying implementations, allowing for easy modification or replacement of components without affecting external consumers. Supports modular design and componentization, enabling the addition or removal of features without disrupting existing functionality.	Achieving a balance between flexibility and stability can be challenging, as frequent changes to the interface may introduce compatibility issues or disrupt existing workflows. Overly complex or customizable interfaces may confuse users and increase the learning curve, detracting from the overall user experience.
Adaptability	Enables adaptation to diverse user needs, preferences, and contexts by providing configurable options, customization capabilities, and personalized experiences. Supports user-driven design principles, allowing interfaces to evolve based on user feedback and changing requirements.	Providing too many customization options or configurations may overwhelm users and increase cognitive load, detracting from usability and simplicity. Adapting interfaces to accommodate diverse user needs may introduce complexity and inconsistency, making it challenging to maintain a cohesive user experience across different contexts or use cases.

(*continued*)

Table 3-5. (*continued*)

Aspect	Advantages	Disadvantages
Accessibility	Enhances accessibility by providing intuitive, user-friendly interfaces that cater to diverse user demographics, including individuals with disabilities or special needs. Supports compliance with accessibility standards and guidelines, ensuring equitable access to information and services for all users.	Ensuring comprehensive accessibility may require additional resources and expertise, particularly in designing interfaces that accommodate various assistive technologies and accessibility features. Overlooking accessibility considerations may result in exclusionary design practices and legal liabilities related to noncompliance with accessibility regulations.
Integration	Facilitates seamless integration with external systems, services, or APIs through well-defined interface contracts and integration points. Enables interoperability between heterogeneous systems and platforms, fostering collaboration and data exchange across organizational boundaries.	Managing complex integration dependencies and versioning conflicts can introduce challenges in maintaining compatibility and consistency across integrated systems. Overly tight coupling between interfaces and underlying implementations may hinder flexibility and scalability, limiting the adaptability of integrated systems to changing requirements.

The Internet of Things encompasses interconnected devices that collect and exchange data, transforming how healthcare providers monitor and manage patient health remotely. Exploring the components of IoT sets the stage for understanding its wide-ranging applications within healthcare systems.

IoT Applications in Healthcare

The Internet of Things has introduced transformative possibilities in healthcare, revolutionizing patient care, clinical operations, and medical research. By seamlessly integrating devices, sensors, and data analytics, IoT applications enhance diagnostic accuracy, streamline workflows, and facilitate remote monitoring, thereby improving patient outcomes and optimizing healthcare delivery. Figure 3-4 depicts the architecture of an IoT healthcare system, consisting of five key components. Product infrastructure includes the hardware devices and equipment used in healthcare, such as mobile devices and patient monitoring tools. Sensors are used to collect health data from patients or the environment, such as wearables or medical sensors. The application platform hosts and supports healthcare applications, allowing for seamless integration of the system. Analytics involves processing and analyzing data to derive meaningful insights, including descriptive, diagnostic, event-based actions, and predictive analytics. Finally, connectivity represents the communication infrastructure (e.g., Wi-Fi, Bluetooth) that ensures the devices and systems can connect and share data effectively. These components work together to enable real-time health monitoring, data analysis, and informed decision-making in the healthcare environment.

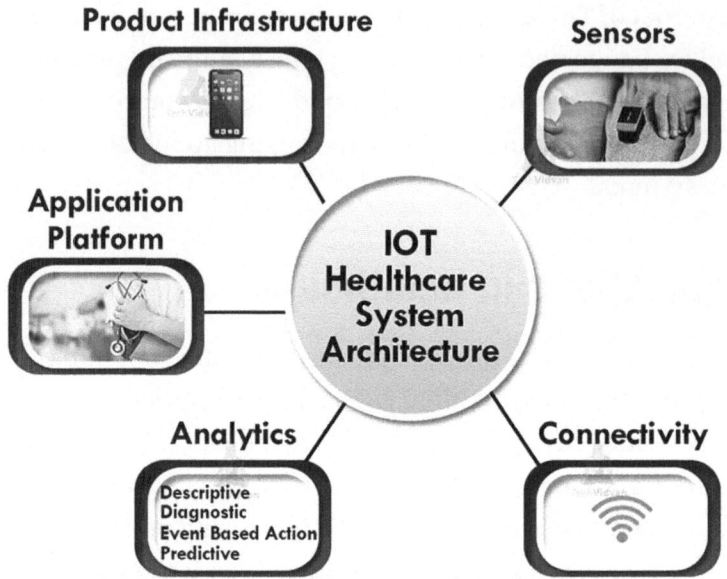

Figure 3-4. *IoT healthcare system architecture*

The diverse applications of IoT in healthcare and their impact on various aspects of the healthcare ecosystem are described in the following list:

- **Remote patient monitoring:** IoT-enabled wearable devices and medical sensors enable continuous monitoring of patients' vital signs, including heart rate, blood pressure, blood glucose levels, and oxygen saturation. These devices transmit real-time data to healthcare providers, allowing for early detection of health issues, timely interventions, and personalized treatment adjustments. Remote patient monitoring is particularly valuable for managing chronic conditions, such as diabetes, hypertension, and heart disease, by empowering patients to actively participate in their care and reducing the need for frequent hospital visits.

- **Telemedicine and virtual consultations:** IoT facilitates telemedicine services by enabling remote consultations between patients and healthcare providers through video conferencing, secure messaging, and virtual health platforms. Telemedicine platforms leverage IoT technologies to collect and transmit patient data, facilitate virtual examinations, and support clinical decision-making. This enables patients to access healthcare services from the comfort of their homes, especially in rural or underserved areas, while reducing healthcare costs and improving access to timely care.

- **Medication adherence monitoring:** IoT devices and smart medication dispensers help monitor patients' medication adherence by tracking medication usage, dosage schedules, and refill reminders. These devices provide notifications to patients and caregivers, alerting them to missed doses or medication errors. By promoting medication adherence, IoT solutions improve treatment effectiveness, reduce medication-related complications, and enhance patient safety, particularly for individuals with chronic conditions or complex medication regimens.

- **Remote diagnostics and imaging:** IoT-enabled medical imaging devices, such as portable ultrasound scanners and digital cameras, facilitate remote diagnostics and imaging consultations. These devices capture high-resolution images and transmit them securely to radiologists and specialists for interpretation and analysis. Remote diagnostic capabilities enhance access to specialized care, accelerate diagnosis timelines, and enable timely interventions, especially in remote or resource-limited settings where access to traditional imaging facilities may be limited.

- **Smart hospitals and healthcare facilities:** IoT transforms hospitals and healthcare facilities into smart environments by integrating connected devices, sensors, and automation systems. Smart hospital solutions monitor and optimize various aspects of facility management, including energy usage, asset tracking, inventory management, and environmental monitoring. By automating routine tasks, optimizing resource allocation, and improving operational efficiency, IoT enhances patient experiences, reduces costs, and enhances overall quality of care delivery.

- **Predictive maintenance and equipment monitoring:** IoT-enabled predictive maintenance solutions monitor the performance and condition of medical equipment, such as MRI machines, X-ray systems, and infusion pumps, in real time. These solutions analyze equipment data, detect anomalies or potential failures, and trigger proactive maintenance alerts to prevent downtime and ensure equipment reliability. By minimizing unplanned equipment failures and optimizing maintenance schedules, IoT improves clinical workflows, reduces operational disruptions, and enhances patient safety.

- **Health and wellness monitoring:** IoT devices and wearables facilitate health and wellness monitoring by tracking individuals' physical activity, sleep patterns, nutrition, and overall lifestyle habits. These devices provide personalized insights and actionable recommendations to promote healthy behaviors, prevent chronic diseases, and improve overall well-being. Health and wellness monitoring solutions empower individuals to take control of their health, make informed lifestyle choices, and engage in preventive care, leading to better health outcomes and reduced healthcare costs over time.

- **Elderly care and aging in place:** IoT technologies support aging-in-place initiatives by monitoring elderly individuals' health and safety in their homes. Smart home devices, such as motion sensors, smart door locks, and fall-detection systems, detect emergencies or changes in daily routines and alert caregivers or healthcare providers accordingly. IoT-enabled elderly care solutions enable seniors to maintain independence, receive timely assistance, and access healthcare services remotely, while providing peace of mind to caregivers and family members.

- **Clinical trials and research:** IoT facilitates data collection and monitoring in clinical trials and research studies by integrating wearable sensors, mobile health apps, and remote monitoring devices. These IoT-enabled solutions enable real-time data capture, patient-reported outcomes, and adherence monitoring, while enhancing participant engagement and retention. By streamlining clinical trial processes, improving data quality, and accelerating data analysis, IoT contributes to the advancement of medical research and the development of new therapies and treatments.

- **Public health surveillance and epidemiology:** IoT supports public health surveillance and epidemiological monitoring by collecting and analyzing data on disease outbreaks, environmental factors, and population health trends. IoT-enabled surveillance systems monitor environmental sensors, water quality sensors, and vector surveillance devices to detect early warning signs of infectious diseases, natural disasters, or environmental hazards. By enabling timely interventions, resource allocation, and public health response efforts, IoT helps mitigate health risks, protect communities, and enhance public health preparedness and resilience.

In conclusion, IoT applications in healthcare offer immense potential to revolutionize patient care, clinical operations, and public health initiatives. By leveraging connected devices, sensors, and data analytics, IoT enables remote monitoring, telemedicine, predictive maintenance, and personalized interventions, thereby improving patient outcomes, enhancing operational efficiency, and advancing medical research. However, realizing the full benefits of IoT in healthcare requires addressing challenges related to data privacy, security, interoperability, and regulatory compliance, while promoting collaboration, innovation, and stakeholder engagement across the healthcare ecosystem. With continued advancements in technology and strategic investments in IoT solutions, healthcare organizations can harness the power of IoT to deliver high-quality, patient-centered care and improve health outcomes for individuals and populations alike.

IoT applications in healthcare span remote patient monitoring, smart medical devices, and real-time health data analytics, revolutionizing care delivery and patient outcomes. With IoT poised to redefine healthcare, it's crucial to examine both the benefits it brings and the challenges it poses to healthcare stakeholders.

Benefits and Challenges of IoT in Healthcare

The adoption of IoT technologies in healthcare holds the promise of transformative benefits (such as those identified in Figure 3-5), but it also presents significant challenges. In this section, we'll explore the advantages and obstacles associated with implementing IoT in healthcare settings.

Figure 3-5 depicts the following benefits of IoT in healthcare:

1. Simultaneous Reporting and Monitoring: This allows healthcare providers to track patient conditions and receive real-time data for informed decision-making.

2. Improved Efficiency: IoT systems can optimize healthcare operations, reduce time spent on manual tasks, and improve overall workflow efficiency.

3. Patient Safety: By enabling continuous monitoring and alerts, IoT helps enhance patient safety, preventing potential health issues or emergencies.

4. Tele-Rehabilitation: This refers to using IoT devices for remote rehabilitation, allowing patients to perform recovery exercises at home while being monitored by healthcare providers.

5. Improved Patient Compliance: IoT systems can help patients follow prescribed treatments by sending reminders or tracking adherence to medical instructions.

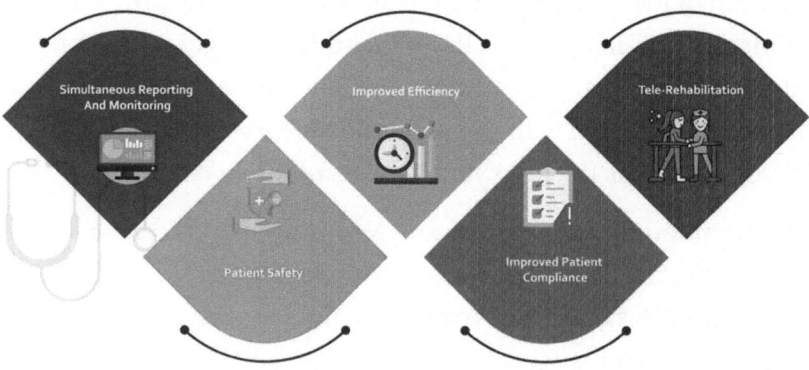

Figure 3-5. *Benefits of IoT in healthcare*

Benefits of IoT in Healthcare

The benefits of incorporating IoT in healthcare include the following:

- **Remote patient monitoring:** IoT enables continuous monitoring of patients' vital signs and health parameters outside of traditional clinical settings. This allows for early detection of health issues, timely interventions, and personalized care, leading to improved patient outcomes and reduced hospital readmissions.

- **Telemedicine and remote consultations:** IoT facilitates remote consultations between patients and healthcare providers, overcoming geographical barriers and improving access to medical expertise. Telemedicine services powered by IoT technologies enable timely diagnosis, treatment, and follow-up care, especially for patients in rural or underserved areas.

- **Improved chronic disease management:** IoT devices and wearables empower patients to actively manage chronic conditions such as diabetes, hypertension, and heart disease. By tracking symptoms, medication adherence, and lifestyle habits, IoT promotes self-management, early intervention, and preventive care, thereby reducing disease complications and healthcare costs.

- **Enhanced operational efficiency:** IoT optimizes clinical workflows, streamlines operations, and reduces administrative burdens in healthcare facilities. Smart hospital solutions monitor equipment usage, manage inventory levels, and automate routine tasks, improving resource allocation, minimizing waste, and enhancing staff productivity.

- **Data-driven insights and decision-making:** IoT generates vast amounts of data from connected devices, enabling healthcare providers to gain valuable insights into patient health trends, treatment effectiveness, and operational performance. Data analytics and machine learning algorithms analyze IoT data to identify patterns, predict outcomes, and inform clinical decision-making, leading to more informed, evidence-based care delivery.

- **Preventive care and wellness monitoring:** IoT facilitates proactive health monitoring and wellness management by tracking individuals' physical activity, sleep patterns, and overall lifestyle behaviors. By providing personalized insights and actionable recommendations, IoT encourages healthy behaviors, prevents disease onset, and promotes overall well-being, reducing healthcare costs and improving population health outcomes.

- **Real-time emergency response:** IoT enables rapid response to medical emergencies by automatically detecting and alerting caregivers or emergency services to critical events. Smart home devices, wearable sensors, and fall-detection systems monitor elderly individuals' safety and well-being, enabling timely assistance and reducing the risk of adverse outcomes.

Challenges of IoT in Healthcare

The challenges of incorporating IoT in healthcare include the following:

- **Data security and privacy:** IoT devices collect and transmit sensitive patient data, raising concerns about data security, privacy breaches, and unauthorized access. Ensuring the confidentiality, integrity, and availability of IoT data requires robust cybersecurity measures, encryption protocols, access controls, and compliance with data protection regulations such as HIPAA and GDPR.

- **Interoperability and integration:** Healthcare organizations often use a multitude of disparate systems, devices, and platforms, posing challenges for IoT integration and interoperability. Ensuring seamless communication and data exchange between IoT devices, electronic health records (EHRs), and clinical systems requires standardized protocols, interoperability frameworks, and collaboration among stakeholders.

- **Regulatory compliance:** IoT applications in healthcare are subject to regulatory requirements and compliance standards governing medical devices, data privacy, and patient safety. Navigating regulatory complexities, obtaining necessary approvals, and ensuring compliance with FDA regulations and industry standards can delay IoT implementation and increase costs for healthcare organizations.

- **Data quality and accuracy:** IoT devices may generate noisy or incomplete data due to environmental factors, sensor errors, or device malfunctions, impacting the reliability and accuracy of clinical insights derived from IoT data. Addressing data quality issues and implementing data validation mechanisms are essential for ensuring the integrity and trustworthiness of IoT-generated data in healthcare applications.

- **Scalability and infrastructure:** Scaling IoT deployments in healthcare settings requires robust infrastructure, network bandwidth, and cloud computing resources to handle large volumes of data generated by connected devices. Healthcare organizations must invest in scalable IoT architectures, edge computing capabilities, and network infrastructure to support growing IoT ecosystems and meet evolving healthcare demands.

- **User acceptance and adoption:** Healthcare professionals and patients may face challenges in adopting and integrating IoT technologies into their workflows and daily routines. Overcoming resistance to change, addressing usability concerns, and providing adequate training and support are essential for fostering user acceptance and engagement with IoT solutions in healthcare.

- **Cost and return on investment (ROI):** Implementing IoT technologies in healthcare involves significant upfront costs for device acquisition, infrastructure deployment, and system integration. Demonstrating the ROI of IoT investments, quantifying the value of improved patient outcomes and operational efficiencies, and securing funding for IoT initiatives are critical challenges for healthcare organizations seeking to justify and sustain IoT adoption.

In conclusion, while IoT offers immense potential to transform healthcare delivery, it also presents formidable challenges that must be addressed to realize its full benefits. By overcoming obstacles related to data security, interoperability, regulatory compliance, and user adoption, healthcare organizations can leverage IoT technologies to enhance patient care, improve operational efficiency, and drive innovation in healthcare delivery. With strategic planning, investment, and collaboration, IoT has the power to revolutionize healthcare and shape the future of medicine for years to come.

Summary

This chapter introduced the concept of IoT and its integral components, emphasizing its transformative impact on healthcare. It explored diverse applications of IoT in healthcare settings, from remote patient monitoring to smart medical devices, highlighting the potential to improve patient outcomes and operational efficiency. The chapter also addressed the benefits of IoT, such as enhanced data collection and patient engagement, alongside challenges like data security and interoperability issues within complex healthcare ecosystems.

In Chapter 4, we will delve into the synergistic relationship between AI and IoT technologies. Chapter 4 will explore how their integration enables real-time data analysis, enhances decision-making processes in healthcare, and anticipates future trends, particularly in the realm of telemedicine.

CHAPTER 4

Integration of AI and IoT in Healthcare 4.0

In Chapter 3, we explored the Internet of Things (IoT) in healthcare, examining its components, applications, and associated benefits and challenges. This chapter focuses on the powerful integration of AI and IoT in Healthcare 4.0, highlighting the synergies between these technologies and their combined impact on healthcare.

Synergies Between AI and IoT in Healthcare

Synergies between AI and IoT in healthcare refer to the complementary and mutually beneficial relationship between these two advanced technologies to improve healthcare delivery, patient outcomes, and operational efficiency.

AI involves the development of intelligent algorithms and systems that can analyze data, learn from patterns, and make decisions or predictions autonomously. As described in depth in Chapter 2, in healthcare, AI algorithms can process vast amounts of patient data, medical images, and clinical records to assist in diagnosis, treatment planning, and personalized medicine.

On the other hand, IoT refers to a network of interconnected physical devices embedded with sensors, actuators, and communication modules that enable them to collect, exchange, and analyze data. In healthcare, IoT devices include wearable sensors, medical devices, remote patient monitoring systems, and smart hospital infrastructure that collect real-time patient data and environmental information.

The integration of AI and IoT in healthcare creates numerous synergies, revolutionizing how medical services are delivered, monitored, and managed. Table 4-1 describes the synergistic integration of AI and IoT in healthcare applications.

Table 4-1. *Synergy Between AI and IoT in Healthcare*

Synergy	Description
Remote patient monitoring	IoT devices equipped with sensors can continuously monitor patients' vital signs, activity levels, and medication adherence. AI algorithms analyze the data collected in real time to detect anomalies or changes in health status, allowing for early intervention and remote healthcare management.
Predictive analytics for disease management	By integrating AI and IoT, healthcare systems can predict disease outbreaks, patient deterioration, or adverse events based on real-time data from IoT sensors. AI algorithms analyze historical patient data, environmental factors, and IoT-generated data to identify patterns and risk factors, enabling proactive interventions and personalized treatment plans.

(continued)

Table 4-1. (*continued*)

Synergy	Description
Personalized medicine and treatment optimization	AI algorithms process data from IoT-connected wearables, genetic tests, and electronic health records to generate personalized treatment recommendations based on individual patient characteristics, medical history, and real-time health data. This synergy enables healthcare providers to tailor therapies, dosages, and interventions to each patient's unique needs, improving treatment outcomes and minimizing adverse reactions.
Enhanced medical imaging and diagnostics	IoT-enabled medical imaging devices capture high-resolution images and transmit them to AI-powered analysis platforms. AI algorithms analyze imaging data to detect subtle abnormalities, assist radiologists in making diagnoses, and prioritize urgent cases. This collaboration accelerates the diagnostic process, improves accuracy, and enhances patient care in areas such as cancer detection, neuroimaging, and cardiovascular imaging.
Smart healthcare facilities management	IoT sensors deployed in healthcare facilities monitor equipment status, occupancy levels, temperature, and humidity. AI algorithms analyze this data to optimize resource allocation, energy consumption, and facility maintenance schedules. By automating routine tasks and predicting equipment failures, this synergy improves operational efficiency, reduces costs, and ensures a safe and comfortable environment for patients and staff.

(*continued*)

Table 4-1. (*continued*)

Synergy	Description
Real-time health monitoring and emergency response	IoT devices worn by patients or embedded in medical equipment transmit real-time health data to AI-driven monitoring systems. AI algorithms continuously analyze the data to detect signs of deterioration, emergencies, or adverse events. In case of emergencies, automated alerts are sent to healthcare providers, enabling rapid response and timely interventions to save lives.
Medication management and adherence	IoT-enabled smart pill dispensers, medication trackers, and wearable devices monitor patients' medication intake and adherence patterns. AI algorithms analyze the data to identify adherence barriers, predict medication adherence levels, and provide personalized reminders or interventions. This collaboration improves medication management, reduces medication errors, and enhances treatment adherence, particularly for patients with chronic conditions.
Health behavior analysis and intervention	IoT devices collect data on patients' behavior, activity levels, sleep patterns, and environmental factors. AI algorithms analyze this data to gain insights into patients' lifestyles, habits, and risk factors for chronic diseases. Healthcare providers use these insights to design personalized behavior modification programs, provide targeted interventions, and empower patients to adopt healthier habits and prevent disease progression.

These synergies demonstrate how the convergence of AI and IoT technologies in healthcare enhances patient care, improves clinical outcomes, and transforms healthcare delivery by enabling personalized, proactive, and data-driven approaches to healthcare management.

The convergence of AI and IoT in healthcare enhances data acquisition, analysis, and decision-making processes, fostering a new era of personalized medicine. Exploring these synergies lays the groundwork for understanding how real-time data analysis drives transformative changes in healthcare delivery.

Real-Time Data Analysis and Decision-Making

Real-time data analysis and decision-making are essential components of modern healthcare systems, enabling timely interventions, personalized care, and optimized clinical workflows (see Figure 4-1).

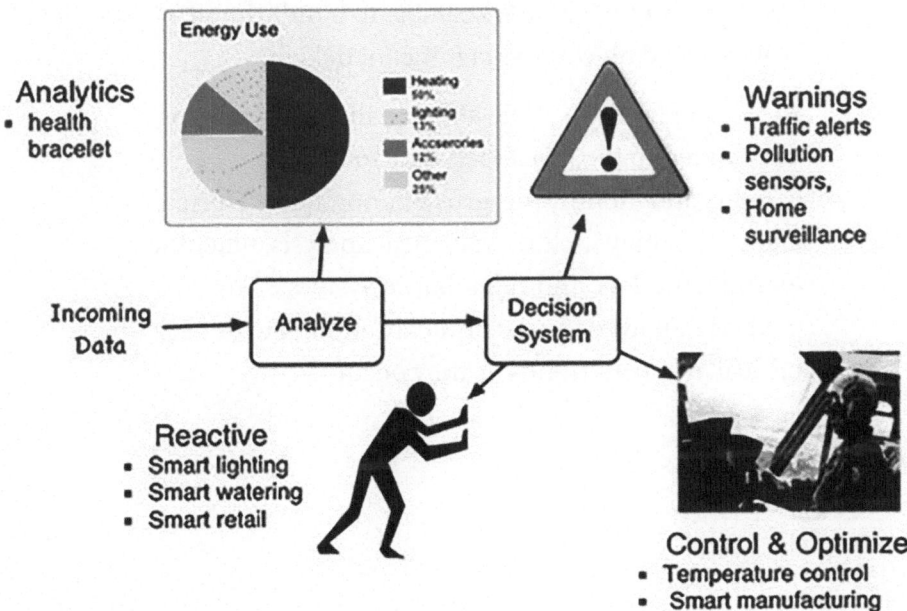

Figure 4-1. *Real-time data analysis*

Here's how these processes are implemented and the benefits they bring to healthcare:

1. **Data collection:** Real-time data analysis in healthcare begins with the collection of data from various sources, including medical devices, electronic health records (EHRs), wearable devices, sensors, and patient monitoring systems. These sources provide a wealth of information, including vital signs, lab results, medication records, patient demographics, and more.

2. **Data processing:** Once the data is collected, it undergoes processing to extract relevant information. This involves cleaning and preprocessing the data, filtering out noise, and transforming the data into a format suitable for analysis. In real-time applications, data processing needs to be efficient and scalable to handle large volumes of data without significant delays.

3. **Real-time analysis:** Real-time analytics algorithms are applied to the processed data to derive insights and identify patterns or anomalies. These algorithms may include statistical analysis, machine learning models, and rules-based systems. The goal is to analyze the data quickly enough to detect critical events or trends as they occur.

4. **Decision-making:** Based on the insights generated by the real-time analysis, decisions are made promptly to respond to changing conditions or events. In healthcare, these decisions can range from adjusting medication dosages to alerting healthcare providers to critical patient conditions, initiating emergency protocols, or recommending treatment options based on patient data.

5. **Automation and integration:** Real-time data analysis and decision-making often involve automation to streamline processes and reduce human intervention. Integration with other systems, such as EHR or communication platforms, ensures that decisions can be quickly communicated and acted upon by relevant stakeholders.

6. **Feedback loop and continuous improvement:** Real-time systems incorporate a feedback loop mechanism to monitor the outcomes of decisions and refine algorithms over time. This continuous improvement process ensures that the system becomes more effective and accurate in its decision-making capabilities.

In healthcare, real-time data analysis and decision-making offer several benefits:

-   **Early detection of medical emergencies:** Real-time analysis enables the early detection of medical emergencies or deteriorating patient conditions, allowing for timely interventions and improved patient outcomes.

- **Personalized treatment recommendations:** Real-time analysis of patient data enables personalized treatment recommendations based on individual patient characteristics, medical history, and real-time monitoring data.

- **Optimization of hospital operations:** Real-time analysis can optimize hospital operations, resource allocation, and patient flow, leading to improved efficiency and reduced wait times.

- **Improved clinical outcomes and patient safety:** Real-time analysis and decision-making contribute to improved clinical outcomes, patient safety, and quality of care by enabling prompt interventions and proactive management of patient conditions.

- **Enhanced efficiency of healthcare delivery:** Real-time analysis streamlines clinical workflows, reduces administrative burdens, and enhances the efficiency and responsiveness of healthcare delivery systems.

Overall, real-time data analysis and decision-making play a crucial role in enabling proactive, data-driven healthcare management, leading to better patient outcomes, enhanced efficiency, and improved quality of care.

Table 4-2 outlines the key advantages and disadvantages of implementing real-time data analysis in organizations.

Table 4-2. *Advantages and Disadvantages of Real-Time Data Analysis*

Advantages	Disadvantages
Immediate response: Real-time data analysis allows for immediate response to events or changes, enabling timely decision-making.	**Complexity:** Implementing real-time data analysis systems can be complex and require significant resources and expertise.
Enhanced accuracy: Real-time analysis reduces the risk of data becoming outdated or irrelevant, leading to more accurate insights and decisions.	**Resource intensive:** Processing large volumes of data in real-time may require substantial computational resources, leading to increased costs.
Proactive problem-solving: Real-time analysis enables proactive identification of issues or opportunities, allowing for preemptive problem-solving and optimization.	**Data quality challenges:** Real-time data may be subject to quality issues, such as incomplete or inconsistent data, which can affect the accuracy of analysis and decisions.
Improved operational efficiency: Real-time insights help optimize processes, resource allocation, and workflows, leading to improved operational efficiency and productivity.	**Overwhelming volume:** The sheer volume of real-time data can be overwhelming, making it challenging to identify relevant patterns or insights amidst the noise.
Competitive advantage: Organizations leveraging real-time data analysis gain a competitive edge by being able to adapt quickly to changing market conditions and customer needs.	**Potential for errors:** Real-time decision-making increases the risk of errors or misinterpretation of data, particularly if decision-makers act hastily without sufficient analysis.

(continued)

Table 4-2. (*continued*)

Advantages	Disadvantages
Enhanced customer experience: Real-time analysis allows organizations to personalize customer experiences, deliver targeted interventions, and address customer needs promptly.	**Security risks:** Real-time data processing introduces security vulnerabilities, such as the risk of data breaches or unauthorized access, if proper security measures are not in place.
Support for predictive analytics: Real-time data can be used to feed predictive analytics models, enabling organizations to forecast future trends, behaviors, or outcomes with greater accuracy.	**Regulatory compliance challenges:** Real-time data analysis may raise compliance concerns regarding data privacy, consent, and regulatory requirements, requiring careful management and governance.
Real-time monitoring and control: Real-time analysis facilitates continuous monitoring and control of systems, equipment, or processes, allowing for rapid intervention and adjustment as needed.	**Scalability issues:** Scaling real-time data analysis systems to accommodate growing data volumes or user demands can be challenging and may require infrastructure upgrades or redesigns.
Agility and adaptability: Real-time insights enable organizations to quickly adapt to market dynamics, emerging trends, or unexpected events, fostering agility and resilience.	**Cultural resistance:** Adopting a real-time decision-making culture may face resistance from stakeholders accustomed to traditional decision-making processes, requiring change management efforts.
Innovation and experimentation: Real-time data analysis encourages experimentation and innovation by providing immediate feedback on new ideas, initiatives, or strategies.	**Dependency on data quality:** Real-time decision-making relies heavily on the quality and reliability of data, necessitating robust data governance and quality assurance practices.

Real-time data analysis facilitated by AI and IoT enables healthcare providers to make informed decisions swiftly, improving diagnostic accuracy and treatment outcomes. Looking forward, the integration of AI and IoT in telemedicine heralds promising trends that are reshaping remote healthcare delivery and patient engagement.

Future Trends in AI and IoT Integration in Telemedicine

The integration of AI and IoT in telemedicine is indeed poised to revolutionize healthcare delivery, offering numerous opportunities for improving patient care, enhancing diagnostic accuracy, and increasing accessibility to medical services. Here's a closer look at the emerging trends shaping the landscape of AI and IoT integration in telemedicine:

- **Remote patient monitoring (RPM) advancements:** RPM solutions will continue to evolve, leveraging IoT sensors and wearable devices to monitor patients' vital signs, symptoms, and medication adherence in real time. AI algorithms will analyze this continuous stream of data to detect abnormalities, predict health trends, and trigger timely interventions, enabling proactive remote healthcare management.

- **AI-driven diagnostic imaging:** AI-powered diagnostic imaging solutions will become more prevalent in telemedicine, enabling healthcare providers to analyze medical images remotely with high accuracy and efficiency. IoT-enabled imaging devices will capture high-quality images, while AI algorithms will assist radiologists in interpreting results, diagnosing conditions, and prioritizing urgent cases, leading to faster diagnoses and treatment decisions.

- **Personalized telemedicine consultations:** AI-driven virtual health assistants will facilitate personalized telemedicine consultations by analyzing patients' medical history, symptoms, and preferences to provide tailored recommendations and treatment plans. IoT-connected devices will enable remote examinations, data collection, and diagnostic tests, enhancing the quality and convenience of virtual healthcare encounters.

- **Edge AI for real-time analytics:** Edge computing combined with AI algorithms will enable real-time analysis of IoT-generated data at the network edge, reducing latency and bandwidth requirements for telemedicine applications. This will facilitate faster decision-making, improved data privacy, and enhanced scalability for remote patient monitoring, diagnostics, and interventions.

- **Predictive healthcare analytics:** AI and IoT integration will enable predictive analytics models to forecast patient outcomes, disease progression, and healthcare resource demands. By analyzing historical patient data, environmental factors, and real-time IoT data, predictive models will help healthcare providers anticipate health risks, optimize treatment strategies, and allocate resources effectively, leading to better healthcare outcomes and cost savings.

- **Enhanced telemedicine security and privacy:**
  As telemedicine adoption grows, there will be an
  increased focus on cybersecurity and privacy measures
  to protect sensitive patient data transmitted over
  IoT networks. AI-driven cybersecurity solutions will
  detect and mitigate security threats, while blockchain
  technology may be utilized to ensure data integrity,
  authentication, and consent management in
  telemedicine transactions.

- **Telemedicine ecosystem integration:** AI and
  IoT integration will foster collaboration and
  interoperability among telemedicine platforms, EHRs,
  medical devices, and healthcare systems. Application
  programming interfaces (APIs) and standardized data
  exchange protocols will enable seamless integration
  of telemedicine services with existing healthcare
  infrastructure, facilitating information sharing, care
  coordination, and continuity of patient care.

These trends signify the growing convergence of AI and IoT
technologies in telemedicine, driving innovation, efficiency, and
accessibility in remote healthcare delivery. As these technologies continue
to mature, they hold the potential to revolutionize the way healthcare is
delivered, making high-quality care more accessible and personalized for
patients worldwide.

Table 4-3 outlines the key advantages and disadvantages of integrating
AI and IoT technologies in telemedicine.

Table 4-3. *Advantages and Disadvantages of AI and IoT Integration in Telemedicine*

Advantages	Disadvantages
Enhanced remote patient monitoring: AI and IoT integration enables more comprehensive and accurate remote patient monitoring, leading to better management of chronic conditions and early detection of health issues.	**Privacy and security concerns:** Integrating AI and IoT in telemedicine raises concerns about the privacy and security of patient data, particularly regarding data breaches, unauthorized access, and potential misuse of personal health information.
Personalized healthcare delivery: AI algorithms analyze patient data from IoT devices to provide personalized treatment plans and recommendations tailored to individual health needs and preferences.	**Data quality and reliability:** Ensuring the quality and reliability of data collected from IoT devices is essential for accurate analysis and decision-making, but IoT sensors may sometimes produce inaccurate or unreliable data, leading to erroneous conclusions or recommendations.
Predictive analytics for health trends: AI-driven predictive analytics models leverage IoT data to forecast health trends, disease outbreaks, or patient-specific outcomes, enabling proactive interventions and resource allocation.	**Integration challenges:** Integrating AI and IoT technologies in telemedicine requires interoperability between different devices, platforms, and data formats, which can be technically challenging and may require standardization efforts across the industry.

(continued)

Table 4-3. (*continued*)

Advantages	Disadvantages
Remote diagnostic imaging: AI-powered diagnostic imaging solutions enhance telemedicine by enabling remote interpretation of medical images captured by IoT-enabled devices, facilitating faster diagnoses and treatment planning.	**Ethical and legal considerations:** The use of AI and IoT in telemedicine raises ethical dilemmas regarding patient autonomy, consent, accountability, and liability, as well as legal issues related to regulatory compliance and liability in case of adverse outcomes.
Improved access to specialized care: AI-enabled telemedicine platforms provide patients in remote or underserved areas with access to specialized healthcare services and expertise that may not be readily available locally, improving healthcare access and equity.	**Technology reliability and connectivity:** Reliance on AI and IoT technologies for telemedicine introduces risks related to technology failures, network connectivity issues, or device malfunctions, which can disrupt healthcare delivery and compromise patient safety.
Cost savings and efficiency gains: AI and IoT integration in telemedicine can lead to cost savings by reducing the need for in-person consultations, hospitalizations, or unnecessary tests, as well as improving operational efficiency and resource utilization.	**Resistance to adoption:** Healthcare professionals and patients may resist adopting AI and IoT technologies in telemedicine due to concerns about job displacement, loss of human touch in healthcare delivery, or unfamiliarity with new technologies.

(*continued*)

Table 4-3. (*continued*)

Advantages	Disadvantages
Remote patient engagement and education: AI-driven virtual health assistants and IoT-enabled educational tools enhance patient engagement by providing personalized health information, self-care tips, and medication reminders, empowering patients to take an active role in their healthcare management.	**Digital divide and accessibility issues:** Disparities in access to AI and IoT technologies, such as limited Internet connectivity or digital literacy, may exacerbate existing healthcare disparities and widen the digital divide, particularly in marginalized or underserved communities.

Summary

This chapter explored the powerful synergies between AI and IoT technologies within healthcare systems. It elucidated how their combined capabilities enable real-time data analysis, facilitating more informed decision-making processes across medical contexts. The chapter also described anticipated future trends in AI and IoT integration, particularly emphasizing their transformative impact on telemedicine practices, aiming to enhance patient care accessibility and quality.

In Chapter 5, we will examine the critical importance of safeguarding healthcare data. Chapter 5 will delve into the regulatory landscape, discuss standards for data protection, and propose strategies to ensure robust data privacy amidst the rapid advancements of Healthcare 4.0 technologies.

Data Security and Privacy in Healthcare 4.0

In Chapter 4, we examined the integration of artificial intelligence (AI) and the Internet of Things (IoT) in Healthcare 4.0, focusing on their synergies, real-time data analysis, and future trends in telemedicine. This chapter shifts attention to the critical issue of data security and privacy in Healthcare 4.0, emphasizing the importance of safeguarding sensitive health information in an increasingly digital landscape.

Data security and privacy in Healthcare 4.0 refer to the measures and practices implemented to protect sensitive patient information and ensure the confidentiality, integrity, and availability of healthcare data in the era of digital transformation and advanced technologies.

In Healthcare 4.0, which encompasses the integration of digital technologies such as AI, IoT, big data analytics, and cloud computing into healthcare delivery, data security and data privacy are paramount due to the increased volume, complexity, and diversity of healthcare data generated and processed.

Data security involves safeguarding healthcare data from unauthorized access, disclosure, alteration, or destruction to prevent data breaches, cyberattacks, and privacy violations. Data security encompasses a range of

Dr. A. K. Srivastav and Dr. P. Das, *Emerging Technologies in Healthcare 4.0*, https://doi.org/10.1007/979-8-8688-1014-5_5

technical, administrative, and physical safeguards, including encryption, access controls, authentication mechanisms, network security, and security monitoring.

Data privacy refers to the protection of patients' rights to control the collection, use, and sharing of their personal health information. It involves ensuring that healthcare data is collected and used in accordance with applicable laws, regulations, and ethical principles, such as patient consent, data minimization, purpose limitation, and transparency. Data privacy measures aim to maintain patient confidentiality, trust, and autonomy while facilitating legitimate healthcare activities and research.

In Healthcare 4.0, data security and privacy are critical considerations given the interconnected nature of digital healthcare systems, the proliferation of electronic health records (EHRs), and the widespread adoption of IoT devices and wearable sensors. Healthcare organizations must implement robust security measures and privacy controls to protect patient data throughout its life cycle, from collection and storage to transmission and disposal.

Key aspects of data security and privacy in Healthcare 4.0 include

- **Secure data storage and transmission:** Healthcare organizations must ensure that patient data is stored securely in electronic systems and transmitted over networks using encryption and secure communication protocols to prevent unauthorized access or interception.

- **Access controls and authentication:** Implementing access controls and authentication mechanisms helps restrict access to sensitive patient information based on user roles, privileges, and authentication factors (e.g., passwords, biometrics) to prevent unauthorized disclosure or misuse.

- **Data encryption:** Encrypting healthcare data at rest and in transit protects it from unauthorized disclosure or tampering by converting it into a scrambled format that can only be decrypted with the appropriate encryption keys.

- **Security monitoring and incident response:** Continuous monitoring of IT systems, networks, and user activities enables healthcare organizations to detect and respond to security incidents, anomalous behavior, or data breaches in a timely manner to minimize the impact on patient data and operations.

- **Compliance with regulations and standards:** Healthcare organizations must comply with data protection laws and regulations, such as the Health Insurance Portability and Accountability Act (HIPAA) in the United States, the General Data Protection Regulation (GDPR) in the European Union, and industry standards for information security, such as the HITRUST Common Security Framework.

- **Privacy by design:** Incorporating privacy considerations into the design and development of healthcare systems, applications, and IoT devices helps minimize privacy risks and ensures that privacy controls are built into the architecture and functionality of digital health solutions from the outset (see Figure 5-1 for an example).

Overall, ensuring data security and privacy in Healthcare 4.0 is essential to protect patient confidentiality, maintain trust in healthcare services, and comply with legal and ethical obligations regarding the handling of sensitive health information in the digital age. By adopting a holistic approach to data protection and privacy management, healthcare organizations can mitigate risks, safeguard patient rights, and foster a culture of trust and accountability in the use of healthcare data.

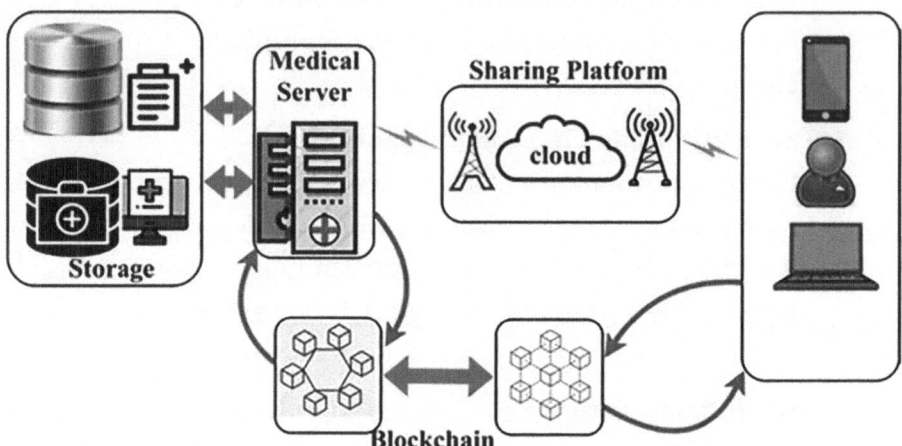

Figure 5-1. *Biomedical security system with blockchain*

Importance of Data Security in Healthcare

Data security is of paramount importance in the healthcare sector due to the sensitive nature of patient information and the potential consequences of data breaches. In this comprehensive analysis, we will delve into the following aspects of data security in healthcare, exploring the reasons why it is crucial and examining the measures and strategies employed to safeguard patient data:

- **Patient confidentiality:** Protecting patient confidentiality is a fundamental ethical principle in healthcare. Patients trust healthcare providers to keep their medical information private and secure. Breaches of confidentiality can have severe consequences, including loss of trust, embarrassment, and discrimination. We will discuss the importance of patient confidentiality and the legal frameworks, such as HIPAA in the United States, that mandate its protection.

- **Prevention of data breaches:** Healthcare organizations are prime targets for cyberattacks due to the valuable patient data they possess. Data breaches can result in significant financial losses, reputational damage, and legal liabilities. This chapter will discuss common cyber threats, such as phishing, and outline strategies for preventing and mitigating data breaches in the healthcare sector.

- **Protection against identity theft:** Medical identity theft is a growing concern in the healthcare sector, where stolen patient information is used to obtain medical services fraudulently. While this chapter focuses primarily on the regulations and standards for data protection, it also highlights the risks posed by medical identity theft and the importance of robust data protection measures in preventing such incidents.

- **Maintaining trust and reputation:** Trust is essential in the doctor–patient relationship and in the healthcare ecosystem as a whole. Data breaches and privacy violations can erode patient trust and damage the reputation of healthcare providers. We will discuss the importance of maintaining trust and transparency in handling patient data and strategies for rebuilding trust after a security incident.

- **Compliance with regulatory requirements:**
  Healthcare organizations must comply with various
  regulatory requirements and standards related
  to data security and privacy. We will examine key
  regulations such as HIPAA, GDPR, and other national
  and international laws governing data protection in
  healthcare. We will also discuss the implications of
  noncompliance and the steps organizations can take to
  ensure compliance.

- **Facilitation of research and innovation:** Secure
  access to healthcare data is essential for medical
  research, clinical trials, and healthcare innovation.
  We will explore the role of data security in facilitating
  research while protecting patient privacy and
  confidentiality. We will also discuss emerging
  technologies and methodologies for securely sharing
  and analyzing healthcare data for research purposes.

- **Prevention of medical errors:** Accurate and secure
  patient data is critical for providing safe and effective
  medical care. We will examine the role of data security
  in preventing medical errors, such as misdiagnoses
  and incorrect treatments, and discuss strategies
  for ensuring the integrity and reliability of patient
  information.

- **Cybersecurity preparedness:** Healthcare organizations
  must be prepared to defend against evolving cyber
  threats through robust cybersecurity measures and
  proactive security practices. We will explore best
  practices for cybersecurity preparedness, including
  risk assessment, employee training, incident response
  planning, and continuous monitoring and improvement.

By addressing these key aspects of data security in healthcare, organizations can effectively protect patient information, maintain trust, comply with regulations, facilitate research and innovation, prevent medical errors, and defend against cyber threats. Implementing a comprehensive data security strategy is essential for safeguarding patient data and upholding the highest standards of care in the healthcare sector.

Data security is crucial in Healthcare 4.0, where sensitive patient information must be safeguarded against unauthorized access and breaches. Understanding the importance of data security sets the stage for exploring the regulatory landscape and standards governing data protection in healthcare.

Regulations and Standards for Data Protection

In today's digital age, where vast amounts of sensitive data are collected, stored, and transmitted, regulations and standards governing data protection are essential to safeguarding individuals' privacy and ensuring the security of sensitive information. In sensitive sectors like healthcare, where the confidentiality and integrity of patient data are paramount, adherence to data protection regulations is particularly crucial.

Here, we will explore in depth some of the most prominent regulations and standards governing data protection in healthcare:

- **Health Insurance Portability and Accountability Act (HIPAA):**

    - HIPAA is a landmark U.S. federal law enacted in 1996 to address the security and privacy of protected health information (PHI).

- The Privacy Rule of HIPAA establishes standards for the use and disclosure of PHI by covered entities, such as healthcare providers, health plans, and healthcare clearinghouses.

- The Security Rule of HIPAA outlines administrative, physical, and technical safeguards that covered entities and their business associates must implement to protect electronic PHI (ePHI).

- HIPAA also includes provisions for breach notification, patient rights, and enforcement mechanisms.

- **General Data Protection Regulation (GDPR) (see Figure 5-2):**

  - GDPR is a comprehensive data protection regulation enacted by the European Union (EU) in 2018.

  - GDPR applies to organizations that process personal data of individuals within the EU and the European Economic Area (EEA), regardless of the organization's location.

  - GDPR imposes stringent requirements on data controllers and processors, including healthcare organizations, regarding data processing, consent management, data subject rights, data minimization, and security measures.

  - GDPR also mandates notification of data breaches and provides for significant penalties for noncompliance.

Figure 5-2. General Data Protection Regulation (GDPR)

- **Health Information Technology for Economic and Clinical Health Act (HITECH Act):**

  - The HITECH Act was enacted as part of the American Recovery and Reinvestment Act (ARRA) of 2009 to promote the adoption and meaningful use of health information technology (HIT).

  - HITECH Act strengthens HIPAA's enforcement mechanisms by expanding its scope, increasing penalties for non-compliance, and introducing breach notification requirements.

  - HITECH Act incentivizes healthcare organizations to adopt EHRs and other HIT systems to improve healthcare quality, efficiency, and security.

- **HITRUST Common Security Framework (HITRUST CSF):**

  - HITRUST is a nonprofit organization that developed the HITRUST CSF, a widely adopted common security framework for healthcare organizations.

  - HITRUST CSF provides a comprehensive set of controls and requirements aligned with various regulations and standards, including HIPAA, GDPR, and NIST Cybersecurity Framework.

  - HITRUST certification demonstrates an organization's commitment to data security and compliance with multiple regulatory requirements.

- **The NIST Cybersecurity Framework (CSF 2.0):**

  - The NIST Cybersecurity Framework is a voluntary framework developed by the U.S. National Institute of Standards and Technology to help organizations manage and improve their cybersecurity risk management processes.

  - The NIST Cybersecurity Framework provides guidance on identifying, protecting, detecting, responding to, and recovering from cybersecurity threats and incidents.

  - NIST Cybersecurity Framework is widely used by healthcare organizations to enhance their cybersecurity posture and align with regulatory requirements.

- **ISO/IEC 27001:**

  - ISO/IEC 27001 is an international standard for information security management systems (ISMSs) published by the International Organization for Standardization (ISO) and the International Electrotechnical Commission (IEC).

  - ISO/IEC 27001 provides a systematic approach to managing sensitive company information, including healthcare data, ensuring its confidentiality, integrity, and availability.

  - ISO/IEC 27001 certification demonstrates an organization's commitment to information security best practices and compliance with international standards.

- **Payment Card Industry Data Security Standard (PCI DSS):**

  - PCI DSS is a set of security standards designed to ensure the secure handling of payment card data by organizations that process, store, or transmit payment card information.

  - While primarily focused on payment card data security, PCI DSS may also be relevant to healthcare organizations that handle payment card information for services rendered.

  - Compliance with PCI DSS helps healthcare organizations mitigate the risk of data breaches and financial fraud associated with payment card transactions.

141

CHAPTER 5   DATA SECURITY AND PRIVACY INHEALTHCARE 4.0

- **Data protection laws:**

  - Various countries and states have enacted data protection laws governing the collection, use, and disclosure of personal data, including healthcare data.

  - Examples include the California Consumer Privacy Act (CCPA) in the United States, the Personal Information Protection and Electronic Documents Act (PIPEDA) in Canada, and the Data Protection Act (DPA) in the United Kingdom.

  - These laws impose requirements on organizations regarding data processing, consent management, data subject rights, breach notification, and accountability.

The implementation of robust data protection measures in compliance with these regulations and standards is essential for healthcare organizations to safeguard patient information, maintain trust, mitigate legal and financial risks, and uphold the highest standards of data protection and privacy. By adhering to these requirements, healthcare organizations can demonstrate their commitment to protecting patient confidentiality, ensuring data security, and complying with legal and regulatory obligations.

Aspects of the GDPR of Particular Relevance to Healthcare

General Data Protection Regulation (GDPR).

Transparency

Transparency plays a pivotal role in data protection regulations, particularly under the General Data Protection Regulation, which mandates that individuals have the right to understand how their personal data is being processed. This principle is especially crucial in the context of healthcare, where sensitive patient information is routinely collected, stored, and utilized for various purposes. To ensure compliance with GDPR requirements, healthcare organizations must provide clear and accessible information to patients regarding the processing of their personal data. This includes not only informing patients about the purpose and legal basis for processing their data but also addressing additional points outlined in the organization's privacy policy.

One effective approach recommended by the Data Protection Commission (DPC) is to make this information readily available to patients through summary leaflets and posters strategically placed in the admissions areas of hospitals and medical offices. These notices serve as a means to inform patients about how their personal data is being utilized, the purposes for which it is being processed, and their rights in relation to data protection. By providing concise and easy-to-understand summaries, patients can gain insight into the handling of their personal data without being overwhelmed by technical jargon or legal terminology.

The content of these summary leaflets and posters should cover essential aspects of data processing, including the purposes for which personal data is collected, the legal basis for processing, and any additional uses such as training, service evaluation, or clinical audit. Moreover, patients should be informed about their rights under the GDPR, including the right to access their data, rectify inaccuracies, and lodge complaints with supervisory authorities. Clear instructions should also be provided on how patients can access the organization's full privacy policy and whom to contact for inquiries or concerns regarding their personal data, typically the Data Protection Officer (DPO).

In crafting these summary materials, healthcare organizations must strike a balance between comprehensiveness and readability. While it is essential to convey key information accurately, the language and format should be accessible to patients of varying literacy levels and cultural backgrounds.

Visual aids, such as diagrams or infographics, can help simplify complex concepts, while plain language and clear headings enhance readability.

Furthermore, the placement of summary leaflets and posters in high-traffic areas of hospital admissions ensures maximum visibility and accessibility to patients. These materials serve as a proactive measure to inform patients about their data protection rights and foster trust between healthcare providers and individuals entrusting them with their personal information. By promoting transparency and accountability in data processing practices, healthcare organizations not only comply with regulatory requirements but also demonstrate a commitment to patient privacy and confidentiality.

In addition to the provision of summary materials, healthcare organizations should also ensure that patients have easy access to the full privacy policy, either through physical copies available upon request or via digital channels such as the organization's website. The privacy policy serves as a comprehensive resource detailing the organization's data protection practices, including data retention periods, security measures, and procedures for exercising data subject rights. By making this information readily accessible, patients can make informed decisions about their personal data and understand how it is managed throughout the healthcare process.

Moreover, healthcare organizations should designate a dedicated point of contact, such as the DPO, to address patient inquiries or concerns regarding data protection. Patients should be provided with clear contact information for the DPO, along with instructions on how to reach out for assistance or clarification on data-related matters. This ensures that patients have a direct channel for addressing any queries or issues regarding their personal data, further enhancing transparency and accountability in data processing practices.

In summary, transparency in the processing of patient personal data is a fundamental principle of data protection regulations, particularly under the GDPR. Healthcare organizations must take proactive measures to inform patients about how their personal data is being processed, including the purposes, legal basis, and additional uses such as training or clinical audit. Summary leaflets and posters placed in hospital admissions areas serve as effective tools for conveying this information in a clear and accessible manner. Additionally, patients should have easy access to the organization's full privacy policy and a designated point of contact for addressing data-related inquiries or concerns. By promoting transparency and accountability in data processing practices, healthcare organizations can build trust with patients and uphold their privacy rights in the healthcare setting.

Legal Basis for Processing of Special Categories of Personal Data

Under data protection legislation, the processing of personal data requires a legal basis, and the GDPR provides specific conditions for processing health-related data. These conditions encompass various aspects of healthcare, including preventive or occupational medicine, medical diagnosis, provision of healthcare, management of healthcare systems and services, contracts with health professionals, public health, ensuring high standards of quality of healthcare, and protecting the vital interests of the data subject. The latter refers to situations where processing is necessary to protect someone's life, especially when the individual is incapable of giving consent and no less-intrusive method is feasible.

When relying on these legal bases, organizations must implement "suitable and specific measures" to safeguard the fundamental rights and freedoms of patients. The Data Protection Act outlines several such measures, including limitations on access to personal data, strict time limits for erasure, targeted training for personnel, logging and verification mechanisms proportional to the risk to privacy, processing by healthcare practitioners or those bound by confidentiality, pseudonymization, encryption, and obtaining explicit consent from patients.

Consent plays a crucial role in data processing, as it must be freely given, informed, and unambiguous, reflecting an individual's wishes. Passive acceptance or failure to object does not constitute valid consent, and data controllers must demonstrate that consent was obtained legitimately. Moreover, individuals have the right to withdraw their consent easily, and data controllers must inform them of this right. Personal data should be retained only for as long as necessary and must be stored in a format that allows identification of data subjects.

To ensure compliance with these principles, organizations should establish robust data protection policies and procedures. Transparency is paramount, and patients must be provided with clear information about the processing of their personal data at the point of collection. Privacy policies should cover various aspects, including the purpose and legal basis for processing, as well as specific measures taken to protect patient rights. As previously discussed, the Data Protection Commission (DPC) recommends disseminating this information through summary leaflets and posters in hospital admissions areas, ensuring patients are aware of how their data is used and whom to contact with any queries.

Effective measures for safeguarding patient rights include restricting access to personal data, implementing time limits for data erasure, providing targeted training to personnel, and employing encryption and pseudonymization techniques. Consent should be actively obtained, ensuring individuals understand the implications and can withdraw consent if desired. Additionally, organizations should regularly review and update their data protection measures to adapt to evolving risks and regulatory requirements.

Overall, adherence to legal bases and appropriate data protection measures is essential for maintaining patient trust, ensuring compliance with regulations, and safeguarding individuals' rights to privacy and data protection in the healthcare sector.

Data Subjects' Rights

Data subjects' rights are significantly bolstered under the GDPR, affording individuals greater control over their personal data. For medical professionals, understanding and adhering to these rights are paramount, particularly concerning patients' rights of access and rectification and the right to be forgotten.

Firstly, patients possess the right of access to information regarding the processing of their personal data, as well as the right to obtain a copy of any personal data held by the data controller. This right empowers patients to understand how their data is being used and to verify its accuracy and lawfulness. The data controller is obligated to fulfill such requests within one month, with the possibility of a two-month extension if the request is particularly complex or extensive. This timeframe ensures timely access to information while allowing controllers sufficient time to gather and prepare the necessary data.

Secondly, patients have the right to rectify any inaccuracies in their personal data without undue delay. This right is crucial for maintaining the integrity and accuracy of patient records, ensuring that medical professionals have access to reliable information for effective healthcare provision. Prompt rectification of inaccuracies mitigates the risk of erroneous diagnoses or treatment decisions, promoting patient safety and well-being.

Additionally, the right to be forgotten grants patients the ability to request the deletion of their personal data held by the data controller. While this right is not absolute and is subject to certain conditions, such as the withdrawal of consent or unlawful processing, it nonetheless affords individuals greater autonomy over their data. Patients may invoke this right to safeguard their privacy, particularly in cases where data processing is no longer necessary or where consent has been revoked.

For medical professionals, ensuring compliance with these rights necessitates robust data management practices and transparent communication with patients. Data controllers must establish efficient procedures for handling access and rectification requests, including mechanisms for verifying the identity of data subjects and promptly addressing any inaccuracies or concerns. Moreover, controllers should maintain comprehensive records of data processing activities to facilitate compliance monitoring and demonstrate accountability.

Educating patients about their rights under the GDPR is also essential, fostering trust and transparency in the healthcare relationship. Informing patients about how their data is processed, their rights to access and rectify information, and the conditions under which data may be deleted empowers them to assert control over their personal information. Furthermore, healthcare organizations should provide accessible channels for patients to exercise their rights, such as online portals or dedicated contact points, streamlining the request process and enhancing user experience.

In conclusion, respecting and upholding patients' rights under the GDPR is integral to ethical and responsible data management in healthcare. By recognizing and facilitating patients' rights of access, rectification, and the right to be forgotten, medical professionals can promote patient-centric care, protect privacy, and foster trust in the handling of personal data. Compliance with these rights not only ensures legal adherence but also contributes to the delivery of high-quality, patient-centered healthcare services.

Data Controller Obligations

The obligations under the GDPR primarily rest with the Data Controller. For example, if a doctor is in private practice, they act as the Data Controller. In a hospital setting, the employer (e.g., the hospital) is the Data Controller. The Data Controller must ensure that appropriate technical and security measures are implemented within the organization. While healthcare organizations play a role in supporting compliance, individuals, regardless of their role, are still responsible for their actions in handling personal data.

Privacy Policy

As previously discussed, transparency is a fundamental principle of the GDPR, requiring organizations to provide clear and accessible information to individuals about the processing of their personal data. In a healthcare context, meeting transparency obligations to patients can be effectively achieved through the implementation of a comprehensive privacy policy. This privacy policy serves as a key document outlining the organization's data handling practices and ensuring patients are informed about how their personal data is collected, stored, and used.

A well-crafted privacy policy should be easy to read and concise, providing patients with essential information about various aspects of data processing. Firstly, it should detail the types of personal data collected and stored by the organization. In a medical context, this may include sensitive health information, demographic details, and contact information necessary for providing healthcare services. Patients should have a clear understanding of what data is being collected about them and why.

Furthermore, the privacy policy should elucidate the purposes for which personal data will be used. In addition to the primary purpose of providing healthcare, it may include the use of data for training healthcare professionals, conducting service evaluations, and clinical audits to improve the quality of care. Patients should be aware of how their data contributes to these secondary purposes and the safeguards in place to protect their privacy.

Additionally, the privacy policy should outline any potential categories of third parties with whom personal data may be shared. This could include healthcare providers, insurance companies, research institutions, or regulatory bodies involved in the provision or oversight of healthcare services. Patients should understand the circumstances under which their data may be disclosed and the measures taken to ensure confidentiality and security.

The criteria used to determine the data retention period should also be transparently communicated in the privacy policy. Patients should know how long their data will be retained and the rationale behind these retention periods. This helps manage patient expectations and ensures compliance with legal requirements while minimizing the risk of unnecessary data retention.

Moreover, the privacy policy must specify the legal basis for processing personal data. This could include consent, contractual necessity, compliance with legal obligations, or legitimate interests pursued by the organization. Patients have the right to know the legal grounds on which their data is being processed and the implications of each basis for their privacy rights.

The privacy policy should also comprehensively outline data subjects' rights under the GDPR. This includes rights such as the right of access, rectification, erasure, restriction of processing, data portability, and the right to object to processing. Patients should be informed of their rights and provided with guidance on how to exercise them effectively.

Furthermore, the privacy policy should prominently feature the contact details of the data controller, typically the healthcare organization responsible for data processing activities. Additionally, it should include the name and contact details of the Data Protection Officer (DPO), who serves as a point of contact for privacy-related inquiries and ensures compliance with data protection regulations. Patients should know whom to contact if they have questions or concerns about the handling of their personal data.

In line with GDPR transparency obligations, as previously mentioned, the DPC recommends making the privacy policy freely available to patients in short format, such as posters or leaflets in waiting rooms, as well as on the hospital website. This short format should include basic information about data processing practices, how to access the full privacy policy, and the contact details of the DPO. By providing patients with accessible and understandable information about their privacy rights and data processing practices, healthcare organizations can foster trust, promote transparency, and uphold compliance with data protection regulations.

Records of Processing Activities

In healthcare settings, data controllers are obligated to maintain comprehensive records of processing activities to ensure compliance with data protection regulations, particularly under the GDPR. These records serve as a vital tool for documenting and managing data processing activities within the organization. The key components of records of processing activities include the following:

- **Name and contact details:** This section should include the name and contact details of the data controller, typically the healthcare organization responsible for determining the purposes and means of processing personal data. Additionally, the contact details of the DPO, who oversees data protection compliance within the organization, should be provided.

- **Categories of data subjects:** Data controllers must document the categories of individuals whose personal data is processed within the organization. In a healthcare setting, this may include patients, healthcare professionals, administrative staff, and other individuals involved in the provision of healthcare services.

- **Categories of personal data:** This component entails categorizing the types of personal data processed by the organization. In healthcare, this may encompass sensitive health information, demographic data, contact details, medical history, diagnostic records, and other relevant information necessary for providing healthcare services.

- **Purposes of processing:** Data controllers must specify the purposes for which personal data is processed within the organization. This may include purposes such as providing healthcare services, managing patient records, conducting research, billing and administrative purposes, and complying with legal obligations.

- **Categories of recipients:** Documentation should detail the categories of recipients to whom personal data is disclosed or will be disclosed. Recipients may include healthcare professionals, insurance providers, regulatory authorities, research institutions, and other entities involved in the provision or oversight of healthcare services.

- **Transfer of personal data to third countries:** If personal data is transferred to countries outside the European Economic Area (EEA), data controllers must document details of such transfers and the measures in place to ensure the protection of personal data. This includes documenting any safeguards implemented, such as standard contractual clauses or binding corporate rules.

- **Technical and organizational security measures:**
  Data controllers are required to provide a general
  description of the technical and organizational security
  measures implemented to protect personal data
  against unauthorized access, disclosure, alteration,
  or destruction. This may include measures such
  as encryption, access controls, regular security
  assessments, staff training, and incident response
  procedures.

Maintaining accurate and up-to-date records of processing activities is
essential for demonstrating compliance with data protection regulations,
facilitating accountability, and ensuring the protection of individuals'
rights to privacy and data protection. By documenting key aspects of data
processing activities, healthcare organizations can effectively manage
risks, respond to regulatory inquiries, and build trust with patients and
stakeholders.

Data Processing Contracts

When a data processor is engaged to support healthcare provision
activities, it is imperative to establish a contract between the data
controller (typically the healthcare organization) and the service provider
(the data processor). This contract serves to delineate the terms and
conditions of the data processing arrangement, ensuring compliance with
data protection regulations and safeguarding the rights of data subjects.
The contract should include the following key elements:

- **Subject matter and duration of processing:** The contract should clearly define the subject matter, outlining the specific services or activities that the data processor will undertake on behalf of the data controller. Additionally, it should specify the duration of the processing, including the start and end dates of the contract or any provisions for renewal or termination.

- **Nature and purpose of processing:** It is essential to articulate the nature and purpose of the processing activities that the data processor will perform. This involves detailing the specific tasks, operations, or functions that the data processor will carry out with regard to the personal data entrusted to them by the data controller. For example, the processing activities may include data storage, analysis, maintenance, or transmission necessary to support healthcare provision.

- **Type of personal data and categories of data subjects:** The contract should identify the types of personal data that will be processed by the data processor on behalf of the data controller. This includes specifying the categories of data subjects whose personal data will be processed, such as patients, healthcare professionals, or administrative staff. Clearly defining the scope of personal data ensures that both parties have a mutual understanding of their obligations and responsibilities.

- **Obligations and rights of the data controller:** The contract should delineate the respective obligations and rights of the data controller and the data processor. This may include specifying the data controller's obligation to provide instructions to the data processor regarding data processing activities, adherence to data protection principles and regulations, and the right to monitor and audit the data processor's compliance with the contract and applicable laws. Additionally, the contract should outline the data processor's obligations to implement appropriate technical and organizational measures to ensure the security and confidentiality of personal data, comply with instructions from the data controller, and notify the data controller of any data breaches or incidents promptly.

By incorporating these essential elements into the contract between the data controller and the data processor, healthcare organizations can establish a clear framework for data processing activities, mitigate risks, and ensure accountability and compliance with data protection laws. This contractual agreement serves to protect the interests of data subjects, maintain the integrity and confidentiality of personal data, and foster trust and transparency in data processing practices within the healthcare sector.

Data Protection Officer

Healthcare organizations, due to the nature of their core activities involving the processing of data concerning health, are mandated to appoint a Data Protection Officer under the GDPR. The DPO plays a crucial role in ensuring compliance with data protection laws and regulations, as well as safeguarding the rights and interests of data subjects. The responsibilities of the DPO include

- **Monitoring internal compliance:** The DPO is tasked with monitoring the organization's internal compliance with data protection laws and regulations. This involves conducting regular assessments and audits to ensure that data processing activities adhere to legal requirements and organizational policies.

- **Ensuring staff training on data protection:** The DPO is responsible for ensuring that staff members receive adequate training and education on data protection principles, regulations, and best practices. This includes raising awareness about privacy risks, implementing security measures, and promoting a culture of data protection within the organization.

- **Supporting data protection impact assessments (DPIAs):** DPIAs are conducted to assess and mitigate privacy risks associated with new projects, systems, or processes involving the processing of personal data. The DPO plays a key role in supporting and facilitating DPIAs, providing expertise and guidance on privacy considerations and compliance requirements.

- **Advising on data protection obligations:** The DPO advises the organization on its data protection obligations, including those specific to healthcare settings. This may involve providing guidance on legal requirements related to health research, patient confidentiality, data sharing, and consent management.

- **Acting as a contact point for data subjects and the Data Protection Commission:** The DPO serves as the primary point of contact for data subjects (i.e., individuals whose personal data is processed) and the DPC (or relevant supervisory authority). Data subjects can reach out to the DPO to exercise their rights under data protection laws, seek clarification on data processing practices, or raise concerns about privacy issues. Similarly, the DPO liaises with the DPC regarding regulatory matters, data breaches, and compliance inquiries.

Importantly, the DPO is bound by secrecy and confidentiality obligations, ensuring the protection of personal data and sensitive information. As such, the DPO should be granted access to personal data and be actively involved in all aspects of data protection within the organization. This includes participating in decision-making processes related to data processing, providing guidance on privacy-enhancing measures, and ensuring that privacy considerations are integrated into business operations and strategies.

Overall, the role of the DPO is critical in promoting accountability, transparency, and trust in data processing activities within healthcare organizations. By fulfilling their responsibilities effectively, DPOs contribute to the protection of individuals' privacy rights, the prevention of data breaches, and the establishment of a robust data protection framework that aligns with legal requirements and ethical standards.

Security Obligations

Data controllers and data processors in healthcare settings bear a significant responsibility to implement robust technical and organizational measures to safeguard patient personal data in accordance with the

GDPR. Recognizing the unique sensitivity and confidentiality of health data, the DPC recommends specific security measures tailored to the healthcare sector to mitigate risks and protect patient privacy.

One key measure is *pseudonymization*, a technique that involves replacing identifying information with pseudonyms to prevent direct association with an individual. By pseudonymizing patient data, healthcare organizations can minimize the risk of unauthorized access or disclosure while still allowing for effective data processing for medical purposes. Additionally, encryption is essential for securing data both at rest and in transit, ensuring that only authorized individuals can access and decipher sensitive information. Encryption techniques, such as end-to-end encryption for electronic communications and data encryption for storage, provide an extra layer of protection against data breaches and unauthorized access.

Physical security measures are also crucial in healthcare settings to prevent unauthorized access to restricted areas and sensitive patient information. Secure door access systems, including keycard or biometric entry systems, limit access to designated areas, such as patient records rooms or laboratories, to authorized personnel only. Regular reviews of swipe card access every six months help ensure that access permissions are up-to-date and aligned with staff roles and responsibilities. Similarly, changing key codes periodically strengthens security by reducing the risk of unauthorized entry through compromised codes or keys.

Moreover, organizational measures play a vital role in enhancing data security within healthcare organizations. Implementing policies and procedures that promote secure data handling practices is essential, such as setting computers to lock automatically after a period of inactivity to prevent unauthorized access in shared work environments. Prohibiting the sharing of user accounts to access personal data maintains accountability and traceability of data access and usage, reducing the risk of data breaches due to unauthorized access or misuse.

Physical documents containing personal data, such as patient records or medical charts, must also be securely managed to prevent loss, theft, or unauthorized disclosure. Securely locking filing cabinets used to store personal data and implementing protocols to avoid patients carrying medical charts from one part of a hospital to another help minimize the risk of physical data breaches and ensure confidentiality.

Regular information security audits are essential to evaluate the effectiveness of implemented security measures and identify any vulnerabilities or areas for improvement. By conducting periodic assessments, healthcare organizations can proactively identify and address security risks, enhance data protection practices, and maintain compliance with regulatory requirements. Information security audits provide assurance to patients and stakeholders that appropriate measures are in place to protect their personal data and uphold their privacy rights.

In conclusion, the implementation of appropriate technical and organizational security measures is imperative for healthcare organizations to protect patient personal data and mitigate risks of data breaches. By adhering to recommendations from the DPC and undertaking regular security audits, healthcare organizations can enhance data security, maintain patient trust, and uphold compliance with data protection regulations. Effective security measures not only protect patient privacy but also contribute to the overall integrity and quality of healthcare services.

Data Breach Notifications

Data breach notifications are a critical aspect of data protection management, particularly in healthcare settings, where the confidentiality and integrity of patient personal data are paramount. A personal data breach refers to any breach of security resulting in the accidental or unlawful disclosure, alteration, loss, or destruction of personal data. Given the sensitive nature of health data, breaches involving patient information can have serious implications for individuals' privacy rights and must be addressed promptly and effectively.

Under the GDPR, healthcare organizations are obligated to report personal data breaches to the DPC if the breach poses any risk to the privacy rights of patients. Moreover, if the breach poses a high risk to patient privacy and there are no feasible measures to mitigate the risk, affected patients must be promptly informed. This notification requirement underscores the importance of transparency and accountability in managing data breaches, ensuring that individuals are informed about potential risks to their personal data and empowered to take necessary precautions.

In the context of healthcare, where data breaches often involve sensitive health information classified as Special Categories of Personal Data by the GDPR, the level of risk associated with a breach must be carefully assessed. Healthcare organizations must consider the potential impact on patient confidentiality, the sensitivity of the information exposed, and the likelihood of harm or adverse consequences to affected individuals. This risk assessment informs decision-making regarding breach notification and mitigation efforts, guiding organizations in their response to data security incidents.

Central to effective breach management is the maintenance of a comprehensive log of all personal data breaches, regardless of whether they meet the reporting threshold. This log serves as a record of incidents, detailing the nature of the breach, the extent of the impact, the actions taken in response, and any remedial measures implemented to prevent recurrence. By maintaining a systematic record of breaches, healthcare organizations can demonstrate accountability, track patterns or trends in data security incidents, and assess the effectiveness of their security measures over time.

To facilitate timely and appropriate responses to data breaches, the DPC recommends that healthcare organizations establish protocols for handling such incidents. These protocols should outline the steps to be taken in the event of a breach, including notification procedures, internal reporting mechanisms, and coordination with relevant stakeholders. Additionally, all staff members should receive training on breach response protocols and their responsibilities in safeguarding patient data. Training programs should cover topics such as recognizing signs of a breach, reporting procedures, and the importance of maintaining confidentiality and data security.

In conclusion, data breach notifications are a critical aspect of data protection governance in healthcare organizations, ensuring transparency, accountability, and effective risk management. By promptly identifying and responding to breaches, organizations can mitigate the impact on patient privacy and uphold their obligations under the GDPR. Establishing robust breach response protocols and providing comprehensive staff training are essential steps in building a culture of data security and safeguarding patient trust in the healthcare sector. Ultimately, proactive measures to prevent, detect, and respond to data breaches are essential for maintaining the integrity and confidentiality of patient information in healthcare settings.

Sharing Personal Health Data

When using or disclosing personal data, different considerations will arise for different situations. Therefore, it is critical that there is clarity on the following points:

- The purpose of the disclosure (which is of utmost importance as it determines the rules that apply)
- The legal basis for the disclosure
- The patient's right to transparency
- The duty of confidentiality to the patient

Sharing Patient Data with Other Organizations for Provision of Healthcare

In the realm of medical diagnostics, particularly within laboratory settings, the processing of patient personal data is integral to the diagnostic and treatment process. When a patient undergoes a consultation with a healthcare professional for medical diagnosis or treatment, there should be an explicit agreement for their personal data to be processed, typically in the form of a document that the patient reads and signs.

This agreement is essential, as it enables healthcare professionals to effectively assess and diagnose medical conditions, prescribe appropriate treatments, and monitor patient health outcomes. Within internal laboratory settings, such as those operated within hospitals or healthcare facilities, patient personal data is routinely processed as part of laboratory consultations and diagnostic procedures. This includes the collection, analysis, and storage of biological samples, test results, and other medical information necessary for accurate diagnosis and treatment planning.

In situations where specialized testing or analysis is required, healthcare providers may engage external laboratories to perform diagnostic services. In such cases, it is imperative for the data controller, whether it be a hospital or private practitioner, to establish a written contract with the external laboratory and ensure the presence of a data sharing agreement. These contractual arrangements serve to clarify the terms of data processing, delineate the responsibilities of both parties, and ensure compliance with data protection regulations. Additionally, the data controller must verify that the external laboratory, acting as a data processor, has implemented appropriate technical and organizational measures to safeguard patient data. These measures include ensuring ongoing confidentiality, integrity, and availability of processing services, as well as the ability to promptly restore access to personal data in the event of a security incident or data breach. A robust process for evaluating the effectiveness of these measures is also essential to maintain data security and regulatory compliance.

Furthermore, when engaging international laboratories located outside the European Economic Area, additional considerations come into play regarding data protection. The data controller must ascertain whether the country in which the laboratory is located provides an adequate level of data protection in accordance with EU standards. If the country does not meet these standards, the data controller must implement alternative safeguards, such as utilizing model contracts containing standard contractual clauses approved by regulatory authorities. These clauses ensure that adequate data protection measures are in place and provide legal mechanisms for transferring personal data to countries outside the EEA while maintaining compliance with data protection regulations.

In summary, the processing of patient personal data within medical diagnostics, including laboratory consultations and external testing services, is essential for providing high-quality healthcare and facilitating accurate diagnosis and treatment. Data controllers must establish clear contractual agreements and ensure the implementation of robust security measures when engaging external laboratories. Additionally, when transferring data to international laboratories, adequate safeguards must be implemented to protect patient privacy and comply with data protection laws. By adhering to these principles, healthcare organizations can uphold patient confidentiality, safeguard sensitive medical information, and maintain trust in the healthcare system.

Sharing Patient Data with Other Medical Professionals

In the healthcare landscape, the sharing of patient data among medical professionals and institutions plays a crucial role in ensuring comprehensive and effective patient care. When allowing personal data to be processed or reviewed by other healthcare professionals who uphold a duty of confidentiality to the patient, it is essential to maintain transparency and adhere to data protection principles. The privacy policy of healthcare organizations should clearly outline the potential for personal data, especially health-related information, to be shared in this manner. Transparency ensures that patients are informed about the purposes and extent of data sharing, fostering trust and accountability in the healthcare system. Additionally, data disclosure should be limited to the minimum number of recipients necessary to achieve the intended purpose, thereby minimizing privacy risks and ensuring compliance with data protection regulations.

When it comes to sharing patient data with other hospitals or healthcare institutions, it is crucial to recognize that such actions constitute data processing under data protection laws. Therefore, all types of data processing, including sharing or transferring personal data, require a lawful basis for doing so, such as obtaining the patient's consent or relying on another lawful basis provided for in data protection regulations. Both the hospital sharing the patient data and the hospital receiving the data must have a lawful basis for their respective processing activities. Patients should be made aware that their health data may be shared with other hospitals and informed about the general purposes for such sharing, such as during patient transfers or for laboratory services.

In scenarios where the receiving hospital becomes a data controller of the patient data, holding the data for its own purposes rather than on behalf of the original hospital, it is not strictly necessary to establish a written contract between the parties to comply with the GDPR. However, it is advisable and prudent to have a data sharing agreement in place between hospitals. This agreement outlines the responsibilities and obligations of each party concerning data protection and privacy, including informing patients about how their data will be used and ensuring compliance with relevant data protection laws and regulations. By formalizing data sharing arrangements through such agreements, hospitals can demonstrate their commitment to protecting patient privacy and maintaining data security throughout the sharing process.

In summary, the sharing of patient data among healthcare professionals and institutions is essential for delivering high-quality patient care and improving health outcomes. However, it is imperative to uphold principles of transparency, accountability, and data protection when engaging in data sharing activities. By ensuring that data sharing practices are conducted lawfully, transparently, and with due regard for patient privacy rights, healthcare organizations can build patient trust, facilitate collaborative care efforts, and enhance the overall quality of healthcare delivery.

Sharing Patient Data with Insurance Companies and Lawyers

Sharing patient data with insurance companies and lawyers involves the processing of personal data, which must adhere to data protection laws and the GDPR. Like all types of data processing, insurance companies and lawyers must have a lawful basis for processing patient data under the GDPR. One such lawful basis is the necessity of processing for the establishment, exercise, or defense of legal claims, or in connection with legal proceedings or potential legal proceedings. This legal framework allows for the sharing of patient data with insurance companies and lawyers when it is relevant to the resolution of legal matters, such as insurance claims or legal disputes.

To ensure transparency and compliance with data protection obligations, healthcare organizations must outline in their privacy policy the potential for sharing patient data with insurance companies and lawyers. Transparency is essential to inform patients about the circumstances under which their personal data may be disclosed and to uphold their privacy rights. Insurance companies and lawyers, as data controllers in their own right, process patient data for specific purposes, such as claims handling or providing legal advice. As such, they must also comply with data protection laws and regulations governing the processing of personal data.

While sharing patient data with data controllers such as insurance companies and lawyers may not always require a formal contract between the parties, a written release of records signed by the patient is typically necessary to ensure compliance with the GDPR. Healthcare organizations must share only the information that is relevant and proportionate to the purpose for which it is being shared, such as handling an insurance claim or providing legal advice. This principle of data minimization helps mitigate privacy risks and ensures compliance with data protection principles, such as purpose limitation and data minimization.

Moreover, healthcare organizations have a responsibility to safeguard patient privacy and confidentiality when sharing data with insurance companies and lawyers. This includes implementing appropriate security measures to protect the confidentiality, integrity, and availability of patient data during transmission and processing. By implementing robust data protection measures and ensuring the lawful and transparent sharing of patient data with insurance companies and lawyers, healthcare organizations can uphold patient trust, protect privacy rights, and facilitate the resolution of legal matters in an ethical and responsible manner.

In summary, sharing patient data with insurance companies and lawyers requires adherence to data protection laws, transparency with patients, and careful consideration of data minimization principles. By outlining the potential for data sharing in their privacy policy and exercising caution when sharing patient data, healthcare organizations can fulfill their legal and ethical obligations while facilitating the resolution of legal claims and proceedings. Effective data protection measures and transparency in data processing practices are essential to maintaining patient trust and confidentiality in the healthcare system.

Special Considerations when Sharing Patient Data

When it comes to sharing patient data, several special considerations must be taken into account to ensure compliance with data protection regulations and safeguard patient privacy. One such consideration pertains to the handling of children's data, which requires specific protection due to their potential vulnerability and limited understanding of data privacy risks. While children's personal data for medical purposes can be shared under the same legal basis as adult health data, the GDPR imposes additional safeguards to protect children's rights and interests. Healthcare providers have a responsibility to help children understand the implications of data sharing, ensuring that they are aware of how their information will be transferred and used.

In the context of e-mail communication and data transfer, healthcare organizations must implement appropriate technical and organizational measures to mitigate risks to patient privacy. Utilizing secure communication channels, such as the healthmail.ie service provided by the Health Service Executive (HSE), is recommended for sharing clinical information between health professionals. Healthmail.ie offers a secure platform for transmitting sensitive medical data, ensuring confidentiality and integrity throughout the communication process. In the United States, it is common practice for medical organizations to provide a secure patient portal, which patients can access with a username and password, often supplemented by a one-time password (sent via text or email) for added security. However, in situations where the use of healthmail.ie or secure patient portals is not feasible, alternative measures must be taken to secure e-mail communications.

Encrypting and password-protecting e-mail attachments are essential steps to safeguard patient data during transmission. Additionally, sending passwords separately, preferably via a different communication channel, adds an extra layer of security to prevent unauthorized access to sensitive information. Human error, such as sending e-mails to the wrong recipient, poses a significant risk of data breaches and must be minimized through proactive measures. Disabling auto-complete of e-mail addresses can help mitigate the risk of inadvertently sending personal data to the wrong recipient, reducing the likelihood of data breaches and ensuring compliance with data protection requirements.

Furthermore, when communicating with patients via e-mail, it is essential to verify the authenticity of the e-mail address through means other than the provided e-mail address. This verification process helps mitigate the risk of phishing attacks or fraudulent communications, ensuring that patient data is only disclosed to authorized recipients. By implementing these measures, healthcare organizations can enhance the security of e-mail communications and data transfer, protect patient confidentiality, and mitigate the risk of data breaches.

In summary, special considerations must be taken into account when sharing patient data, particularly concerning children's data and e-mail communication. Healthcare providers must adhere to data protection regulations, implement appropriate security measures, and ensure transparency and accountability in data handling practices. By prioritizing patient privacy and implementing robust data protection measures, healthcare organizations can maintain trust and confidence in their services while safeguarding sensitive medical information from unauthorized access or disclosure.

What Are the Implications of the Data Protection Legislation on Health Research?

The Data Protection Act 2018 (Section 36(2)) (Health Research) Regulations 2018 is specific to Ireland. It aligns with the GDPR but introduces additional safeguards for health research, such as informed consent and pseudonymization. These regulations provide specific rules for processing personal data in health research in Ireland. The UK Data Protection Act, referenced earlier, applies to the UK and incorporates the GDPR with provisions specific to the UK post-Brexit.

The term "health research" encompasses a broad spectrum of scientific inquiries aimed at advancing understanding, diagnosis, treatment, and prevention of human health issues. This includes research focused on elucidating the normal and abnormal functioning of the human body, developing innovative strategies for disease diagnosis, treatment, and prevention, as well as endeavors to improve healthcare delivery, rehabilitation, and population health outcomes. Health research also encompasses investigations into the social, cultural, environmental, and economic determinants of health, with the overarching goal of enhancing overall well-being and quality of life.

Under Article 9(2)(j) of the GDPR, when scientific research involves processing special categories of personal data (SCD), such as health-related information, specific safeguards must be implemented to ensure compliance with data protection principles. These safeguards include ensuring that data processing is proportionate to the research objectives, respects the essence of the right to data protection, and incorporates suitable and specific measures to safeguard the fundamental rights and interests of data subjects. While the GDPR does not explicitly define what constitutes "suitable and specific measures," Section 36(1) of the 2018 Data Protection Act offers a non-exhaustive list of potential measures that controllers may adopt when processing personal data for research purposes.

Moreover, Section 36(2) of the Data Protection Act 2018 empowers regulators to promulgate additional regulations identifying further suitable and specific measures for research data processing. These measures may encompass a range of technical, organizational, and procedural safeguards tailored to the specific context and objectives of health research activities. Additionally, regulators may specify mandatory measures in certain cases to enhance data protection and ensure compliance with regulatory requirements.

In summary, the Health Research Regulations 2018 represent a significant regulatory framework governing the processing of personal data for health research purposes. By delineating mandatory safeguards and specifying suitable and specific measures for research data processing, these regulations aim to strike a balance between promoting scientific inquiry and protecting individuals' rights to privacy and data protection. Compliance with these regulations is essential for healthcare organizations and research institutions engaged in health research to uphold ethical standards, maintain data security, and safeguard the interests of research participants and data subjects.

Is Obtaining Consent to Use Personal Data Always Necessary when Providing Medical Care?

Under the GDPR, obtaining a legal basis is imperative for processing the personal data of patients. While consent is commonly recognized as a legal basis, it is not the sole option available for the utilization of patient personal data, particularly in the context of providing medical care. Instead, the GDPR outlines various rules under Articles 6 and 9 that collectively serve as the legal framework for processing patient data.

Article 6 of the GDPR establishes the grounds for processing "normal" personal data, encompassing several scenarios where data processing is deemed necessary and lawful. Firstly, Article 6.1(c) stipulates that processing is permissible when it is necessary for compliance with a legal obligation. This legal basis ensures that healthcare providers can lawfully process patient data to fulfill their statutory obligations, such as maintaining medical records or reporting certain health information to regulatory authorities.

Furthermore, Article 6.1(d) allows for data processing when it is necessary to protect the vital interests of the data subject or another natural person. This provision enables healthcare professionals to access and utilize patient data in emergency situations or when immediate medical intervention is required to safeguard the life or health of the individual or others. It serves as a critical legal basis for processing patient data in situations where obtaining explicit consent may not be feasible or practical.

Additionally, Article 6.1(e) permits data processing when it is necessary for the performance of a task carried out in the public interest or in the exercise of official authority vested in the controller. This provision recognizes the essential role of healthcare providers in delivering public health services and ensuring the well-being of individuals and communities. It authorizes the processing of patient data for purposes such as disease surveillance, public health research, and healthcare planning, aligning with broader societal interests and healthcare objectives.

In conjunction with Article 6, Article 9 of the GDPR provides specific conditions for processing special categories of personal data, including health-related information. While consent remains one potential legal basis under Article 9(2)(a), healthcare providers often rely on alternative grounds for processing patient health data. These include Article 9(2)(c), "processing is necessary to protect the vital interests of the data subject or of another natural person where the data subject is physically or legally incapable of giving consent," and Article 9(2)(h), "processing is necessary for the purposes of preventive or occupational medicine, for the assessment of the working capacity of the employee, medical diagnosis, the provision of health or social care, or treatment or the management of health or social care systems and services on the basis...."

In summary, obtaining a legal basis for processing patient data is essential for healthcare providers to ensure compliance with data protection regulations and uphold patient privacy rights. While consent is one available option, Articles 6 and 9 of the GDPR offer a comprehensive framework of legal grounds that enable lawful data processing for medical care provision, public health purposes, and protection of individuals' vital interests. By adhering to these legal provisions, healthcare organizations can effectively manage patient data in a manner that prioritizes privacy, confidentiality, and ethical standards in healthcare delivery.

Regulatory frameworks and standards such as HIPAA and GDPR play a crucial role in ensuring compliance and protecting patient data privacy in healthcare settings. Delving into these regulations paves the way for discussing effective strategies that healthcare organizations can implement to uphold data privacy amidst evolving technological landscapes.

Strategies for Ensuring Data Privacy in Healthcare 4.0

Healthcare 4.0, characterized by the integration of digital technologies such as AI, IoT, big data analytics, and cloud computing into healthcare delivery, presents both opportunities and challenges for data privacy. Here are several strategies for ensuring data privacy in Healthcare 4.0:

- **Implement robust data encryption:** A strategy document for implementing robust data encryption should include the following:

  - An explanation of encryption techniques and algorithms used to protect patient data

  - A description of the importance of encryption at rest and in transit

  - Key management practices to ensure the security of encryption keys

  - Case studies or examples illustrating the effectiveness of data encryption in healthcare settings

- **Adopt access controls and authentication mechanisms:**

  - Role-based access control (RBAC) and its application in healthcare organizations

  - Multi-factor authentication (MFA) and biometric authentication for enhanced security

  - Best practices for user authentication and authorization in Healthcare 4.0

  - Real-world examples of access control implementations in healthcare systems

- **Monitor and audit data access:**

  - Importance of logging and auditing mechanisms in detecting unauthorized access

  - Tools and technologies for monitoring data access and analyzing audit logs

  - Case studies demonstrating the use of data access monitoring in identifying security incidents

  - Best practices for conducting security audits and reviewing audit logs

- **Secure IoT devices and networks:**

  - Security challenges associated with IoT devices in healthcare

  - Strategies for securing IoT devices, including firmware updates and network segmentation

- Network monitoring techniques for detecting and mitigating IoT-related security threats

- Case studies showcasing successful IoT security implementations in healthcare environments

- **Ensure compliance with regulatory requirements:**

  - Overview of key data protection regulations and standards applicable to healthcare, such as HIPAA and GDPR

  - Steps for conducting data privacy impact assessments (DPIAs) and compliance audits

  - Practical guidance for addressing regulatory requirements and maintaining compliance

  - Examples of regulatory enforcement actions and their implications for healthcare organizations

- **Implement data minimization and de-identification techniques:**

  - Explanation of data minimization principles and their importance in reducing privacy risks

  - Techniques for de-identifying patient data while preserving its utility for analysis and research

  - Challenges and best practices for implementing data minimization and de-identification in Healthcare 4.0

  - Case studies illustrating the application of de-identification techniques in healthcare data management

- **Partner with trusted vendors and service providers:**

  - Considerations for evaluating the security practices and compliance of third-party vendors

  - Contractual arrangements and service level agreements (SLAs) to ensure data privacy and security

  - Examples of vendor risk management programs and criteria for vendor selection

  - Real-world scenarios highlighting the importance of vendor trustworthiness in healthcare partnerships

- **Promote data privacy awareness and culture:**

  - Importance of fostering a culture of data privacy and security within healthcare organizations

  - Training programs and awareness initiatives for employees, contractors, and partners

  - Strategies for promoting employee engagement and accountability in data privacy practices

  - Measurement and evaluation of data privacy awareness initiatives' effectiveness

By documenting each of these strategies in depth, including their implementation challenges, best practices, and real-world examples, healthcare organizations can gain a comprehensive understanding of how to ensure data privacy in the era of Healthcare 4.0. With a proactive and holistic approach to data privacy, healthcare organizations can harness the transformative potential of digital technologies while safeguarding patient information and maintaining trust in the healthcare ecosystem.

Summary

This chapter underscored the paramount importance of maintaining robust data security measures within healthcare systems. It examined the critical need for protecting sensitive patient information amidst the evolving landscape of Healthcare 4.0. The chapter delved into existing regulations and standards governing data protection, highlighting compliance requirements and best practices. It explored strategies for ensuring data privacy in Healthcare 4.0, focusing on encryption, access control, and patient consent mechanisms to mitigate risks and uphold confidentiality.

In Chapter 6, we will explore how AI and IoT technologies are revolutionizing remote patient care. Chapter 6 will discuss their roles in enhancing monitoring capabilities through wearable devices and sensors, thereby improving patient outcomes and expanding access to healthcare services beyond traditional clinical settings.

CHAPTER 6

AI and IoT in Remote Patient Monitoring

In Chapter 5, we discussed the importance of data security and privacy in Healthcare 4.0, covering key regulations, standards, and strategies for data protection. This chapter explores the pivotal role of artificial intelligence (AI) and the Internet of Things (IoT) in remote patient monitoring (RPM), highlighting how these technologies enhance patient care outside traditional clinical settings.

Role of AI and IoT in Remote Patient Monitoring (RPM)

The role of AI and IoT in remote monitoring is pivotal in modern healthcare, revolutionizing the way patient care is delivered and managed. Remote monitoring refers to the continuous monitoring of patient health outside of traditional clinical settings, enabling healthcare providers to track vital signs, symptoms, and other health metrics remotely. The integration of AI and IoT in remote monitoring enables real-time data collection, analysis, and decision-making, enhancing the quality of care, improving patient outcomes, and reducing healthcare costs (see Figure 6-1).

Dr. A. K. Srivastav and Dr. P. Das, *Emerging Technologies in Healthcare 4.0*, https://doi.org/10.1007/979-8-8688-1014-5_6

Figure 6-1 illustrates the architecture of a remote patient monitoring system utilizing AI, IoT, and machine learning. At the top of the system is the cloud data center, which manages large-scale data storage and complex computations. Data flows down to the fog nodes, which serve as intermediary processors, handling data pre-processing before it's sent to the cloud. Below the fog nodes are the edge nodes, which are located closest to the patient and their IoT devices, enabling real-time data collection and initial processing. These IoT devices, shown at the bottom of the figure, are essential for patient monitoring, gathering critical data on vital signs and physical activities. The data from these devices are analyzed using machine learning models to predict vital signs and classify physical activities. Furthermore, federated learning allows the machine learning models to be trained on local devices, such as smartphones or wearables, without transferring sensitive patient data to the cloud. This process preserves privacy while improving model accuracy through collaboration across multiple devices. Lastly, reinforcement learning is used in this system to enable AI-based decision-making, where the agent (software system) learns from actions and rewards to improve patient care decisions over time. Together, these components form an integrated system for efficient and secure remote patient monitoring.

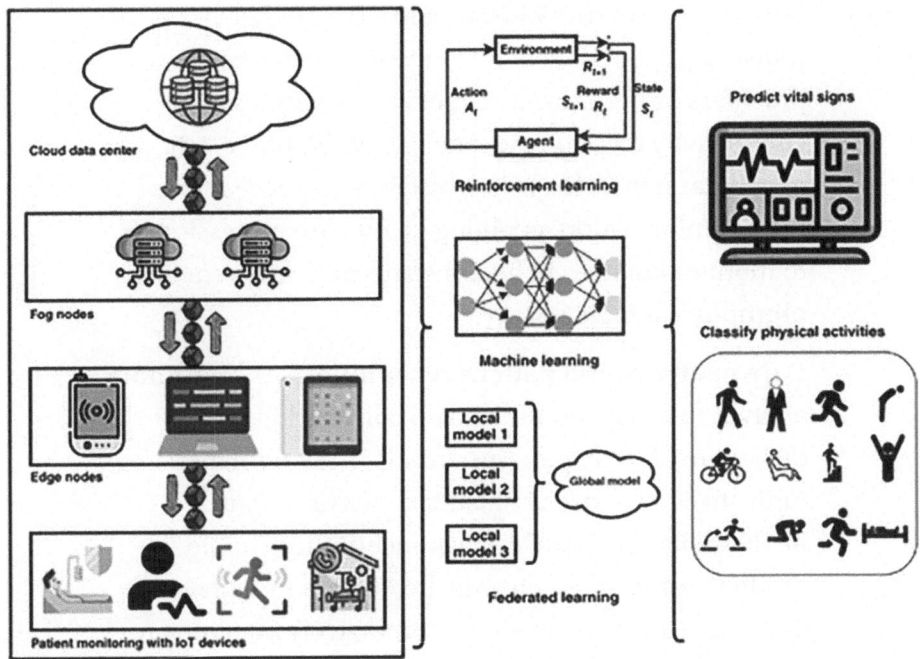

Figure 6-1. *Artificial intelligence–enabled remote patient monitoring architectures*

Here's an overview of the role of AI and IoT in remote monitoring:

- **Continuous data collection:** IoT devices equipped with sensors and wearable technologies enable the continuous collection of patient health data, including vital signs such as heart rate, blood pressure, temperature, and oxygen saturation levels. These devices seamlessly integrate into patients' daily lives, allowing for unobtrusive monitoring over extended periods.

- **Real-time data transmission:** IoT-enabled devices transmit patient data in real time to healthcare providers or monitoring centers using wireless connectivity technologies such as Wi-Fi, Bluetooth, or cellular networks. This ensures timely access to patient information, enabling healthcare professionals to monitor changes in health status and intervene promptly when necessary.

- **Data analytics and pattern recognition:** AI algorithms analyze the vast amount of data collected from IoT devices to identify patterns, trends, and anomalies indicative of changes in health status or potential health risks. Machine learning techniques enable predictive analytics, allowing healthcare providers to anticipate adverse events and proactively intervene to prevent complications.

- **Early warning systems:** AI-powered remote monitoring systems can serve as early warning systems by detecting deviations from normal health parameters or predefined thresholds. Automated alerts and notifications can be generated when abnormal patterns are detected, prompting healthcare providers to take appropriate actions, such as adjusting medication dosages or scheduling follow-up appointments.

- **Personalized healthcare interventions:** AI algorithms can analyze patient data to personalize healthcare interventions based on individual health profiles, preferences, and risk factors. By considering each patient's unique characteristics and medical history, healthcare providers can tailor treatment plans and interventions to optimize outcomes and enhance patient satisfaction.

- **Remote patient engagement and education:** IoT devices equipped with AI-driven virtual assistants or interactive interfaces can engage patients in self-monitoring activities and provide real-time feedback, coaching, and education. These tools empower patients to take an active role in managing their health and adhering to treatment plans, leading to better health outcomes and improved self-management skills.

- **Chronic disease management:** Remote monitoring powered by AI and IoT technologies is particularly beneficial for managing chronic diseases such as diabetes, hypertension, and heart failure. Continuous monitoring of relevant health parameters allows healthcare providers to detect early signs of deterioration, optimize medication regimens, and prevent disease exacerbations, reducing hospitalizations and improving quality of life for patients.

- **Enhanced care coordination and telemedicine:** AI and IoT facilitate seamless care coordination and telemedicine by enabling remote consultations, virtual visits, and remote diagnostics. Healthcare providers can remotely review patient data, conduct virtual assessments, and communicate with patients in real time, eliminating geographical barriers and improving access to specialized care.

- **Population health management:** AI-driven analytics applied to data collected from IoT devices support population health management initiatives by identifying high-risk patient populations, predicting disease outbreaks, and targeting interventions to improve health outcomes at the community level. By analyzing aggregated data from multiple patients, healthcare organizations can identify trends, allocate resources efficiently, and implement preventive strategies to promote population health.

- **Security and privacy considerations:** As with any healthcare technology, ensuring the security and privacy of patient data is paramount in remote monitoring systems. AI and IoT solutions must implement robust security measures, such as encryption, access controls, authentication mechanisms, and regular security audits, to protect patient information from unauthorized access, data breaches, and cyber threats.

In summary, the integration of AI and IoT in remote monitoring holds tremendous potential to transform healthcare delivery by enabling continuous monitoring, personalized interventions, early detection of health risks, and improved patient engagement. By harnessing the power of these technologies, healthcare providers can deliver more proactive, efficient, and patient-centered care, ultimately leading to better health outcomes and enhanced quality of life for patients. However, as discussed in detail in Chapter 5, it is essential to address security and privacy concerns and ensure that AI and IoT solutions comply with regulatory requirements to safeguard patient information and maintain trust in remote monitoring systems.

Synergy Between AI and IoT Technologies

The synergy between AI and IoT technologies represents a transformative force reshaping numerous industries and facets of daily life. At its core, this synergy leverages the capabilities of AI to process vast amounts of data generated by IoT devices, thereby extracting valuable insights, making intelligent decisions, and enhancing overall system performance. This integration heralds a new era of connectivity, automation, and intelligence, with profound implications across diverse domains.

In the realm of healthcare, the amalgamation of AI and IoT facilitates advanced patient monitoring and personalized healthcare delivery. Wearable devices equipped with sensors collect real-time health data, which is then analyzed by AI algorithms to detect anomalies and predict potential health risks. Remote patient monitoring systems enable healthcare providers to deliver timely interventions and optimize treatment plans, leading to improved patient outcomes and reduced healthcare costs. Additionally, AI-driven diagnostic tools empower medical professionals to interpret medical imaging scans more accurately and efficiently, aiding in early disease detection and diagnosis.

In the agricultural sector, AI-enabled IoT solutions optimize crop management practices and improve overall farm productivity. Smart sensors deployed across agricultural fields collect data on soil moisture levels, temperature, and crop health, enabling farmers to make data-driven decisions regarding irrigation, fertilization, and pest control. AI algorithms analyze this data to provide actionable insights, such as optimal planting times and crop yield predictions, thereby maximizing agricultural yields while minimizing resource usage and environmental impact. Furthermore, autonomous drones equipped with AI capabilities can monitor large swathes of farmland, identifying areas requiring attention and facilitating targeted interventions.

In manufacturing and industry, the convergence of AI and IoT technologies revolutionizes traditional processes, paving the way for smart factories and predictive maintenance systems. IoT-enabled sensors embedded within industrial equipment collect real-time performance data, which is then analyzed by AI algorithms to detect anomalies and predict equipment failures before they occur. This proactive approach to maintenance minimizes downtime, reduces maintenance costs, and extends the lifespan of machinery. Moreover, AI-powered predictive analytics optimize production schedules and supply chain management, improving operational efficiency and responsiveness to market demands.

In the realm of smart cities, AI-driven IoT solutions enhance urban infrastructure management and public services delivery. Intelligent transportation systems utilize IoT sensors and AI algorithms to optimize traffic flow, reduce congestion, and enhance road safety. Smart energy grids leverage AI to balance supply and demand, integrate renewable energy sources, and optimize energy distribution, leading to greater energy efficiency and sustainability. Additionally, AI-powered surveillance systems enhance public safety by analyzing video feeds in real time to detect suspicious activities and alert authorities to potential security threats.

Despite the myriad benefits offered by the synergy between AI and IoT technologies, several challenges and considerations must be addressed to fully realize its potential. Data privacy and security concerns loom large, particularly given the sensitive nature of the data collected by IoT devices and processed by AI algorithms. Robust cybersecurity measures, encryption protocols, and data anonymization techniques are essential to safeguarding personal and proprietary information against unauthorized access and cyber threats.

Interoperability and standardization also pose significant challenges, as the proliferation of IoT devices and platforms has led to fragmentation and compatibility issues within the ecosystem. Establishing common protocols and standards for data exchange and communication is critical to ensuring seamless interoperability and integration across diverse systems and devices. Moreover, ethical considerations surrounding the development and deployment of AI algorithms, such as bias and fairness, demand careful scrutiny and regulatory oversight to mitigate potential risks and ensure equitable outcomes.

Looking ahead, the synergy between AI and IoT technologies holds immense promise for driving innovation, efficiency, and sustainability across various sectors. Advancements in edge computing and distributed AI enable more efficient processing of IoT data at the network edge, reducing latency and bandwidth requirements while enhancing privacy and security. Additionally, the integration of blockchain technology with AI and IoT offers novel solutions for data integrity, transparency, and trust in decentralized networks, opening up new avenues for applications such as supply chain management, asset tracking, and decentralized autonomous organizations (DAOs).

In conclusion, the synergy between AI and IoT technologies represents a paradigm shift in how we collect, analyze, and leverage data to drive informed decision-making and intelligent automation. From healthcare and agriculture to manufacturing and smart cities, this convergence holds the potential to revolutionize industries, enhance quality of life, and address pressing societal challenges. However, realizing this potential requires concerted efforts to address technical, ethical, and regulatory challenges, while fostering collaboration and innovation across stakeholders. By harnessing the power of AI and IoT in concert, we can unlock new opportunities for innovation, growth, and human advancement in the digital age.

Benefits of AI and IoT in Remote Monitoring

The benefits of AI and IoT in remote monitoring include improved patient outcomes, enhanced efficiency and cost savings, and early detection of health issues.

Improved Patient Outcomes

The synergy between AI and IoT technologies has significantly contributed to improving patient outcomes in healthcare. By leveraging AI algorithms to analyze data collected from IoT-enabled devices, healthcare providers can offer more personalized and timely interventions, leading to better health outcomes for patients.

One key area where this synergy has made a substantial impact is in remote patient monitoring. IoT devices such as wearable sensors, smartwatches, and medical implants continuously gather vital health metrics, including heart rate, blood pressure, and glucose levels. AI algorithms analyze this streaming data in real time, detecting patterns and abnormalities that may indicate deteriorating health conditions. By remotely monitoring patients' health status, healthcare providers can intervene proactively, preventing adverse events such as heart attacks or diabetic crises. This proactive approach not only improves patient safety but also reduces hospital readmissions and healthcare costs.

Furthermore, AI-powered diagnostic tools enhance the accuracy and efficiency of medical diagnosis, leading to faster treatment initiation and improved patient outcomes. Medical imaging technologies, such as MRI and CT scans, generate vast amounts of data that can be challenging for human radiologists to interpret accurately. AI algorithms trained on large datasets can analyze these images with unprecedented speed and accuracy, assisting radiologists in detecting subtle abnormalities or early signs of disease. Consequently, patients receive timely diagnoses and appropriate treatments, improving their chances of recovery and survival.

Moreover, AI-driven predictive analytics enable healthcare providers to identify patients at high risk of developing chronic conditions or complications. By analyzing electronic health records (EHRs), genetic data, and lifestyle factors, AI algorithms can stratify patients based on their risk profiles and recommend personalized preventive interventions. For example, patients with a family history of cardiovascular disease may receive tailored lifestyle recommendations and preventive medications to mitigate their risk. By intervening early and targeting high-risk individuals, healthcare providers can prevent the onset of chronic diseases and improve long-term health outcomes.

In addition to individual patient care, AI and IoT technologies are also transforming population health management strategies. By aggregating and analyzing health data from diverse sources, including EHRs, wearable devices, and public health databases, AI algorithms can identify disease trends, outbreaks, and disparities in healthcare access. These population-level insights enable policymakers and public health officials to develop targeted interventions and allocate resources more effectively, ultimately improving health outcomes at the community level.

Overall, the synergy between AI and IoT technologies holds tremendous promise for improving patient outcomes in healthcare. By harnessing the power of data analytics, machine learning, and real-time monitoring, healthcare providers can deliver more personalized, proactive, and efficient care, leading to better health outcomes and enhanced quality of life for patients.

Enhanced Efficiency and Cost Savings

The integration of AI and IoT technologies has brought about enhanced efficiency and substantial cost savings across various industries, particularly in manufacturing, logistics, and infrastructure management. By combining the capabilities of AI-driven analytics with the data collection and connectivity of IoT devices, organizations can optimize processes, reduce waste, and streamline operations, leading to significant improvements in efficiency and cost-effectiveness.

In manufacturing, AI-powered IoT systems enable predictive maintenance, a proactive approach that helps prevent equipment failures and minimize costly downtime. IoT sensors embedded within machinery continuously monitor key performance indicators such

187

as temperature, vibration, and energy consumption. This data is then analyzed by AI algorithms to detect patterns indicative of potential malfunctions or breakdowns. By identifying maintenance needs before they escalate into costly issues, organizations can schedule repairs during planned downtime, avoiding unexpected production halts and reducing maintenance costs.

Furthermore, AI-driven predictive analytics optimize production processes, inventory management, and supply chain logistics, leading to improved efficiency and cost savings. By analyzing historical production data, market demand forecasts, and supply chain dynamics, AI algorithms can identify inefficiencies, bottlenecks, and opportunities for optimization. For example, AI-powered demand forecasting models help organizations anticipate fluctuations in customer demand, enabling them to adjust production schedules and inventory levels accordingly, thereby reducing excess inventory holding costs and minimizing stockouts.

Moreover, AI and IoT technologies facilitate the implementation of smart energy management systems, enabling organizations to optimize energy usage, reduce utility costs, and minimize environmental impact. IoT sensors installed in buildings, factories, and infrastructure assets collect real-time data on energy consumption, occupancy patterns, and environmental conditions. AI algorithms analyze this data to identify opportunities for energy efficiency improvements, such as optimizing HVAC systems, scheduling equipment usage during off-peak hours, and implementing renewable energy solutions. By reducing energy waste and optimizing resource utilization, organizations can lower operating costs and achieve sustainability goals.

In logistics and transportation, AI-powered IoT solutions optimize route planning, vehicle maintenance, and fleet management, leading to improved operational efficiency and cost savings. IoT-enabled sensors installed in vehicles track factors such as location, speed, fuel consumption, and vehicle health status in real time. AI algorithms analyze this data to optimize route selection, minimize fuel consumption, and predict maintenance needs, thereby reducing fuel costs, vehicle downtime, and maintenance expenses. Additionally, AI-driven predictive analytics enable organizations to anticipate demand fluctuations, optimize warehouse operations, and streamline last-mile delivery processes, leading to improved customer satisfaction and reduced logistics costs.

Overall, the synergy between AI and IoT technologies enables organizations to achieve significant efficiency gains and cost savings across various sectors. By harnessing the power of data analytics, machine learning, and real-time monitoring, organizations can optimize processes, enhance decision-making, and drive continuous improvement, ultimately improving their bottom line and competitive advantage in the marketplace.

Early Detection of Health Issues

Early detection of health issues is a critical aspect of modern healthcare, and the synergy between AI and IoT technologies has revolutionized this process, enabling proactive monitoring and timely interventions. By combining the data collection capabilities of IoT devices with the analytical power of AI algorithms, healthcare providers can detect subtle signs of illness before symptoms manifest, leading to earlier diagnosis and more effective treatments. This paradigm shift has profound implications for patient outcomes, healthcare costs, and population health management.

One of the key contributions of AI-powered IoT devices to early detection is continuous monitoring of physiological parameters. Wearable devices equipped with sensors for heart rate, blood pressure, and glucose levels, among others, collect real-time data on patients' health status. AI algorithms analyze this data to detect abnormalities or deviations from baseline levels, which may indicate the onset of health issues such as cardiovascular disease, hypertension, or diabetes. By monitoring patients continuously, healthcare providers can identify subtle changes in health metrics and intervene promptly, potentially preventing the progression of disease and reducing the risk of complications.

Furthermore, AI-driven predictive analytics enable healthcare providers to identify individuals at high risk of developing certain health conditions based on a combination of demographic, clinical, and behavioral factors. By analyzing electronic health records, genetic data, and lifestyle information, AI algorithms can stratify patients into risk categories and identify those who may benefit from targeted preventive interventions. For example, individuals with a family history of cancer or a high body mass index may be flagged for closer monitoring or early screening tests, allowing for the detection of cancer at an earlier, more treatable stage.

Moreover, AI-powered diagnostic tools enhance the accuracy and efficiency of medical imaging interpretation, facilitating the early detection of tumors, lesions, and other abnormalities. Medical imaging modalities such as MRI, CT, and ultrasound generate vast amounts of data that can be challenging for human radiologists to analyze thoroughly. AI algorithms trained on large datasets can process these images rapidly and accurately, detecting subtle abnormalities that may be missed by human observers. By assisting radiologists in the interpretation of imaging studies, AI-driven diagnostic tools enable earlier detection of diseases such as cancer, stroke, and cardiovascular disease, leading to more timely interventions and improved patient outcomes.

In addition to individual patient care, AI and IoT technologies also play a crucial role in population health management by analyzing large-scale health data to identify disease trends, outbreaks, and disparities in healthcare access. By aggregating data from electronic health records, wearable devices, and public health databases, AI algorithms can detect patterns and correlations that may signal emerging health threats or areas of unmet healthcare need. For example, AI-powered analytics can identify clusters of individuals with similar symptoms or demographic characteristics, which may indicate the spread of infectious diseases or underlying social determinants of health.

Furthermore, AI-driven predictive modeling enables healthcare providers to forecast future healthcare utilization and allocate resources more efficiently. By analyzing historical healthcare data, including hospital admissions, emergency department visits, and outpatient appointments, AI algorithms can identify patterns and trends that may influence future demand for healthcare services. This predictive insight enables healthcare organizations to adjust staffing levels, bed capacities, and supply chain logistics proactively, ensuring that resources are deployed where they are most needed and avoiding potential bottlenecks or shortages.

Overall, the synergy between AI and IoT technologies has transformed the landscape of early detection in healthcare, enabling proactive monitoring, timely interventions, and population-level insights. By harnessing the power of continuous data collection, real-time monitoring, and predictive analytics, healthcare providers can detect health issues at their earliest stages, leading to improved patient outcomes, reduced healthcare costs, and enhanced population health. As these technologies continue to evolve and become more widely adopted, the potential for early detection to transform healthcare delivery and improve patient outcomes will only continue to grow.

Challenges and Considerations of AI and IoT in Remote Monitoring

The challenges and considerations of AI and IoT in remote monitoring include data privacy and security concerns, regulatory compliance, technical challenges, and infrastructure requirements.

Data Privacy and Security Concerns

Data privacy and security concerns represent critical challenges in the era of rapid technological advancement, particularly with the proliferation of interconnected devices and the vast volumes of data generated and exchanged. The synergy between AI and IoT technologies exacerbates these concerns, as the integration of AI-driven analytics with IoT devices amplifies the potential risks associated with data breaches, unauthorized access, and misuse of personal information. As such, addressing data privacy and security concerns is paramount to fostering trust, safeguarding user rights, and ensuring the responsible deployment of AI and IoT technologies.

One of the primary data privacy concerns in the context of AI and IoT is the collection and storage of sensitive personal data by interconnected devices. IoT devices, ranging from smart thermostats and wearable fitness trackers to connected cars and home assistants, collect a wealth of personal information, including biometric data, location history, and behavioral patterns. This data is often transmitted over networks to centralized servers or cloud platforms for processing and analysis. However, the collection and storage of such sensitive data raise significant privacy risks, as it can be susceptible to unauthorized access, data breaches, or misuse by malicious actors.

Furthermore, the integration of AI algorithms with IoT devices introduces additional privacy considerations, as AI-driven analytics often require access to large datasets for training and model development. In many cases, this training data may contain personally identifiable information (PII) or sensitive health data, raising concerns about data anonymization, consent, and user control. Moreover, the use of machine learning algorithms introduces the risk of algorithmic bias, whereby AI models may inadvertently perpetuate or amplify existing biases present in the training data, leading to discriminatory outcomes or privacy violations.

Another data privacy concern associated with AI and IoT technologies is the potential for covert surveillance and invasion of privacy. IoT devices equipped with cameras, microphones, and sensors can capture audio, video, and environmental data from users' surroundings, raising concerns about unauthorized surveillance or data collection without user consent. Moreover, the proliferation of smart home devices and

192

wearables further blurs the boundaries between public and private spaces, as personal data is collected and transmitted both inside and outside the home environment. This constant monitoring and data collection pose significant privacy risks, as users may be unaware of the extent to which their activities are being recorded and analyzed.

Additionally, the interconnected nature of IoT ecosystems introduces challenges related to data ownership, control, and accountability. With multiple stakeholders involved in the deployment and operation of IoT devices, including device manufacturers, service providers, and third-party developers, determining ownership rights and responsibilities over collected data becomes increasingly complex. Moreover, the lack of standardized protocols for data sharing and interoperability exacerbates these challenges, as data may be siloed or fragmented across different platforms and ecosystems, hindering users' ability to control and manage their data effectively.

Addressing data privacy and security concerns in the context of AI and IoT requires a multifaceted approach encompassing technological, regulatory, and organizational measures. Technological solutions such as encryption, anonymization, and secure authentication protocols can help mitigate the risk of data breaches and unauthorized access. Moreover, the implementation of privacy-preserving AI techniques, such as federated learning (discussed a bit later) and differential privacy, can enable AI models to be trained on decentralized data sources without compromising user privacy.

From a regulatory perspective, policymakers must enact robust data protection laws and regulations to safeguard user rights and hold organizations accountable for data privacy violations. Measures such as the General Data Protection Regulation (GDPR) in the European Union and the California Consumer Privacy Act (CCPA) and Health Insurance Portability and Accountability Act (HIPAA) in the United States impose strict requirements on data collection, processing, and consent, providing users with greater transparency and control over their personal information. Moreover, regulatory frameworks should address emerging challenges such as algorithmic transparency, accountability, and fairness to ensure that AI-driven decision-making processes are ethical and equitable.

Organizations deploying AI and IoT technologies must also prioritize privacy and security by implementing privacy-by-design principles and conducting comprehensive privacy impact assessments. This involves integrating privacy and security considerations into the design, development, and deployment of AI and IoT systems from the outset, rather than as an afterthought. Additionally, organizations should adopt transparent data governance practices, including clear data usage policies, data access controls, and user consent mechanisms, to build trust and accountability with users.

In conclusion, data privacy and security concerns represent significant challenges in the integration of AI and IoT technologies, as the collection, analysis, and sharing of sensitive personal data raise risks of unauthorized access, surveillance, and privacy violations. Addressing these concerns requires a concerted effort from technology developers, policymakers, and organizations to implement robust technical safeguards, enact comprehensive regulatory frameworks, and foster a culture of privacy and accountability. By prioritizing privacy and security in the design and deployment of AI and IoT systems, we can ensure that these transformative technologies contribute to positive societal outcomes while safeguarding user rights and protecting privacy in the digital age.

Regulatory Compliance

Regulatory compliance is a cornerstone of various industries, ensuring adherence to laws, standards, and guidelines set forth by governing bodies. In the context of emerging technologies like AI and IoT, regulatory compliance becomes increasingly complex due to the rapid pace of innovation, potential risks, and ethical considerations involved. As AI and

IoT applications permeate diverse sectors such as healthcare, finance, and transportation, regulatory frameworks play a crucial role in safeguarding consumer rights, promoting fair competition, and addressing societal concerns.

At the heart of regulatory compliance in AI and IoT is the protection of data privacy and security. With the proliferation of IoT devices collecting vast amounts of personal and sensitive data, coupled with AI algorithms analyzing this data for insights, the risk of data breaches, unauthorized access, and misuse becomes a significant concern. Regulatory bodies worldwide have responded by enacting stringent data protection laws such as the previously mentioned GDPR, CCPA, and HIPAA. These regulations impose obligations on organizations to implement robust security measures, obtain explicit consent for data collection and processing, and provide individuals with transparency and control over their data.

Moreover, regulatory compliance in AI and IoT extends to ethical considerations surrounding algorithmic transparency, fairness, and accountability. AI algorithms, trained on large datasets, have the potential to perpetuate biases, discriminate against certain demographics, or make decisions with unintended consequences. To address these concerns, regulatory bodies and industry organizations have proposed guidelines such as the Ethical AI Principles by the European Commission and the AI Principles by the Institute of Electrical and Electronics Engineers (IEEE). These principles advocate for transparency in AI decision-making, fairness in algorithmic outcomes, and accountability for the ethical implications of AI systems.

Furthermore, regulatory compliance in AI and IoT encompasses standards and certifications aimed at ensuring interoperability, reliability, and safety of interconnected devices and systems. In the IoT space, standards bodies such as the International Organization for Standardization (ISO) and the Institute of Electrical and Electronics Engineers (IEEE) develop guidelines for device interoperability, data exchange protocols, and cybersecurity best practices. Similarly, in AI, organizations like the Partnership on AI (PAI) and ISO work toward developing standards for AI ethics, transparency, and governance. Compliance with these standards not only enhances the trustworthiness of AI and IoT systems but also facilitates interoperability and seamless integration across diverse platforms and ecosystems.

Moreover, regulatory compliance in AI and IoT involves addressing legal and liability issues arising from the use of autonomous systems and decision-making algorithms. As AI-powered autonomous vehicles, drones, and robotic systems become increasingly prevalent, questions regarding liability in the event of accidents, errors, or malfunctions emerge. Regulatory bodies and policymakers are tasked with developing frameworks for assigning responsibility, allocating liability, and ensuring accountability in cases where AI systems cause harm or damage. Additionally, regulations governing liability insurance, product safety, and consumer protection may need to be updated to account for the unique risks posed by AI and IoT technologies.

Furthermore, regulatory compliance in AI and IoT requires organizations to navigate complex intellectual property (IP) and data ownership issues. With AI algorithms trained on proprietary datasets and IoT devices generating valuable data streams, disputes over ownership, licensing, and use rights may arise. Regulatory frameworks governing IP rights, data sharing agreements, and technology licensing play a crucial role in defining the rights and obligations of stakeholders involved in AI and IoT ecosystems. Additionally, regulations governing data sovereignty, cross-border data transfers, and jurisdictional issues may pose challenges for organizations operating in global markets.

In conclusion, regulatory compliance in AI and IoT is essential for ensuring the responsible development, deployment, and use of these transformative technologies. By addressing data privacy and security concerns, promoting ethical AI principles, establishing interoperability standards, and addressing legal and liability issues, regulatory frameworks play a vital role in fostering trust, innovation, and societal benefit. As AI and IoT continue to evolve and permeate various industries, regulatory bodies and policymakers must adapt and collaborate with industry stakeholders to develop flexible, forward-thinking regulatory frameworks that balance innovation with the protection of consumer rights and public interest.

Technical Challenges and Infrastructure Requirements

The integration of AI and IoT technologies presents a myriad of technical challenges and infrastructure requirements that must be addressed to realize the full potential of this convergence. From data management and processing to connectivity and scalability, addressing these challenges is crucial for the successful deployment and operation of AI-driven IoT systems across diverse applications and industries.

One of the primary technical challenges in AI and IoT integration is data management and processing. IoT devices generate vast volumes of data in real time, including sensor readings, telemetry data, and multimedia streams. Processing and analyzing this data in a timely manner to extract actionable insights require robust computational infrastructure and advanced data analytics capabilities. Traditional cloud-based architectures may face limitations in handling the volume, velocity, and variety of IoT data streams, leading to latency issues and scalability concerns. To address these challenges, edge computing technologies, which enable data processing and analysis at or near the source of data generation, are increasingly being leveraged in AI-driven IoT deployments. By distributing computational resources closer to IoT devices, edge computing reduces latency, minimizes bandwidth requirements, and enhances data privacy and security.

Furthermore, ensuring interoperability and compatibility among diverse IoT devices and platforms poses significant technical challenges in AI and IoT integration. The proliferation of proprietary protocols, communication standards, and vendor-specific implementations may hinder seamless data exchange and integration within IoT ecosystems. Developing open standards and protocols for device communication, data interchange, and interoperability is essential to enable seamless integration and interoperability across heterogeneous IoT environments. The Digital Twin Consortium (DTC) and the Open Connectivity Foundation (OCF) are two prominent organizations dedicated to enhancing interoperability and standardization in the Internet of Things (IoT) sector.

Moreover, addressing cybersecurity threats and vulnerabilities is paramount in AI-driven IoT deployments. IoT devices, often deployed in uncontrolled or hostile environments, are vulnerable to a wide range of security threats, including malware, ransomware, and distributed denial-of-service (DDoS) attacks. Compromised IoT devices can not only compromise data privacy and integrity but also pose risks to physical safety and critical infrastructure. Implementing robust security measures, including device authentication, data encryption, and intrusion detection systems, is essential to mitigate cybersecurity risks in AI-driven IoT deployments. Additionally, continuous monitoring, threat intelligence, and security updates are necessary to proactively detect and respond to emerging security threats in real-time.

Furthermore, addressing the scalability and resource constraints of IoT devices poses technical challenges in AI and IoT integration. Many IoT devices operate with limited computational resources, memory, and battery life, making it challenging to deploy resource-intensive AI algorithms directly on these devices. Federated learning, a decentralized machine learning approach where AI models are trained collaboratively across distributed IoT devices, offers a promising solution to address scalability and resource constraints in AI-driven IoT deployments. By leveraging federated learning, AI models can be trained directly on IoT devices using local data without the need for centralized data aggregation or heavy computational resources, enabling scalable and privacy-preserving AI deployments in IoT environments.

In addition to technical challenges, addressing infrastructure requirements is essential for the successful deployment and operation of AI-driven IoT systems. Deploying IoT devices at scale requires robust network infrastructure, including high-speed Internet connectivity, low-latency communication protocols, and edge computing resources. Investing in network infrastructure upgrades, such as 5G wireless networks and edge computing infrastructure, is essential to support the growing demands of AI-driven IoT deployments. Additionally, ensuring adequate power supply, backup systems, and physical security measures for IoT devices are essential to maintain uninterrupted operation and protect against physical tampering or sabotage.

In conclusion, addressing technical challenges and infrastructure requirements is essential for the successful integration of AI and IoT technologies. From data management and processing to interoperability, cybersecurity, and scalability, overcoming these challenges requires collaboration among stakeholders, investment in research and development, and adherence to best practices and standards. By addressing these challenges, organizations can unlock the full potential of AI-driven IoT systems to drive innovation, improve efficiency, and address pressing societal challenges across diverse applications and industries.

AI and IoT technologies have revolutionized remote patient monitoring by enabling continuous data collection and analysis, enhancing healthcare providers' ability to monitor patient health remotely. Exploring the role of AI and IoT lays the foundation for examining the specific technologies, such as wearable devices and sensors, that facilitate remote monitoring in real-time.

Wearable Devices and Sensors for Remote Monitoring

In addition to the common types of wearable devices and sensors previously described in this chapter, emerging technologies and advancements in remote monitoring are expanding the capabilities and applications of wearables in healthcare (see Figure 6-2).

Figure 6-2 illustrates a remote patient monitoring system consisting of several interconnected components. The Cardiovascular Measurement Unit uses on-body electrodes to measure ECG (Electrocardiogram) and HR (Heart Rate), providing vital cardiovascular data. The Knee Joint Monitoring Unit tracks knee activity through IMUs (Inertial Measurement Units), which include GSR (Galvanic Skin Response), temperature, and pressure sensors, offering insights into joint health. The PPG Measurement Unit employs LEDs (Light Emitting Diodes) and Photodiodes (PD) to measure PPG (Photoplethysmogram) signals, monitoring SpO2 (blood oxygen level), pulse, and blood pressure (BP). The Activity Monitoring Unit uses IMUs to detect activity-related signals, aiding in fall prediction and gait pattern recognition. Data from all these units are collected by the Central BSN (Body Sensor Network) Node, which has limited processing capabilities and transmits the data to the Home Gateway. The Home Gateway monitors, stores, analyzes, and displays the data while transmitting it to healthcare providers over the internet. The healthcare provider can then monitor the patient remotely, enabling timely interventions and personalized care. This integrated system allows for continuous, real-time monitoring of a patient's health, facilitating early detection and improving overall patient outcomes.

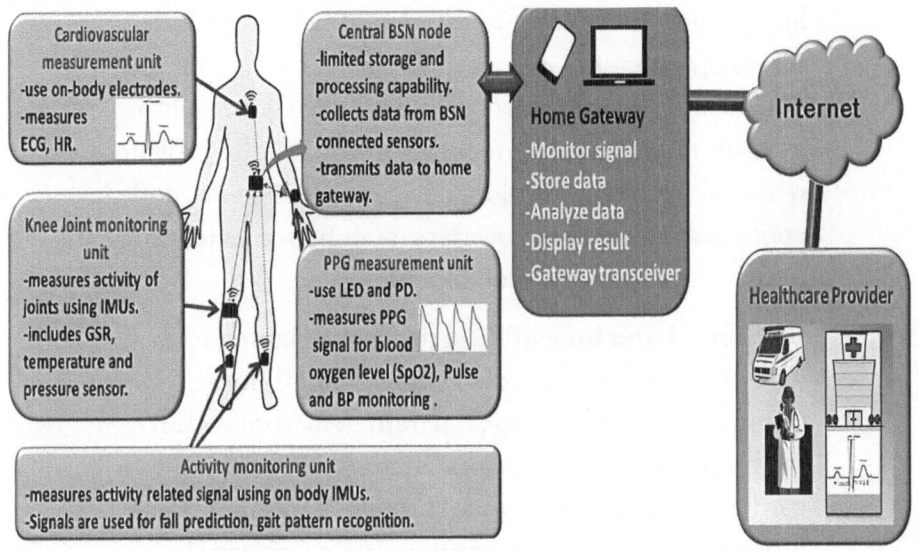

Figure 6-2. *General overview of the remote health monitoring system*

Here are some notable trends and innovations in wearable devices and sensors for remote monitoring:

- **Smart clothing and textiles:** Smart clothing embedded with flexible sensors and conductive fabrics enables noninvasive monitoring of vital signs, posture, movement, and physiological parameters. These wearable textiles seamlessly integrate into everyday apparel, providing continuous monitoring without the need for additional devices or accessories. Smart clothing applications range from athletic performance monitoring and rehabilitation to medical-grade monitoring for chronic disease management and telemedicine.

- **Smart contact lenses and eyewear:** Smart contact lenses equipped with miniature sensors and electronics enable noninvasive monitoring of intraocular pressure, glucose levels, and other ocular parameters. These smart lenses offer continuous monitoring of eye health and disease progression in conditions such as glaucoma and diabetes. Similarly, smart eyewear devices with built-in sensors and augmented reality (AR) capabilities provide real-time data visualization, navigation assistance, and contextual information overlays for enhanced situational awareness and remote collaboration.

- **Implanted and ingestible sensors:** Implanted and ingestible sensors offer discreet and continuous monitoring of physiological parameters from within the body. Implanted sensors, such as pacemakers, cardiac monitors, and neural implants, monitor organ function, cardiac activity, and neurological signals to detect abnormalities and deliver targeted therapies. Ingestible sensors, in the form of swallowable capsules or pills, transmit data on medication adherence, gastrointestinal transit time, and biomarker levels, providing insights into digestive health, medication efficacy, and disease progression.

- **Biosensing tattoos and implants:** Biosensing tattoos and implants utilize biocompatible materials and microelectronics to monitor biomarkers, metabolites, and biochemical processes in the body. These wearable bioelectronics offer minimally invasive monitoring of physiological and biochemical parameters, such as glucose levels, lactate concentrations, and hydration status. Biosensing tattoos and implants enable personalized health monitoring, performance optimization, and disease management, with potential applications in sports medicine, military personnel health, and remote healthcare delivery.

- **Neurofeedback and brain–computer interfaces (BCIs):** Neurofeedback devices and BCIs enable real-time monitoring and modulation of brain activity for cognitive enhancement, neurorehabilitation, and mental health management. These wearable devices use electroencephalography (EEG) sensors and signal processing algorithms to detect brainwave patterns associated with attention, relaxation, or emotional states. Neurofeedback training and BCI-based interventions offer non-pharmacological approaches to managing stress, anxiety, depression, and neurological disorders, empowering users to self-regulate brain function and improve cognitive performance.

- **Ambient and contextual sensing:** Ambient and contextual sensing technologies leverage IoT-enabled environmental sensors and machine learning algorithms to monitor environmental factors, social interactions, and contextual cues influencing health and well-being. These sensors collect data on ambient temperature, humidity, air quality, noise levels, light exposure, and social interactions to assess their impact on health outcomes, stress levels, and productivity. Ambient and contextual sensing systems provide personalized insights and recommendations for optimizing indoor environments, promoting healthy behaviors, and enhancing user experience in home, work, and healthcare settings.

- **Blockchain-enabled wearables:** Blockchain-enabled wearable devices leverage distributed ledger technology to secure and validate data transactions, ensuring the integrity, privacy, and traceability of health data generated by wearables. These blockchain-based platforms enable secure sharing, storage, and monetization of wearable-generated health data while preserving user privacy and control over their personal information. Blockchain-enabled wearables facilitate data interoperability, incentivize data sharing, and support decentralized health ecosystems, empowering users to monetize their health data and participate in research, clinical trials, and wellness programs.

- **AI-powered wearable assistants:** AI-powered wearable assistants combine natural language processing, machine learning, and sensor fusion techniques to provide personalized health coaching, virtual assistance, and remote monitoring services. These wearable AI assistants analyze user behavior, biometric data, and contextual information to deliver proactive health insights, personalized recommendations, and actionable feedback in real time. These AI-powered wearables serve as virtual health coaches, companions, and caregivers, supporting users in achieving health goals, managing chronic conditions, and making informed lifestyle choices.

Overall, the convergence of wearable technology, AI, IoT, and biomedical engineering is driving innovation and transformation in remote monitoring, enabling personalized, proactive, and participatory approaches to healthcare. These emerging trends and advancements in wearable devices and sensors hold promise for improving health outcomes, enhancing patient engagement, and revolutionizing healthcare delivery in the digital age.

Applications of Wearable Devices and Sensors in Remote Monitoring

Among the many applications of wearable devices and sensors in remote monitoring are chronic disease management, elderly care, remote patient monitoring, and fitness and wellness tracking.

Chronic Disease Management

Chronic diseases, often referred to as noncommunicable diseases (NCDs), are long-term medical conditions that generally progress slowly and persist over time. Unlike acute illnesses, which have a sudden onset and typically resolve within a relatively short period, chronic diseases require ongoing management to control symptoms, prevent complications, and maintain quality of life. The World Health Organization (WHO) identifies four main types of chronic diseases that account for the majority of NCD-related deaths globally: cardiovascular diseases, cancer, chronic respiratory diseases, and diabetes.

Cardiovascular diseases, including coronary artery disease, stroke, and heart failure, are the leading cause of mortality worldwide, responsible for an estimated 17.9 million deaths annually. Risk factors for cardiovascular diseases include hypertension, high cholesterol, obesity, smoking, and sedentary lifestyle. Cancer, characterized by the uncontrolled growth and spread of abnormal cells, is another major contributor to the global disease burden, with approximately 10 million deaths attributed to cancer each year. Common risk factors for cancer include tobacco use, unhealthy diet, physical inactivity, and exposure to carcinogens.

Chronic respiratory diseases, such as chronic obstructive pulmonary disease (COPD) and asthma, affect the airways and lungs, leading to symptoms such as coughing, wheezing, and shortness of breath. COPD alone is responsible for over 3 million deaths annually, with smoking being the primary risk factor. Finally, diabetes, a metabolic disorder characterized by elevated blood sugar levels, affects over 400 million people worldwide and is a leading cause of complications such as cardiovascular disease, kidney failure, and blindness. Risk factors for diabetes include obesity, unhealthy diet, physical inactivity, and genetics.

Managing chronic diseases poses several challenges for healthcare systems, providers, and patients alike. One significant challenge is the rising prevalence of chronic conditions, driven in part by aging populations, urbanization, unhealthy lifestyles, and inadequate access to healthcare. The increasing burden of chronic diseases places strain on healthcare resources, leading to higher costs, longer waiting times, and overwhelmed healthcare facilities.

Another challenge is the complexity of chronic disease management, which often requires a multidisciplinary approach involving various healthcare professionals, including physicians, nurses, pharmacists, dietitians, and social workers. Coordinating care among these different providers can be challenging, particularly in fragmented healthcare systems where communication and collaboration may be lacking.

Furthermore, many chronic diseases are associated with modifiable risk factors such as smoking, poor diet, physical inactivity, and alcohol consumption. Addressing these risk factors through lifestyle modifications is essential for preventing and managing chronic conditions. However, changing behavior is notoriously difficult, and healthcare providers often struggle to effectively motivate patients to adopt healthier habits.

Moreover, disparities in healthcare access and quality contribute to inequalities in chronic disease outcomes, with marginalized populations facing greater barriers to prevention, diagnosis, and treatment. Socioeconomic factors such as income, education, race, and ethnicity play a significant role in determining health outcomes, highlighting the need for interventions that address underlying social determinants of health.

Preventing and managing chronic diseases requires a multifaceted approach that addresses both individual-level risk factors and broader societal determinants of health. Key strategies include health promotion, early detection, evidence-based treatment, patient education, and self-management support.

Health promotion efforts aim to reduce the prevalence of modifiable risk factors through public awareness campaigns, community-based interventions, and policy changes. For example, tobacco control measures such as tobacco taxes, smoke-free laws, and anti-smoking campaigns have been successful in reducing smoking rates and lowering the incidence of tobacco-related diseases.

Similarly, initiatives to promote healthy eating and physical activity can help prevent obesity, diabetes, and cardiovascular diseases. These efforts may include nutrition education programs, urban planning policies that support active transportation, and school-based interventions to encourage physical activity among children and adolescents.

Early detection of chronic diseases is crucial for initiating timely treatment and preventing complications. Screening programs, such as mammography for breast cancer, Pap smears for cervical cancer, and blood pressure monitoring for hypertension, can help identify individuals at risk before symptoms develop. Furthermore, advances in medical technology have enabled the development of noninvasive diagnostic tests and biomarkers that facilitate early detection and risk stratification.

Once a chronic disease is diagnosed, evidence-based treatment strategies aimed at controlling symptoms, slowing disease progression, and reducing complications are essential. This may involve pharmacological interventions, such as medications to lower blood pressure or manage blood sugar levels, as well as lifestyle modifications, including diet and exercise counseling.

In addition to medical interventions, patient education plays a critical role in chronic disease management. Providing patients with information about their condition, treatment options, and self-care strategies empowers them to take an active role in managing their health. Health literacy initiatives can help patients understand complex medical concepts, adhere to treatment regimens, and make informed decisions about their care.

Self-management support programs, such as chronic disease self-management workshops and telehealth services, offer tools and resources to help patients monitor their symptoms, track their progress, and communicate with healthcare providers remotely. These programs promote self-efficacy and enable patients to better cope with the challenges of living with a chronic condition.

The Role of Healthcare Providers

Healthcare providers play a central role in chronic disease management, serving as educators, diagnosticians, treatment coordinators, and advocates for their patients. Physicians, in particular, are responsible for diagnosing chronic conditions, developing treatment plans, and monitoring disease progression. They must stay abreast of the latest clinical guidelines and evidence-based practices to deliver high-quality care.

Nurses also play a critical role in chronic disease management, providing hands-on care, conducting assessments, administering medications, and educating patients about their conditions. Nurse practitioners and physician assistants may take on expanded roles in primary care settings, helping to bridge gaps in access to healthcare, particularly in underserved communities.

Pharmacists contribute to chronic disease management by ensuring safe and appropriate medication use, conducting medication therapy management (MTM) services, and counseling patients on proper medication administration and potential side effects. They also collaborate with other members of the healthcare team to optimize treatment regimens and promote medication adherence.

Dietitians and nutritionists play a vital role in helping patients manage chronic conditions such as diabetes, obesity, and cardiovascular diseases through dietary interventions. They provide personalized nutrition counseling, develop meal plans, and offer guidance on healthy eating habits to support overall health and well-being.

Social workers and care coordinators assist patients in navigating the complexities of the healthcare system, accessing community resources, and addressing social determinants of health that may impact their ability to manage chronic conditions effectively. They advocate for patients' needs and facilitate communication between patients, families, and healthcare providers.

Interprofessional collaboration is essential in chronic disease management, as it allows for comprehensive and coordinated care that addresses the diverse needs of patients. By working together as a team, healthcare providers can leverage their unique skills and perspectives to develop holistic treatment plans that optimize patient outcomes and improve quality of life.

Patient Education and Self-Management

Empowering patients to actively participate in their care is a cornerstone of effective chronic disease management. Patient education programs aim to equip individuals with the knowledge, skills, and confidence they need to make informed decisions about their health and engage in self-care activities.

Patient education begins at the time of diagnosis and continues throughout the course of the illness, covering topics such as disease pathology, treatment options, medication management, symptom recognition, and lifestyle modifications. Healthcare providers use various educational strategies, including verbal instruction, written materials, visual aids, and digital resources, to convey information in a manner that is accessible and understandable to patients.

In addition to providing information, healthcare providers must support patients in developing self-management skills that enable them to take an active role in managing their conditions on a day-to-day basis. This may involve teaching patients how to monitor their symptoms, track their medications, adhere to treatment regimens, and make healthy lifestyle choices.

Self-management support goes beyond education to encompass ongoing guidance, encouragement, and problem-solving assistance tailored to the individual needs and preferences of each patient. Healthcare providers can facilitate self-management by fostering a collaborative relationship with patients, eliciting their goals and preferences, and helping them develop personalized strategies for overcoming barriers to adherence and behavior change.

Technology plays an increasingly prominent role in supporting self-management efforts, with a growing array of digital tools and mobile health applications designed to help patients track their health metrics, set goals, receive reminders, and communicate with their healthcare providers remotely. Telehealth platforms offer opportunities for virtual consultations, remote monitoring, and real-time feedback, enhancing access to care for patients with chronic conditions, particularly those in rural or underserved areas.

Elderly Care

The elderly population, typically defined as individuals aged 65 and older, experiences a range of physical, cognitive, and psychosocial changes that can impact their quality of life and independence. Chronic conditions such as arthritis, hypertension, diabetes, and dementia become more prevalent with age, often requiring ongoing medical management and support. Mobility issues, sensory impairments, and functional limitations can also affect older adults' ability to perform activities of daily living (ADLs), such as bathing, dressing, and cooking.

Mental health concerns are common among the elderly, with depression, anxiety, and cognitive decline posing significant challenges. Social isolation and loneliness, exacerbated by factors such as retirement, loss of loved ones, and reduced mobility, further contribute to poor mental well-being among older adults. Economic insecurity, including inadequate retirement savings, limited access to affordable healthcare, and high healthcare costs, adds to the vulnerability of aging populations, particularly those with limited financial resources.

Models of Elderly Care

Various models of elderly care have been developed to meet the diverse needs of aging populations and their families. These models range from institutionalized care settings, such as nursing homes and assisted living facilities, to community-based programs and home care services.

Nursing homes provide 24-hour skilled nursing care for older adults who require assistance with ADLs and medical supervision. These facilities offer a range of services, including medication management, rehabilitation therapy, and social activities, tailored to the individual needs of residents. Assisted living facilities offer a less intensive level of care than nursing homes, providing assistance with tasks such as meal preparation, housekeeping, and medication reminders while promoting independence and autonomy.

Home care services allow older adults to age in place while receiving support from healthcare professionals and caregivers in the comfort of their own homes. Home health aides, nurses, and therapists provide assistance with personal care, medical treatments, and rehabilitation exercises, allowing seniors to maintain their independence and dignity while receiving necessary care. Telehealth and remote monitoring technologies offer additional support for home-bound individuals, enabling virtual consultations, medication reminders, and health status monitoring.

Community-based programs, such as senior centers, adult day care centers, and meal delivery services, provide socialization opportunities, recreational activities, and nutritional support for older adults living in the community. These programs promote social engagement, prevent social isolation, and enhance the overall well-being of seniors by fostering connections with peers and access to supportive services.

Role of Healthcare Professionals and Caregivers

Healthcare professionals, including physicians, nurses, social workers, and therapists, play a crucial role in providing comprehensive care for the elderly. Physicians oversee medical management, coordinate care among specialists, and address the complex health needs of older adults, including chronic conditions, medication management, and end-of-life care planning. Nurses provide hands-on care, administer treatments, and educate patients and families about disease management, symptom recognition, and healthy aging strategies.

Social workers assist older adults and their families in navigating the healthcare system, accessing community resources, and addressing psychosocial needs such as housing, financial assistance, and long-term care planning. Therapists, including physical therapists, occupational therapists, and speech-language pathologists, help older adults maintain mobility, independence, and cognitive function through rehabilitation interventions tailored to their individual needs.

Caregivers, including family members, friends, and professional caregivers, play a vital role in supporting older adults' daily needs and promoting their well-being. Family caregivers often juggle multiple responsibilities, including providing hands-on care, managing medications, coordinating appointments, and advocating for their loved ones' needs within the healthcare system. Professional caregivers offer respite care, companionship, and assistance with ADLs, allowing family caregivers to take breaks and attend to their own needs.

Community Engagement and Policy Interventions

Community engagement and policy interventions are essential for creating age-friendly environments that support the health, safety, and well-being of older adults. Age-friendly communities prioritize accessible housing, transportation, healthcare services, and recreational facilities that accommodate the needs of older residents. They also promote social inclusion, intergenerational interactions, and opportunities for lifelong learning and civic engagement.

Policy interventions at the local, national, and international levels can help address systemic barriers to healthy aging and promote equity in elderly care. Policies related to healthcare financing, long-term care insurance, and retirement savings can improve older adults' economic security and access to essential services. Legislation aimed at preventing elder abuse, neglect, and financial exploitation protects vulnerable seniors from harm and ensures their rights and dignity are upheld.

Furthermore, investments in geriatric workforce training, research on aging-related issues, and innovative care delivery models can enhance the capacity of healthcare systems to meet the needs of aging populations effectively. Interdisciplinary collaboration, data sharing, and quality improvement initiatives promote best practices in elderly care and drive continuous innovation and improvement in the field.

Elderly care is a complex and multifaceted endeavor that requires a holistic approach addressing the diverse needs of aging populations. By understanding the unique challenges faced by older adults and implementing comprehensive models of care delivery, healthcare professionals, caregivers, communities, and policymakers can promote healthy aging, enhance quality of life, and ensure dignity and respect for older adults throughout the aging process. Through collaborative efforts and targeted interventions, we can build age-friendly societies that support the well-being and flourishing of older adults worldwide.

Applications of Remote Patient Monitoring

Remote patient monitoring has applications across a wide range of medical specialties and patient populations. In cardiology, for example, RPM allows for the remote monitoring of patients with cardiovascular conditions such as hypertension, congestive heart failure, and arrhythmias. Wearable devices equipped with electrocardiogram (ECG) sensors can detect abnormal heart rhythms and alert healthcare providers to potential cardiac events, enabling early intervention and prevention of adverse outcomes.

Similarly, in respiratory care, RPM facilitates the remote monitoring of patients with chronic respiratory diseases such as COPD and asthma. Spirometers, pulse oximeters, and respiratory rate monitors can track changes in lung function and oxygen saturation levels, allowing healthcare providers to adjust treatment regimens and provide timely interventions to prevent exacerbations.

In diabetes management, RPM enables continuous monitoring of blood glucose levels, insulin usage, and lifestyle factors such as diet and exercise. Connected glucometers and insulin pumps can transmit data to healthcare providers in real-time, allowing for personalized adjustments to insulin dosing, medication regimens, and lifestyle recommendations to optimize glycemic control and reduce the risk of diabetic complications.

Beyond chronic disease management, remote patient monitoring has applications in post-surgical care, rehabilitation, mental health, and geriatric care. For example, RPM can facilitate remote monitoring of patients recovering from surgery or injury, enabling healthcare providers to track healing progress, manage pain, and identify complications early. In geriatric care, RPM allows for the remote monitoring of elderly patients living independently at home, providing peace of mind to caregivers and enabling timely interventions in case of falls, medication nonadherence, or changes in health status.

Benefits and Challenges of Remote Patient Monitoring

The adoption of remote patient monitoring offers numerous benefits to patients, healthcare providers, and healthcare systems alike. For patients, RPM provides greater convenience and flexibility by allowing them to receive care in the comfort of their own homes, reducing the need for frequent clinic visits and hospitalizations. This can be particularly beneficial for patients with mobility limitations, transportation barriers, or chronic conditions that require ongoing monitoring and management.

Furthermore, RPM empowers patients to take a more active role in managing their health by providing them with access to real-time health data, personalized feedback, and self-management tools. By enabling patients to track their progress, monitor their symptoms, and receive timely interventions, RPM promotes patient engagement, adherence to treatment regimens, and overall health literacy.

For healthcare providers, remote patient monitoring offers opportunities to deliver more proactive, patient-centered care that is tailored to the individual needs and preferences of each patient. By monitoring patients' health status remotely, healthcare providers can identify trends, detect early warning signs, and intervene before health issues escalate, leading to better outcomes and reduced healthcare costs.

Additionally, RPM facilitates care coordination and collaboration among members of the healthcare team, enabling seamless communication, data sharing, and decision-making. By providing access to real-time patient data, RPM enables healthcare providers to make more informed clinical judgments, optimize treatment plans, and prioritize resources effectively.

From a healthcare system perspective, remote patient monitoring has the potential to reduce healthcare costs by preventing unnecessary hospitalizations, emergency department visits, and complications associated with untreated or poorly managed conditions. By shifting care delivery from expensive inpatient settings to more cost-effective outpatient and home-based settings, RPM can help healthcare systems achieve greater efficiency, improve resource allocation, and enhance the overall value of care.

Despite its numerous benefits, remote patient monitoring also presents several challenges and considerations that must be addressed to realize its full potential. One significant challenge is the need for robust infrastructure and technology to support remote monitoring activities, including secure data transmission, interoperability between devices and EHR systems, and integration with existing workflows.

Furthermore, ensuring data privacy and security is paramount in remote patient monitoring, given the sensitive nature of health information and the potential risks associated with unauthorized access or breaches. Healthcare organizations must implement appropriate safeguards, such as encryption, authentication, and access controls, to protect patient data and comply with regulatory requirements, such as the Health Insurance Portability and Accountability Act (HIPAA).

Another challenge is ensuring equitable access to remote patient monitoring technology and services, particularly among underserved populations, including rural communities, low-income individuals, and older adults. Addressing barriers to adoption, such as digital literacy, Internet connectivity, and affordability, is essential to prevent exacerbating existing health disparities and ensure that all patients have access to the benefits of RPM.

Moreover, integrating remote patient monitoring into existing care delivery models requires changes in clinical workflows, care protocols, and reimbursement mechanisms. Healthcare organizations must invest in training and education for healthcare providers and staff to ensure they are proficient in using RPM technology and incorporating remote monitoring data into clinical decision-making effectively.

Furthermore, establishing clear guidelines and protocols for remote patient monitoring is essential to ensure the safe and effective use of RPM technology. This includes defining the roles and responsibilities of healthcare providers, patients, and caregivers, establishing criteria for patient eligibility and device selection, and specifying protocols for data collection, transmission, and interpretation.

Despite these challenges, the future of remote patient monitoring appears promising, with continued advancements in technology, regulatory support, and reimbursement policies driving its adoption and integration into mainstream healthcare delivery. As wearable sensors become smaller, more affordable, and more accurate, and telehealth platforms become more sophisticated and user-friendly, the potential applications of RPM will continue to expand.

Furthermore, the COVID-19 pandemic has accelerated the adoption of remote patient monitoring, as healthcare organizations seek alternative ways to deliver care while minimizing exposure to infectious diseases. Telehealth visits, remote monitoring, and virtual care platforms have become essential tools for delivering care remotely, enabling patients to receive timely interventions and support while reducing the burden on healthcare facilities.

Looking ahead, remote patient monitoring has the potential to revolutionize healthcare delivery by enabling proactive, personalized, and patient-centered care that transcends the boundaries of traditional clinical settings. By harnessing the power of technology to monitor patients' health status remotely, RPM holds promise for improving outcomes, enhancing access to care, and reducing healthcare costs, ultimately leading to better health and well-being for individuals and populations alike.

Fitness and Wellness Tracking

Fitness and wellness tracking involves the systematic monitoring of various health metrics and behaviors to assess and improve overall health and well-being. This can include tracking physical activity levels, exercise routines, nutritional intake, sleep quality, hydration, stress levels, and other lifestyle factors that impact health. The primary goals of fitness and wellness tracking are to promote awareness, facilitate behavior change, and empower individuals to make informed decisions about their health habits.

Tracking physical activity and exercise is a central component of fitness monitoring, as regular physical activity is associated with numerous health benefits, including improved cardiovascular health, weight management, mood regulation, and overall quality of life. Individuals may use wearable activity trackers, such as fitness bands or smartwatches, to monitor steps taken, distance traveled, calories burned, and active minutes throughout the day.

Nutrition tracking involves monitoring dietary intake to ensure adequate consumption of essential nutrients, maintain energy balance, and support overall health and performance. This may include tracking macronutrient intake (e.g., carbohydrates, proteins, fats), micronutrient intake (e.g., vitamins, minerals), and total calorie consumption using mobile apps, food journals, or online databases.

Sleep tracking involves monitoring sleep duration, quality, and patterns to identify factors that may impact sleep quality and overall well-being. Wearable sleep trackers and mobile apps can provide insights into sleep stages, sleep disturbances, and sleep hygiene practices, such as bedtime routines, screen time exposure, and environmental factors (e.g., noise, light).

Stress tracking involves monitoring physiological and psychological indicators of stress, such as heart rate variability, skin conductance, and self-reported stress levels, to identify triggers and patterns and implement stress management strategies. Biofeedback devices, meditation apps, and stress management programs can help individuals track and manage stress levels effectively.

Benefits of Fitness and Wellness Tracking

The adoption of fitness and wellness tracking offers numerous benefits to individuals seeking to improve their health and well-being. One of the primary benefits is increased awareness and accountability, as tracking health metrics and behaviors provides individuals with real-time feedback on their progress and adherence to health goals. This awareness can motivate individuals to make positive changes to their lifestyle habits and adopt healthier behaviors over time.

Furthermore, fitness and wellness tracking can facilitate behavior change by helping individuals set specific, measurable, achievable, relevant, and time-bound (SMART) goals and track their progress toward these goals. By breaking down larger goals into smaller, more manageable tasks and monitoring progress regularly, individuals can build momentum, stay motivated, and sustain behavior change efforts over the long term.

Moreover, fitness and wellness tracking can improve self-management skills by empowering individuals to take a more active role in managing their health and well-being. By providing individuals with access to personalized data and insights, tracking tools enable them to identify patterns, trends, and areas for improvement and make informed decisions about their health habits and lifestyle choices.

Additionally, fitness and wellness tracking can enhance communication and collaboration between individuals and their healthcare providers, enabling more informed discussions about health goals, progress, and treatment plans. By sharing tracking data with healthcare providers, individuals can receive personalized recommendations, support, and guidance to optimize their health outcomes and prevent or manage chronic conditions.

Furthermore, the social aspect of fitness and wellness tracking can provide individuals with a sense of community, support, and accountability. Many tracking platforms and apps offer features such as social sharing, group challenges, and online communities where individuals can connect with like-minded peers, share experiences, and receive encouragement and support from others on their fitness and wellness journey.

Challenges and Considerations

Despite its numerous benefits, fitness and wellness tracking also presents several challenges and considerations that individuals should be aware of when using tracking tools and technologies. One significant challenge is the accuracy and reliability of tracking devices and data, as not all devices and apps are created equal. Variability in sensor accuracy, data algorithms, and device calibration can lead to discrepancies in tracking metrics, such as step counts, calorie estimates, and sleep duration, which may impact the validity and usefulness of tracking data.

Furthermore, the potential for data overload and information overwhelm is a common challenge associated with fitness and wellness tracking, particularly when individuals are bombarded with a constant stream of data and notifications from multiple tracking devices and apps. Managing and interpreting large volumes of tracking data can be overwhelming and may detract from the overall user experience, leading to disengagement and abandonment of tracking efforts.

Privacy and security concerns are another consideration in fitness and wellness tracking, as individuals may be hesitant to share sensitive health data with third-party apps and platforms due to fears of data breaches, unauthorized access, or misuse of personal information. Ensuring data privacy and security requires robust data encryption, authentication, and access controls, as well as transparent privacy policies and user consent mechanisms.

Moreover, the potential for obsessive tracking behavior and unhealthy fixation on numbers and metrics is a risk associated with fitness and wellness tracking, particularly among individuals with a history of disordered eating, body image concerns, or obsessive-compulsive tendencies. Excessive focus on tracking metrics, such as calorie counts, exercise minutes, or body weight, can lead to stress, anxiety, and unhealthy behaviors, undermining the intended goals of tracking for health and well-being.

Furthermore, the lack of standardization and interoperability among tracking devices and apps poses challenges for individuals who use multiple devices or platforms to track different aspects of their health and wellness. Incompatibility between devices, data silos, and fragmentation of tracking data can hinder data integration, analysis, and interpretation, limiting the utility of tracking data for informing health decisions and behavior change.

Role of Technology in Facilitating Tracking Efforts

Technology plays a central role in facilitating fitness and wellness tracking efforts by providing individuals with access to a wide range of tracking devices, apps, and online platforms that support their health goals. Wearable devices, such as fitness bands, smartwatches, and activity trackers, offer convenient and unobtrusive ways to monitor physical activity, exercise, and other health metrics throughout the day.

Mobile apps and digital platforms provide individuals with tools and resources to track various aspects of their health and wellness, including nutrition, sleep, stress, hydration, and mindfulness. These apps offer features such as food logging, meal planning, recipe databases, sleep tracking, meditation exercises, and mood tracking, allowing individuals to monitor and manage their health habits in a personalized and customizable manner.

Furthermore, advances in data analytics and AI technologies enable individuals to gain deeper insights into their tracking data, identify patterns and trends, and receive personalized recommendations for optimizing their health and well-being. Machine learning algorithms can analyze large volumes of tracking data to provide actionable insights, predictive analytics, and personalized feedback tailored to the individual needs and goals of each user.

Moreover, telehealth and remote monitoring technologies have become increasingly integrated into fitness and wellness tracking efforts, enabling individuals to connect with healthcare providers, wellness coaches, and other support networks remotely. Telehealth platforms offer virtual consultations, coaching sessions, and remote monitoring services that complement traditional in-person care and provide individuals with greater access to support and guidance when and where they need it most.

Additionally, gamification and behavioral economics principles are often employed in fitness and wellness tracking apps to enhance engagement, motivation, and adherence to health goals. Features such as goal setting, progress tracking, rewards, challenges, and social incentives can make tracking more enjoyable and engaging, encouraging individuals to stick with their tracking habits over time.

Benefits of Fitness and Wellness Tracking

The use of fitness and wellness tracking has the potential to have a significant impact on individual health outcomes and behavior change by empowering individuals to take control of their health habits and make informed decisions about their lifestyle choices. By providing individuals with access to personalized data, insights, and support, tracking tools enable them to identify areas for improvement, set achievable goals, and track their progress toward better health and well-being.

Furthermore, by promoting awareness, accountability, and self-management skills, fitness and wellness tracking can facilitate behavior change across a wide range of health domains, including physical activity, nutrition, sleep, stress management, and overall lifestyle habits. Individuals who track their health behaviors are more likely to make positive changes to their habits and sustain these changes over time compared to those who do not track their behaviors.

Moreover, by fostering a sense of community, support, and accountability, fitness and wellness tracking can enhance social connectedness and peer support, which are important determinants of health behavior change. Online communities, group challenges, and social sharing features in tracking apps provide individuals with opportunities to connect with like-minded peers, share experiences, and receive encouragement and support from others on their health and wellness journey.

Additionally, by facilitating communication and collaboration between individuals and their healthcare providers, fitness and wellness tracking can improve healthcare delivery and outcomes. Healthcare providers who have access to tracking data can provide more personalized recommendations, support, and guidance to help individuals achieve their health goals and prevent or manage chronic conditions more effectively.

Furthermore, by leveraging technology to deliver remote coaching, telehealth consultations, and virtual support services, fitness and wellness tracking can overcome barriers to access and engagement, particularly among underserved populations, including rural communities, low-income individuals, and older adults. Remote monitoring and telehealth platforms offer individuals greater flexibility and convenience in accessing care and support, leading to improved health outcomes and satisfaction with care.

Fitness and wellness tracking represents a powerful tool for promoting health awareness, behavior change, and self-management skills among individuals seeking to improve their health and well-being. By harnessing the capabilities of technology, individuals can track various aspects of their health and lifestyle habits, receive personalized feedback and recommendations, and connect with support networks remotely. While there are challenges and considerations associated with fitness and wellness tracking, the potential benefits for individual health outcomes, behavior change, and healthcare delivery are significant. By embracing technology-enabled tracking solutions and fostering a culture of health tracking and self-care, individuals can empower themselves to take control of their health and achieve their wellness goals for a happier, healthier life.

Wearable Devices and Sensors for Remote Monitoring

The challenges and limitations of wearable devices and sensors for remote monitoring include the accuracy and reliability of measurements, user acceptance and adherence, and regulatory compliance.

Accuracy and Reliability of Measurements

Both the accuracy and reliability of measurements are subject to several challenges and limitations, but several strategies are available to help mitigate those challenges and limitations.

Challenges in Ensuring Accuracy and Reliability

- **Instrumentation and calibration:** One of the primary challenges in ensuring accuracy and reliability of measurements lies in the quality and calibration of instrumentation used. Instruments may drift over time, resulting in inaccuracies in measurements if not regularly calibrated and maintained. Furthermore, differences in instrument design, manufacturing tolerances, and sensor technologies can introduce variability and uncertainty in measurements, impacting their accuracy and reliability.

- **Measurement uncertainty:** Measurement uncertainty arises from various sources, including inherent variability in the measurement process, limitations of measurement instruments, and environmental factors such as temperature, humidity, and pressure. Quantifying and managing measurement uncertainty is essential for assessing the reliability of measurements and interpreting results accurately. However, estimating uncertainty can be challenging, particularly in complex measurement systems with multiple sources of variability and error.

- **Human error and bias:** Human error and bias represent significant sources of uncertainty in measurements, stemming from factors such as observer variability, subjective judgment, cognitive biases, and improper measurement techniques. Even with well-calibrated instrumentation and standardized procedures, variations in human perception, interpretation, and execution can introduce errors and inconsistencies, affecting the accuracy and reliability of measurements.

- **Sampling and sample size:** Sampling methods and sample size are critical considerations in many measurement applications, particularly in scientific research, quality control, and statistical analysis. Inadequate sample size or biased sampling techniques can lead to sampling errors and inaccuracies in estimates, compromising the reliability and validity of study findings. Moreover, sampling from heterogeneous populations or nonrepresentative samples can introduce bias and limit the generalizability of results.

- **Environmental factors:** Environmental conditions, such as temperature, humidity, vibration, electromagnetic interference (EMI), and contamination, can impact the performance and accuracy of measurement instruments. Variations in environmental conditions can cause drift, noise, and interference in measurements, leading to inaccuracies and uncertainties in results. Shielding, environmental controls, and calibration procedures are often employed to mitigate the effects of environmental factors on measurement accuracy and reliability.

- **Measurement traceability and standards:** Establishing traceability to recognized measurement standards is essential for ensuring the accuracy and reliability of measurements, particularly in metrology and calibration laboratories. Traceability provides a documented link between measurement results and national or international standards, enabling comparability, consistency, and confidence in measurement data. However, achieving traceability can be challenging, especially in fields where standards are lacking or measurement techniques are evolving rapidly.

- **Data processing and analysis:** Data processing and analysis play a crucial role in extracting meaningful information from measurement data, but they also introduce opportunities for errors and biases. Improper data filtering, normalization, outlier detection, and statistical analysis techniques can lead to distorted results and erroneous conclusions. Moreover, the choice of data analysis methods and algorithms may introduce systematic errors or overlook important patterns and trends in the data, compromising the accuracy and reliability of findings.

- **Measurement system complexity:** The complexity of measurement systems, including multi-sensor arrays, interconnected subsystems, and feedback loops, can pose challenges for ensuring accuracy and reliability.

Interactions between components, nonlinearities, and dynamic behaviors can introduce uncertainties and errors that are difficult to predict and quantify. Furthermore, the integration of multiple measurement technologies and data fusion techniques adds another layer of complexity, requiring careful calibration, validation, and verification to ensure accuracy and reliability.

- **Time-dependent effects:** Some measurements are susceptible to time-dependent effects, such as aging, degradation, drift, and fatigue, which can impact measurement accuracy and reliability over time. Instruments may exhibit changes in performance characteristics due to prolonged use, exposure to environmental conditions, or wear and tear, necessitating regular maintenance, recalibration, and replacement to mitigate the effects of aging and ensure consistent performance.

- **Cost and resource constraints:** Budgetary constraints, resource limitations, and time pressures can present challenges in achieving the desired level of accuracy and reliability in measurements. High-quality instrumentation, rigorous calibration procedures, extensive testing, and validation efforts often require substantial investments of time, money, and expertise. Limited resources may force compromises in measurement quality, leading to trade-offs between accuracy, reliability, and cost-effectiveness.

Limitations of Measurement Techniques

- **Sensitivity and resolution:** Many measurement techniques have inherent limitations in terms of sensitivity and resolution, defined as the smallest detectable change or smallest increment that can be reliably measured. Low sensitivity or resolution can lead to missed signals, measurement noise, or inability to distinguish small variations, limiting the accuracy and precision of measurements, particularly in applications requiring high sensitivity and fine resolution.

- **Measurement range:** The measurement range of an instrument defines the range of values over which it can accurately measure a quantity. Instruments may have limited dynamic range or saturation limits, beyond which measurements become inaccurate or unreliable. Out-of-range measurements may be truncated, clipped, or distorted, leading to inaccuracies and loss of information, particularly in situations with wide-ranging or transient signals.

- **Interference and cross-sensitivity:** Measurement techniques may be susceptible to interference from external sources or cross-sensitivity to other variables, leading to measurement errors and inaccuracies. Common sources of interference include EMI, crosstalk, ambient noise, and cross-reactivity with interfering substances. Minimizing interference and cross-sensitivity requires careful shielding, filtering, and isolation techniques to ensure accurate and reliable measurements.

- **Nonlinearity and hysteresis:** Many measurement systems exhibit nonlinear behavior, where the relationship between input and output is not linear or predictable. Nonlinearities can lead to distortions, inaccuracies, and hysteresis effects, where the measured response depends on the history or path of the input signal. Correcting for nonlinearities and hysteresis requires advanced signal processing techniques, calibration procedures, and mathematical modeling to ensure accurate and reliable measurements across the full operating range of the system.

- **Measurement errors and uncertainties:** All measurement techniques are subject to errors and uncertainties, which can arise from various sources, including random fluctuations, systematic biases, instrumental errors, and environmental factors. Understanding and quantifying measurement errors and uncertainties is essential for assessing the reliability and validity of measurement data and making informed decisions based on the results. However, measuring and characterizing uncertainties can be challenging, particularly in complex measurement systems with multiple sources of error and variability.

- **Invasive and destructive techniques:** Some measurement techniques involve invasive or destructive procedures that may alter or damage the sample or specimen being measured. Invasive techniques, such as biopsies, surgeries, or chemical analyses, can introduce artifacts, contamination, or tissue damage, affecting the accuracy and reliability of measurements. Noninvasive or nondestructive alternatives are often preferred when possible to minimize the impact on the sample and preserve its integrity for subsequent analyses.

- **Limitations in resolution and bandwidth:** Measurement techniques may have limitations in resolution, defined as the smallest discernible change in a measured quantity, and bandwidth, defined as the frequency range over which measurements can be reliably obtained. Limited resolution or bandwidth can constrain the accuracy, sensitivity, and dynamic range of measurements, particularly in applications requiring high-speed or high-resolution data acquisition.

- **Environmental sensitivity:** Some measurement techniques are sensitive to environmental conditions, such as temperature, humidity, pressure, and electromagnetic fields, which can influence measurement accuracy and reliability. Variations in environmental conditions can cause drift, noise, and interference in measurements, leading to inaccuracies and uncertainties in results. Environmental controls, calibration procedures, and shielding techniques are often employed to mitigate the effects of environmental sensitivity on measurement quality.

- **Complexity:** The complexity of measurement techniques vary widely, ranging from simple, direct methods to sophisticated, multistep procedures requiring specialized equipment and expertise. Complex measurement techniques may be difficult to implement, interpret, and validate, requiring extensive training, resources, and quality assurance measures to ensure accuracy and reliability. Simplifying measurement techniques and standardizing procedures can help reduce complexity and improve consistency and reproducibility of measurements across different settings and operators.

- **Trade-offs between accuracy and speed:** In many measurement applications, there is a trade-off between accuracy and speed, where increasing measurement speed may come at the expense of accuracy, and vice versa. Fast measurement techniques, such as rapid screening assays or real-time monitoring systems, may sacrifice precision or sensitivity for rapid data acquisition, leading to compromises in measurement quality. Balancing the need for speed with the requirements for accuracy and reliability is essential for optimizing measurement performance and meeting the specific needs of each application.

Strategies to Mitigate Challenges and Limitations

- **Instrumentation selection and calibration:** Choose high-quality instrumentation with proven accuracy, reliability, and stability, and ensure regular calibration and maintenance to maintain performance over time.

- **Measurement traceability and standards:** Establish traceability to recognized measurement standards and participate in proficiency testing and interlaboratory comparisons to verify measurement accuracy and reliability.

231

- **Quality assurance and quality control:** Implement robust quality assurance and quality control procedures to monitor and verify measurement accuracy, precision, and repeatability, including regular instrument checks, calibration checks, and validation studies.

- **Error analysis and uncertainty estimation:** Conduct comprehensive error analysis and uncertainty estimation to identify sources of measurement error, quantify uncertainties, and assess the reliability of measurement results.

- **Standardization and protocol development:** Standardize measurement protocols, procedures, and data analysis methods to ensure consistency, reproducibility, and comparability of measurements across different operators, instruments, and settings.

- **Environmental controls and stability:** Maintain stable environmental conditions, such as temperature, humidity, and vibration, to minimize variability and interference in measurements and ensure consistent performance of instrumentation.

- **Training and education:** Provide training and education to personnel involved in measurement activities to ensure proper technique, adherence to protocols, and awareness of potential sources of error and bias.

- **Data validation and verification:** Validate measurement data through independent verification, cross-validation, or comparison with reference methods or standards to confirm accuracy, reliability, and consistency of results.

- **Continuous improvement and feedback:**
  Continuously monitor, evaluate, and improve
  measurement processes and procedures based on
  feedback, performance metrics, and lessons learned to
  enhance accuracy, efficiency, and effectiveness.

- **Collaboration and interdisciplinary approaches:**
  Foster collaboration and interdisciplinary approaches
  to measurement science, bringing together experts
  from diverse fields to address complex measurement
  challenges and develop innovative solutions.

User Acceptance and Adherence

User acceptance encompasses the attitudes, beliefs, perceptions, and
intentions of individuals toward a healthcare intervention such as a
recommendation to wear a device or sensor for remote monitoring, reflecting
their willingness and motivation to engage with it. Acceptance is influenced
by various factors, including perceived usefulness, ease of use, compatibility
with existing beliefs and practices, perceived benefits, perceived risks, trust in
the intervention, social norms, and peer influence. Individuals are more likely
to accept interventions that align with their values, preferences, and goals and
perceive them as relevant, beneficial, and compatible with their lifestyle.

User adherence refers to the extent to which individuals follow prescribed
recommendations, instructions, or treatment plans as intended over time.
Adherence behaviors encompass various actions, including medication
adherence, dietary adherence, exercise adherence, appointment attendance,
self-monitoring, lifestyle modifications, and health-seeking behaviors.
Adherence is influenced by a multitude of factors, including individual
characteristics, psychological factors, social support, environmental factors,
healthcare system factors, and intervention-related factors.

Although user acceptance of wearable devices and sensors and adherence to their proper use are challenges in the healthcare field, several strategies exist to enhance acceptance and adherence.

Determinants of User Acceptance

- **Perceived usefulness:** Individuals are more likely to accept healthcare interventions that offer perceived benefits, such as improved health outcomes, symptom relief, quality of life enhancements, or risk reduction. Perceived usefulness reflects individuals' beliefs about the effectiveness and value of the intervention in addressing their health concerns and achieving their health goals.

- **Ease of use:** The perceived ease of use refers to individuals' perceptions of the effort required to adopt and use the intervention. Interventions that are user-friendly, intuitive, accessible, and convenient are more likely to be accepted, as they minimize barriers to engagement and facilitate adoption and adherence.

- **Compatibility:** Compatibility refers to the extent to which the intervention aligns with individuals' existing beliefs, values, practices, habits, and lifestyle. Interventions that fit seamlessly into individuals' daily routines, preferences, and cultural norms are more likely to be accepted and integrated into their lives.

- **Perceived benefits and risks:** Individuals weigh the perceived benefits of the intervention against potential risks, costs, side effects, or inconveniences associated with its use. Interventions with perceived high benefits and low risks are more likely to be accepted, whereas those with perceived high risks or uncertainties may face resistance or skepticism.

- **Trust and credibility:** Trust in the intervention, healthcare provider, or source of information plays a crucial role in user acceptance. Individuals are more likely to accept interventions endorsed by trusted sources, such as healthcare professionals, reputable organizations, or peer testimonials, as they perceive them as credible, reliable, and trustworthy.

- **Social influence and peer support:** Social factors, such as social norms, peer influence, social support, and social networks, can influence user acceptance. Individuals may be more inclined to accept interventions that are endorsed or recommended by peers, family members, or opinion leaders, as they seek social validation, acceptance, and approval.

Determinants of Adherence

- **Individual beliefs and attitudes:** Individual beliefs, attitudes, perceptions, and motivations play a significant role in adherence behaviors. Positive attitudes toward the intervention, perceived benefits, self-efficacy, outcome expectations, and intrinsic motivation are associated with higher adherence, whereas negative attitudes, perceived barriers, misconceptions, and ambivalence may impede adherence.

- **Health literacy and knowledge:** Health literacy, knowledge, and understanding of the intervention and its rationale are essential for informed decision-making and adherence. Individuals with higher health literacy and knowledge levels are better equipped to comprehend, interpret, and adhere to recommendations, whereas those with limited health literacy may struggle to understand instructions, navigate healthcare systems, and make informed choices.

- **Self-management skills:** Self-management skills, including goal-setting, problem-solving, decision-making, self-monitoring, and coping strategies, are crucial for adherence to healthcare interventions. Individuals who possess effective self-management skills are better able to overcome barriers, manage challenges, and sustain behavior change over time, leading to improved adherence and health outcomes.

- **Social support and environment:** Social support from family members, friends, caregivers, healthcare providers, and peers can significantly influence adherence behaviors. Positive social support networks provide encouragement, accountability, practical assistance, and emotional support, facilitating adherence and fostering resilience in the face of challenges.

- **Healthcare provider-patient relationship:** The quality of the healthcare provider–patient relationship, including communication, trust, empathy, collaboration, and shared decision-making, is a key determinant of adherence. A supportive, collaborative relationship with healthcare providers enhances patient engagement, motivation, and commitment to treatment goals, leading to improved adherence and satisfaction with care.

- **Intervention characteristics:** The characteristics of the intervention itself, such as complexity, frequency, duration, mode of delivery, and perceived effectiveness, influence adherence behaviors. Interventions that are simple, flexible, personalized, interactive, and tailored to individuals' needs and preferences are more likely to be adhered to over time.

Strategies to Enhance Acceptance and Adherence

- **Individualized approach:** Tailor interventions to individuals' needs, preferences, goals, and circumstances to enhance acceptance and adherence. Provide personalized recommendations, support, and resources based on individuals' characteristics, motivations, and barriers.

- **Education and health literacy:** Provide clear, understandable, and culturally sensitive education and information about the intervention, its rationale, benefits, risks, and expected outcomes to improve acceptance and adherence. Enhance health literacy and empower individuals to make informed decisions about their health.

- **Behavioral strategies:** Incorporate behavioral change techniques, such as goal-setting, action planning, self-monitoring, feedback, reinforcement, and social support, to promote adherence and sustain behavior change. Empower individuals with self-management skills and coping strategies to overcome barriers and maintain motivation.

- **Communication and support:** Establish open, trustful, and collaborative communication channels between individuals and healthcare providers to enhance acceptance and adherence. Provide ongoing support, encouragement, and guidance to address concerns, reinforce positive behaviors, and troubleshoot challenges.

- **Simplification and convenience:** Simplify interventions and reduce complexity to minimize barriers to acceptance and adherence. Design interventions that are convenient, accessible, and easy to use, with clear instructions and minimal burden on individuals' time, resources, and cognitive load.

- **Integration into daily life:** Integrate interventions into individuals' daily routines, habits, and environments to enhance acceptance and adherence. Promote seamless integration of interventions into existing lifestyle practices, such as incorporating physical activity into daily activities or embedding reminders into daily routines.

- **Social support and peer influence:** Leverage social support networks, peer support groups, and online communities to foster acceptance and adherence. Facilitate peer-to-peer interactions, social sharing, and mutual support to enhance motivation, accountability, and engagement with the intervention.

- **Feedback and reinforcement:** Provide regular feedback, reinforcement, and positive reinforcement to acknowledge progress, celebrate achievements, and motivate continued adherence. Use feedback mechanisms, such as progress trackers, reminders, and rewards, to reinforce desired behaviors and encourage persistence.

Regulatory Compliance

Regulatory compliance for wearable devices and sensors in remote patient monitoring involves adhering to laws and standards that protect patient privacy, ensure safety, and guarantee data accuracy. Devices must comply with privacy regulations like HIPAA and GDPR, and meet safety standards set by organizations such as the FDA. They must also be certified for accuracy in monitoring vital signs and meet cybersecurity standards to protect patient data. Compliance ensures that wearable devices operate ethically, maintain patient trust, and support reliable healthcare delivery.

Key Regulatory Areas in Healthcare

- **Patient privacy and data security:** As discussed in Chapter 5, compliance with laws such as HIPAA and the GDPR is essential for protecting patient privacy and confidentiality. Healthcare organizations must implement safeguards to secure electronic protected health information (ePHI), prevent unauthorized access, and mitigate data breaches.

- **Quality and safety standards:** Compliance with quality and safety standards, such as those established by organizations like The Joint Commission, Centers for Medicare and Medicaid Services (CMS), and World

Health Organization (WHO), is critical for delivering high-quality care and minimizing patient harm. Healthcare organizations must implement evidence-based practices, performance metrics, and quality improvement initiatives to meet accreditation and certification requirements.

- **Billing and coding regulations:** Compliance with billing and coding regulations, such as the International Classification of Diseases (ICD) and Current Procedural Terminology (CPT) code sets, is essential for accurate billing, reimbursement, and claims processing. Healthcare providers must document services accurately, code diagnoses and procedures correctly, and adhere to coding guidelines to prevent fraud, waste, and abuse.

- **Licensure and credentialing requirements:** Compliance with state licensure and professional credentialing requirements is necessary for healthcare providers to practice legally and maintain professional competence. Healthcare organizations must verify credentials, monitor licensure status, and ensure that providers meet ongoing continuing education requirements to uphold regulatory standards.

- **Pharmaceutical and medical device regulations:** Compliance with regulations from agencies such as the US Food and Drug Administration (FDA) and European Medicines Agency (EMA) is essential for ensuring the safety, efficacy, and quality of pharmaceuticals and medical devices. Healthcare organizations must adhere to Good Manufacturing Practices (GMP), conduct clinical trials ethically, and obtain regulatory approvals before marketing products.

Challenges and Considerations in Regulatory Compliance

- **Complex and evolving regulatory landscape:** The
  healthcare regulatory environment is complex,
  multifaceted, and constantly evolving, with numerous
  laws, regulations, standards, and guidelines at the
  federal, state, and international levels. Keeping abreast
  of regulatory changes, interpreting requirements,
  and ensuring compliance across diverse regulatory
  domains pose significant challenges for healthcare
  organizations and providers.

- **Resource constraints:** Limited resources, including
  financial, human, and technological resources, can
  impede compliance efforts, particularly for smaller
  healthcare organizations and providers with limited
  budgets and staffing. Compliance requires investment
  in training, infrastructure, technology, and ongoing
  monitoring and auditing activities, which may strain
  organizational resources and capacity.

- **Interdisciplinary nature of compliance:** Regulatory
  compliance in healthcare requires collaboration and
  coordination across multiple disciplines, including
  clinical, administrative, legal, information technology,
  compliance, and risk management. Ensuring alignment
  and communication among stakeholders with diverse
  expertise and priorities can be challenging, particularly
  in large, complex healthcare organizations.

- **Data security and privacy risks:** Healthcare
  organizations face growing cybersecurity threats
  and privacy risks associated with the proliferation of
  EHRs , interconnected systems, mobile devices, and

241

cloud-based platforms. Safeguarding patient data, preventing unauthorized access, and complying with privacy regulations require robust security measures, encryption protocols, access controls, and employee training.

- **Regulatory interpretation and implementation:** Interpreting regulatory requirements and translating them into actionable policies, procedures, and practices can be challenging, particularly when regulations are vague, ambiguous, or open to interpretation. Healthcare organizations must navigate regulatory nuances, seek guidance from legal experts, regulatory agencies, and industry associations, and tailor compliance strategies to their specific context and needs.

- **Compliance monitoring and auditing:** Ongoing monitoring, auditing, and enforcement of compliance activities are essential for detecting noncompliance, identifying areas for improvement, and mitigating risks of violations and sanctions. However, conducting internal audits, self-assessments, and compliance reviews requires dedicated resources, expertise, and systems for tracking and documenting compliance activities.

- **Cultural and organizational challenges:** Organizational culture, leadership commitment, and workforce attitudes play a crucial role in shaping compliance behaviors and practices. Establishing a culture of compliance, integrity, and accountability requires strong leadership, clear communication, employee training, and incentives for ethical conduct.

Strategies to Navigate Regulatory Compliance

- **Conduct regulatory risk assessments:** Identify and assess regulatory risks and vulnerabilities across key areas of operation, including patient care, data security, billing, and licensure. Prioritize risks based on likelihood, impact, and regulatory requirements, and develop risk mitigation strategies and action plans accordingly.

- **Invest in compliance education and training:** Provide comprehensive education and training programs to healthcare staff at all levels to enhance awareness, understanding, and adherence to regulatory requirements. Offer specialized training on topics such as HIPAA privacy and security, billing compliance, infection control, and ethical conduct.

- **Implement compliance management systems:** Establish formal compliance management systems, policies, and procedures to guide compliance activities, ensure accountability, and promote consistency across the organization. Implement mechanisms for documenting, tracking, and reporting compliance activities, incidents, and corrective actions.

- **Foster collaboration and communication:** Promote collaboration and communication among interdisciplinary teams, departments, and stakeholders involved in compliance efforts. Establish cross-functional compliance committees, task forces, or working groups to facilitate information sharing, problem-solving, and decision-making.

- **Leverage technology solutions:** Utilize technology solutions, such as EHRs, compliance software, data analytics tools, and automated monitoring systems, to streamline compliance activities, enhance data security, and improve documentation and reporting capabilities.

- **Engage external resources and expertise:** Seek guidance, support, and expertise from external consultants, legal counsel, industry associations, and regulatory agencies to navigate complex regulatory requirements, interpret regulations, and address compliance challenges effectively.

- **Conduct regular audits and monitoring:** Conduct regular internal audits, assessments, and monitoring activities to evaluate compliance performance, identify areas of noncompliance or weakness, and implement corrective actions and process improvements proactively.

- **Stay informed and adapt:** Stay abreast of regulatory developments, changes, and updates through regular monitoring of regulatory agencies, industry publications, and professional networks. Continuously evaluate and adapt compliance strategies, policies, and practices in response to evolving regulatory requirements, industry trends, and organizational changes.

Wearable devices equipped with sensors play a pivotal role in collecting biometric data and transmitting it in real time, offering insights into patients' health conditions outside traditional clinical settings. Understanding these technologies leads to a discussion on how remote monitoring improves patient outcomes by facilitating early intervention and personalized healthcare delivery.

Improving Patient Outcomes Through Remote Monitoring

Remote monitoring of patients using wearable devices and other technologies has the potential to significantly improve patient outcomes across various healthcare settings. Here's how remote monitoring can contribute to better patient outcomes:

- **Early detection of health issues:** Remote monitoring allows for continuous tracking of vital signs, symptoms, and disease-specific parameters in real time. By detecting changes or abnormalities early, healthcare providers can intervene promptly to prevent complications, exacerbations, or hospitalizations. For example, remote monitoring of patients with heart failure can detect signs of fluid retention or worsening symptoms, enabling timely adjustments to medication or treatment plans to prevent heart failure exacerbations.

- **Improved disease management:** Remote monitoring enables patients with chronic conditions to actively participate in their own care by providing regular feedback and insights into their health status. By monitoring parameters such as blood pressure, blood glucose levels, or medication adherence remotely, patients can better manage their conditions and make informed decisions about lifestyle changes, medication adjustments, or seeking medical advice when necessary. This proactive approach to disease management can lead to better control of chronic conditions, reduced complications, and improved quality of life for patients.

245

- **Personalized treatment plans:** Remote monitoring data provides healthcare providers with valuable insights into patients' individual health status and response to treatment. By analyzing trends, patterns, and fluctuations in patient data over time, healthcare providers can tailor treatment plans, medication regimens, or lifestyle interventions to meet the unique needs of each patient. Personalized treatment plans based on remote monitoring data can lead to better treatment adherence, improved symptom management, and optimized therapeutic outcomes for patients.

- **Enhanced patient engagement and empowerment:** Remote monitoring promotes active patient engagement in their own care by involving patients in the monitoring process and encouraging them to take ownership of their health. Patients can use wearable devices and mobile apps to track their health metrics, set goals, and receive feedback on their progress. This increased engagement empowers patients to make informed decisions about their health, adhere to treatment plans, and adopt healthier lifestyle behaviors, leading to improved self-management and better health outcomes.

- **Reduced healthcare costs and resource utilization:** Remote monitoring can help reduce healthcare costs by preventing avoidable hospitalizations, emergency room visits, and unnecessary healthcare utilization. By monitoring patients remotely and intervening early to address health issues, healthcare providers can prevent costly complications, reduce the need for in-person visits, and optimize resource allocation.

Remote monitoring also facilitates more efficient use of healthcare resources by focusing attention on patients who need it most, thereby reducing overall healthcare spending and improving healthcare system sustainability.

- **Continuous monitoring and follow-up care:** Remote monitoring enables continuous monitoring of patients' health status beyond the traditional clinical setting. Patients can be monitored in their homes, communities, or other nonclinical environments, allowing for more frequent monitoring and follow-up care. This continuous monitoring provides healthcare providers with a more comprehensive understanding of patients' health trajectories, enabling proactive interventions and personalized care delivery to optimize patient outcomes over time.

Overall, remote monitoring has the potential to revolutionize healthcare delivery by improving patient outcomes, enhancing patient engagement, reducing healthcare costs, and enabling more personalized and proactive approaches to patient care. As technology continues to advance and remote monitoring solutions become more widely adopted, the impact on patient outcomes is expected to grow, leading to better health outcomes and improved quality of life for patients worldwide (see Figure 6-3).

Figure 6-3 provides a visual representation of several benefits of wearable devices and sensors for remote patient monitoring. It differs from the preceding list because it groups these benefits into categories, visually highlighting the various impacts on healthcare, such as improving patient outcomes, reducing healthcare costs, enhancing clinical staff effectiveness, and supporting underserved populations. The list, on the other hand, presents these benefits individually without such groupings. This distinction helps clarify the range of positive effects that remote patient monitoring can have, not only on patients but also on healthcare systems as a whole.

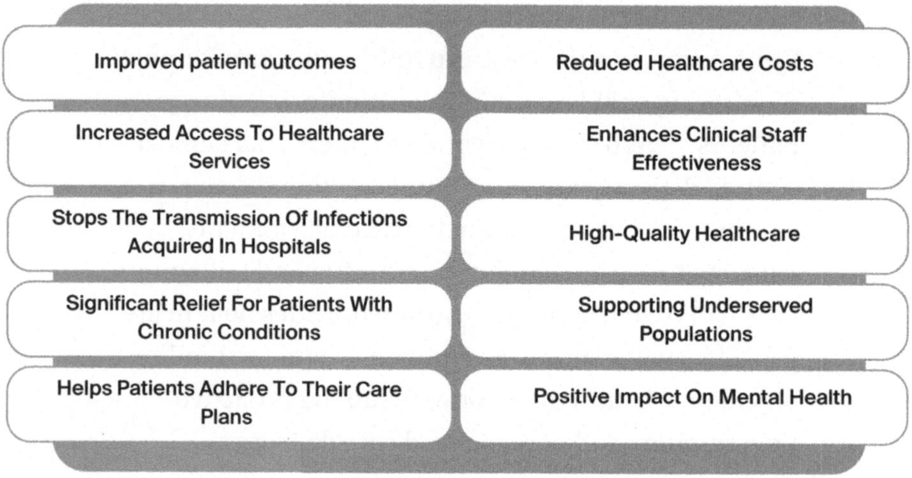

Improved patient outcomes	Reduced Healthcare Costs
Increased Access To Healthcare Services	Enhances Clinical Staff Effectiveness
Stops The Transmission Of Infections Acquired In Hospitals	High-Quality Healthcare
Significant Relief For Patients With Chronic Conditions	Supporting Underserved Populations
Helps Patients Adhere To Their Care Plans	Positive Impact On Mental Health

Figure 6-3. *Benefits of remote patient monitoring and telehealth*

Table 6-1 summarizes the benefits and challenges associated with remote monitoring in healthcare.

Table 6-1. *Advantages and Disadvantages of Remote Monitoring in Healthcare*

Advantages	Disadvantages
Enhanced access to healthcare: Remote monitoring allows patients to receive timely care and support regardless of their location, improving access to healthcare services.	**Technological barriers:** Not all patients may have access to the necessary technology or Internet connectivity required for remote monitoring, limiting its effectiveness and reach.
Early detection of health issues: Remote monitoring enables healthcare providers to detect potential health issues or exacerbations early, allowing for timely interventions and preventive measures.	**Privacy and security concerns:** Remote monitoring involves the transmission and storage of sensitive patient health data, raising concerns about privacy breaches, data security, and confidentiality.
Improved chronic disease management: Remote monitoring facilitates the continuous monitoring of chronic conditions, such as diabetes, hypertension, and heart disease, leading to better disease management and outcomes.	**Reliability of data:** The accuracy and reliability of data collected through remote monitoring devices may vary, leading to inaccuracies in assessment and decision-making if not properly validated or calibrated.
Patient empowerment and engagement: Remote monitoring empowers patients to take an active role in managing their health, providing them with real-time data and insights to make informed decisions and engage in self-care activities.	**Workflow integration challenges:** Integrating remote monitoring data into existing healthcare workflows and EHR systems can be complex and time-consuming, requiring changes in clinical processes and documentation practices.

(*continued*)

249

Table 6-1. (*continued*)

Advantages	Disadvantages
Cost savings and efficiency: Remote monitoring has the potential to reduce healthcare costs by minimizing hospital readmissions, emergency department visits, and unnecessary healthcare utilization through proactive monitoring and early intervention.	**Resistance to change:** Some patients and healthcare providers may be resistant to adopting remote monitoring technologies due to unfamiliarity, skepticism, or concerns about the reliability and effectiveness of remote care.
Personalized care and tailored interventions: Remote monitoring allows for personalized care plans and tailored interventions based on individual patient needs, preferences, and risk profiles, leading to more targeted and effective treatments.	**Liability and legal issues:** Remote monitoring introduces legal and liability considerations related to the interpretation of remote data, clinical decision-making, liability for adverse events, and malpractice claims, requiring clear policies and protocols to mitigate risks.
Continuous monitoring and follow-up: Remote monitoring enables continuous monitoring of patient health metrics and follow-up care, reducing gaps in care and ensuring that patients receive timely interventions and support between healthcare visits.	**Patient compliance and engagement:** Ensuring patient compliance with remote monitoring protocols and maintaining patient engagement over time can be challenging, requiring ongoing education, support, and incentives to promote adherence and motivation.
Scalability and flexibility: Remote monitoring solutions can be scalable and adaptable to accommodate diverse patient populations, healthcare settings, and care delivery models, providing flexibility in implementation and expansion.	**Resource allocation and workload:** Implementing remote monitoring programs may require additional resources, staff training, and infrastructure investments, leading to increased workload and resource allocation challenges for healthcare organizations.

Summary

This chapter explored the transformative impact of AI and IoT technologies on remote healthcare monitoring. It delved into how these technologies play crucial roles in monitoring patient health remotely, utilizing wearable devices and sensors to collect real-time data. The chapter highlighted how remote monitoring improves patient outcomes by enabling proactive healthcare interventions and enhancing continuous care delivery outside of traditional healthcare settings.

In Chapter 7, we will delve deeper into the application of AI and IoT in healthcare. Chapter 7 will focus on AI-based diagnostic tools and IoT-enabled devices used in disease management. We will explore how these technologies contribute to advancing precision medicine, emphasizing personalized treatment approaches and optimizing healthcare outcomes through data-driven insights and innovative technologies.

CHAPTER 7

AI and IoT in Disease Diagnosis and Management

In Chapter 6, we explored the role of artificial intelligence (AI) and the Internet of Things (IoT) in remote patient monitoring, focusing on wearable devices and sensors, and their impact on patient outcomes. This chapter delves into the application of AI and IoT in disease diagnosis and management, showcasing how these technologies are revolutionizing precision medicine by improving the accuracy, efficiency, and effectiveness of diagnosing and managing various medical conditions.

As a quick refresher from earlier chapters, AI involves the development of computer algorithms and systems that can mimic human intelligence, such as learning from data, recognizing patterns, making decisions, and solving problems. In the context of disease diagnosis and management, AI techniques, including machine learning, deep learning, natural language processing, and computer vision, are utilized to analyze medical data, such as imaging scans, laboratory tests, electronic health records (EHRs), and wearable sensor data, to assist healthcare providers in diagnosing diseases, predicting outcomes, and optimizing treatment plans.

IoT refers to the network of interconnected devices embedded with sensors, actuators, and communication modules that collect, transmit, and exchange data over the Internet. In healthcare, IoT devices, such as wearable sensors, medical devices, home monitoring systems, and smart health gadgets, enable continuous monitoring of patients' vital signs, symptoms, and behaviors outside of traditional clinical settings. By integrating IoT data streams with AI algorithms, healthcare providers can gain real-time insights into patients' health status, remotely monitor disease progression, and deliver personalized interventions and treatments.

AI and IoT technologies hold great promise for revolutionizing disease diagnosis and management by leveraging advanced data analytics, predictive modeling, and real-time monitoring capabilities to improve patient outcomes and healthcare delivery efficiency.

In disease diagnosis, AI algorithms can analyze medical imaging scans (e.g., X-rays, MRI, CT scans) and pathology slides to detect abnormalities, identify patterns indicative of specific diseases (e.g., tumors, fractures, infections), and assist radiologists and pathologists in making accurate diagnoses. By leveraging large datasets of annotated medical images, AI-based diagnostic systems can learn to recognize subtle patterns and variations that may not be readily apparent to the human eye, leading to earlier detection, more precise diagnoses, and improved treatment planning.

In disease management, IoT-enabled devices and wearables allow for continuous monitoring of patients' physiological parameters, such as heart rate, blood pressure, blood glucose levels, and activity levels, in real time. These devices can transmit data to healthcare providers' systems or mobile applications, where AI algorithms analyze the data, detect deviations from normal patterns, and provide actionable insights to clinicians. For example, AI-powered decision support systems (DSSs) can alert healthcare providers to abnormal vital signs, medication nonadherence, or signs of disease exacerbation, enabling timely interventions, medication adjustments, or lifestyle recommendations to prevent complications and improve patient outcomes.

Figure 7-1 illustrates a process where wearable sensors collect data, which is processed by an IoT device and analyzed using the GARIC architecture with regression rules. This system helps predict colorectal cancer by assessing symptoms like weight loss, abdominal pain, rectal bleeding, and blood in stool. The data is used to determine the disease stage (from Stage 0 to Stage 4), and AI models are trained to improve prediction accuracy. The system integrates Boltzmann belief network deep learning and genetic data analysis (GWAS) for enhanced disease prediction and early diagnosis.

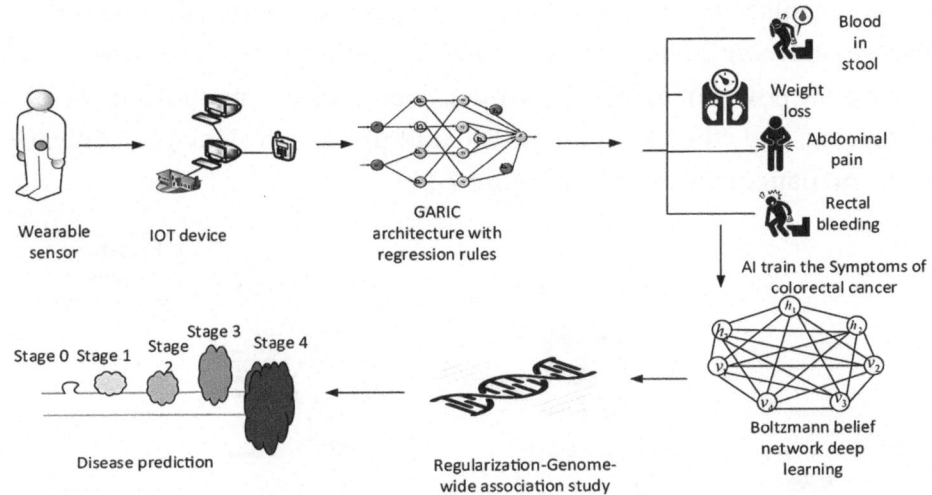

Figure 7-1. *Schematics diagram of IoT with AI-based disease prediction*

Furthermore, AI and IoT technologies facilitate remote patient monitoring, telemedicine consultations, and personalized care delivery, allowing patients to receive high-quality healthcare services from the comfort of their homes, reducing the need for in-person visits to healthcare facilities, and improving access to care, particularly for patients in rural or underserved areas.

Overall, the integration of AI and IoT in disease diagnosis and management represents a paradigm shift in healthcare delivery, offering opportunities to enhance diagnostic accuracy, optimize treatment outcomes, and empower patients to take control of their health through personalized, data-driven interventions and continuous monitoring. By leveraging the synergies between AI and IoT technologies, healthcare providers can transform the way diseases are diagnosed, managed, and prevented, ultimately leading to better health outcomes and improved quality of life for patients.

AI-Based Diagnostic Tools

AI-based diagnostic tools leverage artificial intelligence algorithms to analyze medical data and assist healthcare professionals in diagnosing diseases and conditions more accurately and efficiently. These tools harness the power of machine learning, deep learning, natural language processing, and other AI techniques to interpret medical images, clinical data, and patient histories (see Figure 7-2).

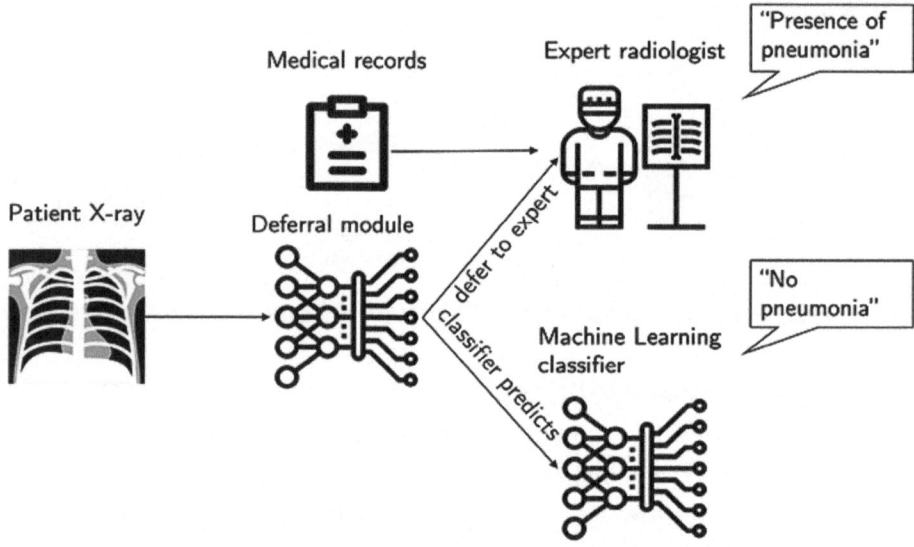

Figure 7-2. *The system either queries the expert to diagnose the patient or AI-based diagnostic tools*

Here are some key examples and applications of AI-based diagnostic tools:

- **Medical imaging analysis:** AI algorithms are used to analyze medical images such as X-rays, MRIs, CT scans, and mammograms to detect abnormalities and assist radiologists in making diagnoses. Convolutional neural networks (CNNs) and deep learning models can accurately identify patterns, lesions, tumors, fractures, and other anomalies in medical images, leading to faster and more accurate diagnoses. AI-based imaging tools have been developed for various medical specialties, including radiology, cardiology, oncology, and pathology.

- **Dermatology diagnosis:** AI-powered dermatology tools analyze images of skin lesions, moles, and rashes to assist dermatologists in diagnosing skin conditions and diseases. These tools use deep learning algorithms to classify skin images, identify malignant or benign lesions, and provide diagnostic recommendations. AI-based dermatology tools have shown promising results in diagnosing skin cancers, such as melanoma, and improving access to dermatological care in underserved areas.

- **Ophthalmology screening:** AI-based tools for ophthalmology analyze retinal images to detect eye diseases and conditions, such as diabetic retinopathy, glaucoma, and age-related macular degeneration (AMD). Deep learning algorithms can identify signs of disease progression, detect abnormalities in retinal blood vessels, and predict the risk of vision loss. AI-enabled ophthalmology screening tools have the potential to improve early detection and treatment of eye diseases, preventing vision loss and blindness.

- **Pathology and histopathology:** AI algorithms analyze histopathology slides and tissue samples to assist pathologists in diagnosing cancer and other diseases. Deep learning models can detect cancerous cells, classify tumor subtypes, and predict disease prognosis based on microscopic images of tissue specimens. AI-based pathology tools enhance the accuracy and efficiency of cancer diagnosis, enabling timely treatment decisions and improved patient outcomes.

- **Diagnostic decision support systems:** AI-based diagnostic DDSs integrate clinical data, laboratory results, imaging findings, and patient histories to provide evidence-based diagnostic recommendations to healthcare providers. These systems use machine learning algorithms to analyze complex datasets, identify relevant clinical patterns, and generate differential diagnoses. AI-based diagnostic DDSs help clinicians make informed decisions, reduce diagnostic errors, and improve patient care.

- **Genomic analysis and precision medicine:** AI-driven genomic analysis tools interpret genetic data to identify disease-causing mutations, predict disease risk, and guide personalized treatment strategies. Machine learning algorithms analyze genomic sequences, gene expression profiles, and genetic variations to tailor treatment plans to individual patients' genetic profiles. AI-based genomic analysis tools facilitate precision medicine approaches, enabling targeted therapies and improving treatment outcomes for patients with genetic disorders, cancer, and rare diseases.

- **Remote diagnostics and telemedicine:** AI-powered remote diagnostic tools enable telemedicine consultations and virtual assessments of patients' health conditions. These tools use AI algorithms to analyze patient-reported symptoms, physiological data from wearable devices, and remote monitoring data to assess patients' health status remotely. AI-based remote diagnostic tools expand access to healthcare services, improve triage decisions, and facilitate remote consultations with specialists, especially in rural or underserved areas.

Overall, AI-based diagnostic tools have the potential to revolutionize healthcare by enhancing diagnostic accuracy, improving patient outcomes, and increasing efficiency in healthcare delivery. As AI technologies continue to advance and integrate into clinical practice, these tools will play an increasingly vital role in diagnosing diseases and improving healthcare outcomes for patients worldwide.

AI-based diagnostic tools leverage machine learning algorithms to analyze medical data and assist healthcare providers in accurate disease diagnosis, improving diagnostic speed and accuracy. Delving into AI-based diagnostic tools sets the stage for exploring how IoT-enabled healthcare devices complement these tools in managing chronic diseases and enhancing patient outcomes.

IoT-Enabled Healthcare Devices for Disease Management

IoT-enabled healthcare devices play a crucial role in disease management by providing continuous monitoring, remote tracking, and personalized interventions for patients with chronic conditions. These devices leverage

IoT technology to collect real-time data on patients' health parameters, deliver actionable insights, and facilitate proactive management of diseases. Here are several examples of IoT-enabled healthcare devices for disease management:

- **Smart wearable devices:** Wearable devices, such as smartwatches, fitness trackers, and biosensors, monitor physiological parameters, activity levels, and health metrics continuously. These devices use built-in sensors to track vital signs like heart rate, blood pressure, blood oxygen saturation (SpO2), and activity patterns. IoT connectivity enables wearable devices to transmit data to mobile apps or cloud platforms for analysis and interpretation. Smart wearables help patients manage chronic conditions such as hypertension, diabetes, obesity, and cardiovascular disease by providing feedback on lifestyle behaviors, encouraging physical activity, and monitoring health trends over time.

- **Connected glucose monitors:** IoT-enabled glucose monitoring devices, such as continuous glucose monitors (CGMs) and smart blood glucose meters, help patients with diabetes monitor their blood sugar levels effectively. These devices use sensors to measure glucose concentrations in interstitial fluid or blood samples and transmit real-time data to smartphones or cloud-based platforms. IoT connectivity enables remote monitoring of glucose levels, trend analysis, and personalized feedback to optimize glycemic control. Connected glucose monitors support self-management of diabetes, facilitate timely adjustments to insulin dosing or medication regimens, and reduce the risk of hypoglycemia or hyperglycemia episodes.

- **Remote blood pressure monitors:** IoT-enabled blood pressure monitors enable remote monitoring of blood pressure readings for patients with hypertension or cardiovascular disease. These devices use cuff-based or cuffless measurement techniques to monitor systolic and diastolic blood pressure levels and transmit data wirelessly to mobile apps or web-based portals. Remote blood pressure monitors provide patients and healthcare providers with insights into blood pressure trends, medication adherence, and lifestyle factors influencing hypertension. By facilitating regular monitoring and timely interventions, IoT-enabled blood pressure monitors help patients achieve better blood pressure control and reduce the risk of hypertension-related complications.

- **Telehealth platforms:** Telehealth platforms integrate IoT-enabled devices, video conferencing tools, and remote monitoring technologies to facilitate virtual consultations and remote care delivery. These platforms enable patients to communicate with healthcare providers, share health data, and receive medical advice from the comfort of their homes. IoT devices such as digital stethoscopes, otoscopes, and pulse oximeters can be integrated into telehealth platforms to enable remote examinations and diagnostic assessments. Telehealth platforms improve access to healthcare services, enhance patient engagement, and support disease management for patients with chronic conditions, acute illnesses, or post-operative care needs.

- **Smart inhalers for asthma and COPD:** Smart inhalers equipped with IoT technology help patients with asthma and chronic obstructive pulmonary disease (COPD) monitor their inhaler usage and track respiratory symptoms. These devices attach to standard metered-dose inhalers (MDIs) or dry powder inhalers (DPIs) and record the date, time, and dosage of each inhalation. IoT connectivity allows smart inhalers to sync data with mobile apps or cloud platforms, providing patients with insights into medication adherence, inhaler technique, and asthma/COPD triggers. Smart inhalers support self-management of respiratory conditions, optimize medication usage, and reduce the frequency of asthma/COPD exacerbations.

- **Implantable medical devices:** Implantable medical devices, such as cardiac pacemakers, defibrillators, and neurostimulators, are increasingly equipped with IoT connectivity for remote monitoring and management of chronic conditions. These devices monitor physiological parameters, deliver therapeutic interventions, and transmit data to healthcare providers for remote analysis. IoT-enabled implantable devices enable proactive monitoring of cardiac arrhythmias, heart failure, epilepsy, and other chronic conditions, allowing healthcare providers to adjust device settings, deliver timely interventions, and prevent adverse events.

- **Smart pill dispensers:** Smart pill dispensers with IoT connectivity help patients manage complex medication regimens and improve medication adherence for chronic conditions. These devices dispense medications according to prescribed schedules, remind patients to take their medications, and track adherence in real time. IoT connectivity enables smart pill dispensers to send alerts to patients' smartphones or caregivers' devices if doses are missed or medications need to be refilled. Smart pill dispensers support medication management for patients with chronic diseases such as hypertension, diabetes, HIV/AIDS, and mental health disorders, reducing the risk of medication errors and treatment noncompliance.

Overall, IoT-enabled healthcare devices play a vital role in disease management by providing patients with continuous monitoring, personalized interventions, and remote support for chronic conditions. These devices empower patients to take an active role in their healthcare, improve treatment adherence, and enhance outcomes for patients with chronic diseases. As IoT technology continues to evolve, the potential for innovative healthcare solutions to transform disease management and patient care remains promising.

IoT-enabled healthcare devices, such as smart insulin pumps and connected glucometers, empower patients and healthcare providers with real-time data monitoring and management of chronic conditions. Examining these devices leads to a discussion on how AI and IoT synergistically advance precision medicine, tailoring treatments based on individual patient data for more effective and personalized healthcare delivery.

Enhancing Precision Medicine Through AI and IoT

Precision medicine aims to tailor medical treatment and interventions to individual patients based on their unique genetic makeup, environment, and lifestyle factors. The integration of AI and IoT holds immense potential for advancing precision medicine by enabling personalized healthcare delivery, predictive analytics, and real-time monitoring of patients' health status. Here's how AI and IoT can enhance precision medicine:

- **Genomic analysis and personalized treatments:** AI algorithms can analyze vast amounts of genomic data to identify genetic variations associated with disease risk, drug response, and treatment outcomes. IoT devices, such as genetic sequencers and wearable sensors, enable the collection of genomic data and real-time monitoring of patients' health metrics. By integrating genomic data with real-time physiological data, AI-driven precision medicine platforms can personalize treatment plans, optimize medication dosages, and predict patients' responses to therapies based on their genetic profiles.

- **Remote patient monitoring and telemedicine:** IoT-enabled devices, such as wearable biosensors, connected medical devices, and mobile health apps, enable remote monitoring of patients' vital signs, symptoms, and medication adherence. AI algorithms analyze continuous streams of data from IoT devices to detect early signs of disease progression, identify health risks, and predict adverse events. Telemedicine platforms leverage AI-driven diagnostic tools and virtual consultations to deliver personalized healthcare services, enabling patients to receive timely interventions and treatment recommendations remotely.

- **Predictive analytics for disease prevention:** AI algorithms analyze multimodal data from IoT sensors, EHRs, and environmental sources to identify patterns, trends, and correlations associated with disease risk and progression. By leveraging predictive analytics, AI-driven precision medicine platforms can forecast patients' likelihood of developing certain diseases, stratify individuals based on their risk profiles, and implement targeted interventions to prevent or delay the onset of diseases. Predictive modeling powered by AI and IoT data enables proactive healthcare management and early intervention strategies tailored to individuals' unique risk factors.

- **Drug discovery and development:** AI algorithms accelerate the drug discovery process by analyzing large-scale genomic data, molecular structures, and biological pathways to identify potential drug targets and predict drug efficacy. IoT devices facilitate high-throughput screening, data collection from clinical trials, and real-world evidence generation, enabling researchers to validate AI-driven drug candidates and optimize treatment regimens. AI-enabled precision medicine platforms streamline the drug development pipeline, reduce time-to-market for novel therapeutics, and improve patient access to targeted treatments for complex diseases.

- **Population health management and public health surveillance:** AI and IoT technologies enable population-level analysis of health data to identify epidemiological trends, disease outbreaks, and healthcare disparities. By integrating data from IoT sensors, wearable devices, and public health databases, AI-driven precision medicine platforms can monitor community health indicators, predict disease hotspots, and implement targeted interventions to mitigate public health risks. Population health management powered by AI and IoT supports evidence-based policymaking, resource allocation, and healthcare planning to improve health outcomes and reduce healthcare disparities at the population level.

- **Real-time decision support and clinical decision-making:** AI-driven decision support systems analyze patient data from IoT devices, EHRs, and medical imaging to assist healthcare providers in making timely and informed clinical decisions. By synthesizing patient-specific information, medical literature, and best practice guidelines, AI algorithms provide personalized treatment recommendations, diagnostic insights, and prognostic assessments to support precision medicine initiatives. Real-time decision support powered by AI and IoT enhances clinical workflows, improves diagnostic accuracy, and optimizes treatment strategies tailored to individual patients' needs.

Overall, the integration of AI and IoT technologies has the potential to revolutionize precision medicine by enabling personalized healthcare delivery, predictive analytics, early disease detection, and targeted interventions. By harnessing the power of AI and IoT data analytics, healthcare providers can optimize patient outcomes, enhance healthcare efficiency, and advance our understanding of human health and disease.

Summary

This chapter 7 explored the cutting-edge applications of AI and IoT technologies in revolutionizing healthcare practices. It examined how AI-based diagnostic tools enhance accuracy and efficiency in diagnosing medical conditions, leveraging advanced algorithms and data analytics. The chapter also discussed IoT-enabled healthcare devices that support disease management through continuous monitoring and personalized patient care. Furthermore, it emphasized the role of AI and IoT in advancing precision medicine, tailoring treatment strategies to individual patient profiles for improved therapeutic outcomes.

In Chapter 8, we will explore the pivotal roles of AI and IoT in optimizing hospital operations. Chapter 8 will delve into how AI and IoT streamline processes such as supply chain management, inventory control, and resource allocation within healthcare settings. We will discuss how these technologies enhance efficiency, reduce costs, and improve overall patient care delivery through smart, data-driven operational strategies.

CHAPTER 8

AI and IoT in Healthcare Operations Management

In Chapter 7, we examined the transformative impact of artificial intelligence (AI) and the Internet of Things (IoT) on disease diagnosis and management, highlighting their role in enhancing precision medicine. This chapter focuses on the application of AI and IoT in healthcare operations management, demonstrating how these technologies streamline hospital operations and improve efficiency.

AI involves the use of machine learning algorithms, natural language processing, and other computational techniques to analyze large datasets, extract meaningful insights, and automate decision-making processes. In healthcare operations management, AI can be applied to tasks such as predictive analytics for patient demand forecasting, optimization of scheduling and staffing, predictive maintenance of medical equipment, and predictive modeling for risk assessment and resource allocation. AI-driven solutions help healthcare organizations make data-driven decisions, improve operational efficiency, and enhance overall performance.

© Dr. Alok Kumar Srivastav, Dr. Priyanka Das 2024
Dr. A. K. Srivastav and Dr. P. Das, *Emerging Technologies in Healthcare 4.0*,
https://doi.org/10.1007/979-8-8688-1014-5_8

IoT refers to the network of interconnected devices embedded with sensors, actuators, and communication modules that collect, transmit, and exchange data over the Internet. In healthcare operations management, IoT devices can monitor various aspects of facility operations, including equipment utilization, environmental conditions, patient movement, and inventory levels. IoT-enabled solutions provide real-time visibility into operational processes, enable remote monitoring and control, and facilitate data-driven decision-making to optimize resource utilization, improve workflow efficiency, and ensure regulatory compliance.

Streamlining Hospital Operations with AI and IoT

Streamlining hospital operations is essential for optimizing resource utilization, improving patient care delivery, and enhancing overall operational efficiency. The integration of AI and IoT offers innovative solutions to automate processes, optimize workflows, and provide real-time insights for better decision-making in hospital settings. Here's how AI and IoT can streamline hospital operations:

- **Asset management and tracking:** IoT-enabled asset tracking systems use sensors and radio frequency identification (RFID) tags to monitor the location, status, and usage of medical equipment, devices, and supplies within the hospital. AI algorithms analyze real-time asset data to optimize inventory levels, prevent equipment shortages, and minimize asset downtime. By streamlining asset management processes, hospitals can reduce costs, improve equipment utilization, and ensure the availability of essential resources for patient care.

- **Predictive maintenance for equipment:** AI-powered predictive maintenance models analyze data from IoT-connected medical devices and equipment to predict equipment failures, malfunctions, or maintenance needs before they occur. By monitoring equipment performance metrics, such as temperature, vibration, and usage patterns, predictive maintenance algorithms can identify potential issues early, schedule maintenance proactively, and prevent costly breakdowns. Predictive maintenance minimizes equipment downtime, extends equipment lifespan, and ensures the reliability of critical hospital infrastructure.

- **Patient flow optimization:** IoT sensors and AI analytics can monitor patient flow throughout the hospital, from admission to discharge, to identify bottlenecks, optimize bed allocation, and improve patient throughput. Real-time patient tracking systems use IoT-enabled wearable devices or smart badges to monitor patients' movements, wait times, and care transitions. AI algorithms analyze patient flow data to identify inefficiencies, optimize staffing levels, and allocate resources effectively to reduce patient wait times, enhance care coordination, and improve overall patient experience.

- **Smart facility management:** IoT sensors embedded in hospital infrastructure, such as lighting, HVAC systems, and energy meters, enable smart facility management solutions to optimize energy usage, reduce operational costs, and enhance environmental sustainability. AI algorithms analyze real-time data from IoT sensors to automate energy management, optimize heating and cooling systems, and identify opportunities for energy conservation. Smart facility management systems improve hospital infrastructure efficiency, lower energy expenses, and create more comfortable and sustainable environments for patients and staff.

- **Supply chain optimization:** AI and IoT technologies streamline hospital supply chain management by monitoring inventory levels, tracking product movements, and predicting demand for medical supplies and pharmaceuticals. IoT-enabled inventory management systems use RFID tags, barcode scanners, and sensors to track supply chain processes in real time. AI-driven demand forecasting algorithms analyze historical data, usage patterns, and external factors to predict future supply needs accurately. Supply chain optimization improves inventory accuracy, reduces stockouts, and ensures timely delivery of essential supplies to support patient care.

- **Clinical decision support systems:** AI-powered clinical decision support systems leverage data from EHRs, medical imaging, and IoT devices to provide evidence-based recommendations, diagnostic insights, and treatment guidelines to healthcare providers. By analyzing patient data, medical literature, and best practice guidelines, AI algorithms assist clinicians in making informed decisions about patient care. Clinical DSSs improve diagnostic accuracy, reduce medical errors, and enhance patient safety by providing timely, personalized recommendations tailored to individual patient needs.

- **Patient monitoring and telemedicine:** IoT-enabled remote patient monitoring solutions use wearable devices, home health kits, and telemedicine platforms to monitor patients' health status outside of traditional clinical settings. AI algorithms analyze real-time patient data, such as vital signs, symptoms, and medication adherence, to detect health anomalies, predict disease progression, and trigger timely interventions. Remote patient monitoring and telemedicine services improve access to care, reduce hospital readmissions, and enable early interventions for chronic conditions, improving patient outcomes and reducing healthcare costs.

By leveraging AI and IoT technologies, hospitals can streamline operations, optimize resource utilization, and improve patient care delivery across various departments and functions. From asset management and patient flow optimization to supply chain management and clinical decision support, AI and IoT solutions enable hospitals to achieve greater efficiency, cost-effectiveness, and quality of care, ultimately enhancing the overall patient experience and healthcare outcomes (see Figure 8-1).

Figure 8-1 illustrates the architecture of a remote healthcare system, where healthcare professionals are connected to patients via medical IoT devices and a smartphone gateway. The smartphone gateway, which connects to medical devices through Bluetooth and Wi-Fi, collects data from patients and transmits it over the internet. This data is then processed through a fog server and can be accessed by healthcare professionals, who may use a clinical decision support system (external applications) to assist in diagnosis and decision-making. The system integrates data from various diversified healthcare data repositories, allowing for more informed and real-time decision-making. This architecture supports continuous monitoring and enhances the efficiency of healthcare delivery by leveraging IoT technologies and remote connectivity.

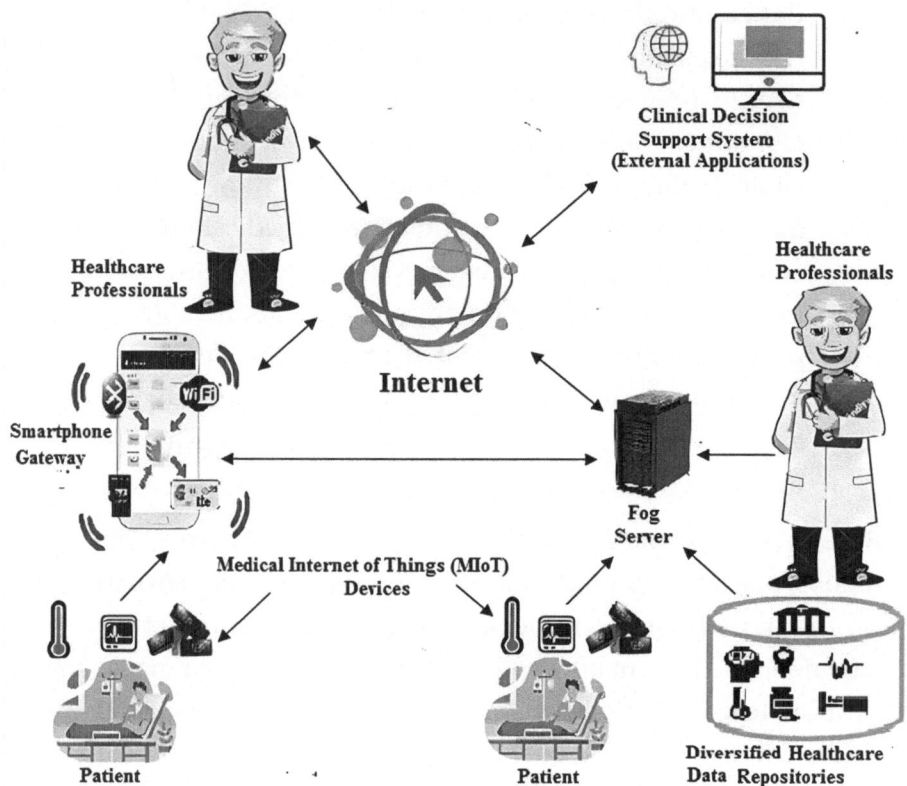

Figure 8-1. *Hospital operations with AI and IoT*

Table 8-1 summarizes the benefits and challenges associated with the integration of AI and IoT technologies in healthcare settings.

Table 8-1. *Advantages and Disadvantages of AI and IoT Technologies in Healthcare*

Advantages	Disadvantages
Enhanced efficiency: AI and IoT technologies enable automation of routine tasks, streamlining hospital operations and reducing manual workload.	**Initial investment:** Implementation of AI and IoT solutions requires significant upfront investment in technology infrastructure, software development, and staff training, which can be costly.
Improved patient care: AI-driven analytics and IoT devices facilitate real-time monitoring of patient health data, leading to early detection of issues, personalized treatment plans, and improved patient outcomes.	**Data security risks:** Connectivity and data exchange between IoT devices and AI systems may introduce vulnerabilities, increasing the risk of cyberattacks, data breaches, and unauthorized access to sensitive patient information.
Optimal resource allocation: AI algorithms analyze data to optimize resource allocation, such as staff scheduling, bed management, and equipment utilization, ensuring efficient use of hospital resources and reducing waste.	**Integration challenges:** Integrating diverse AI and IoT systems with existing hospital infrastructure and EHR systems can be complex and require interoperability standards to ensure seamless data exchange and communication.
Predictive maintenance: IoT sensors monitor equipment health and performance in real time, enabling predictive maintenance to prevent breakdowns, reduce downtime, and extend the lifespan of critical medical devices.	**Staff training requirements:** Healthcare staff need training to operate and interpret data from AI and IoT systems effectively, requiring investment in education and ongoing support to ensure adoption and proficiency.

(continued)

Table 8-1. (*continued*)

Advantages	Disadvantages
Data-driven decision-making: AI algorithms analyze vast amounts of patient data to provide insights and recommendations for clinical decision-making, treatment planning, and population health management, improving healthcare outcomes.	**Ethical and privacy concerns:** Use of AI and IoT technologies raises ethical dilemmas regarding patient consent, data ownership, algorithm bias, and the responsible use of predictive analytics, requiring careful consideration and ethical frameworks.
Remote monitoring and telemedicine: IoT-enabled devices and AI-driven telemedicine platforms enable remote monitoring of patients, virtual consultations, and telehealth services, expanding access to healthcare and reducing the need for in-person visits.	**Dependency on technology:** Hospitals may become overly reliant on AI and IoT systems, leading to potential disruptions in case of system failures, technical glitches, or network outages, necessitating backup plans and contingency measures.
Continuous improvement: AI algorithms learn from data over time, enabling continuous optimization of processes, algorithms, and treatment protocols based on real-world feedback and outcomes, driving continuous improvement in hospital operations and patient care.	**Regulatory compliance challenges:** Healthcare organizations must navigate complex regulatory requirements and compliance standards related to data privacy, patient safety, medical device regulations, and healthcare laws when implementing AI and IoT solutions, ensuring adherence to legal and ethical guidelines.

AI and IoT technologies streamline hospital operations by automating tasks, optimizing workflows, and enhancing operational efficiency across departments. Exploring how AI and IoT streamline operations sets the stage for examining their role in supply chain management and ensuring efficient inventory control within healthcare facilities.

Supply Chain Management and Inventory Control

Supply chain management and inventory control are critical aspects of hospital operations, ensuring that healthcare facilities have access to essential supplies, medications, and medical equipment to deliver high-quality patient care. The integration of AI and IoT can streamline supply chain management processes, optimize inventory control, and enhance operational efficiency in hospitals (see Figure 8-2).Here's how AI and IoT technologies can transform supply chain management and inventory control in healthcare settings:

- **Predictive demand forecasting:** AI algorithms analyze historical data, patient admission rates, procedure schedules, and other relevant factors to predict future demand for medical supplies and equipment. IoT sensors installed in storage areas and medical devices monitor inventory levels, usage patterns, and expiration dates in real time. By combining AI-driven demand forecasting with IoT-enabled inventory monitoring, hospitals can anticipate supply needs, prevent stockouts, and optimize inventory levels to meet patient care demands efficiently.

- **Automated inventory management:** IoT-connected RFID tags, barcode scanners, and smart shelves automate inventory tracking and management processes, reducing manual labor and human error. These IoT devices capture real-time data on inventory movements, asset locations, and stock replenishment needs. AI algorithms analyze this data to optimize inventory replenishment schedules, prioritize critical items, and minimize excess stock levels. Automated inventory management powered by AI and IoT enhances accuracy, visibility, and traceability across the supply chain, improving inventory control and operational efficiency in hospitals.

- **Dynamic supply chain optimization:** AI algorithms optimize supply chain logistics by analyzing multiple variables, such as supplier performance, transportation costs, lead times, and inventory levels. IoT sensors embedded in delivery vehicles, storage facilities, and medical equipment monitor environmental conditions, shipment statuses, and delivery routes in real time. AI-driven supply chain optimization models dynamically adjust procurement strategies, transportation routes, and inventory storage locations to minimize costs, reduce delays, and ensure timely delivery of critical supplies to healthcare facilities.

- **Supplier relationship management:** AI-powered analytics evaluate supplier performance metrics, contract terms, and pricing agreements to assess supplier reliability and compliance with service level agreements (SLAs). IoT-enabled supply chain visibility tools track supplier shipments, quality certifications, and product recalls to ensure compliance with regulatory requirements. AI-driven supplier relationship management platforms identify opportunities for cost savings, negotiate favorable terms, and foster collaboration with strategic suppliers to improve supply chain resilience and mitigate supply chain risks.

- **Predictive maintenance for medical equipment:** IoT sensors embedded in medical devices and equipment monitor equipment usage, performance metrics, and maintenance schedules in real time. AI algorithms analyze equipment data to predict potential failures, identify maintenance needs, and schedule preventive maintenance activities proactively. Predictive maintenance powered by AI and IoT minimizes equipment downtime, extends asset lifespan, and ensures the availability of critical medical devices for patient care, enhancing operational reliability and reducing maintenance costs for hospitals.

- **Regulatory compliance and quality assurance:** AI-driven analytics assess compliance with regulatory standards, accreditation requirements, and quality control protocols across the supply chain. IoT-enabled quality monitoring systems track product quality, temperature-sensitive medications, and sterile storage conditions to ensure compliance with industry regulations and quality standards. AI and IoT technologies facilitate audit trails, documentation management, and real-time reporting to regulatory authorities, enhancing transparency, accountability, and regulatory compliance in hospital supply chain operations.

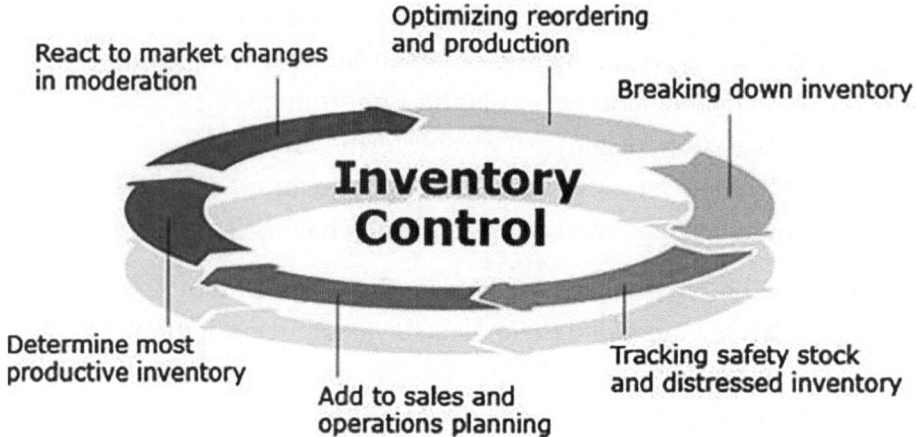

Figure 8-2. *Inventory control*

Overall, the integration of AI and IoT technologies offers significant opportunities to streamline hospital operations, improve supply chain management, and optimize inventory control in healthcare settings. By leveraging AI-driven analytics and IoT-enabled solutions, hospitals can enhance supply chain visibility, efficiency, and resilience, ultimately delivering better patient care and driving operational excellence in healthcare delivery.

Table 8-2 outlines the benefits and challenges associated with implementing advanced supply chain management and inventory control systems in healthcare.

Table 8-2. *Advantages and Disadvantages of Advanced Supply Chain Management in Healthcare*

Advantages	Disadvantages
Enhanced efficiency: Automation of supply chain processes through technology improves efficiency by reducing manual errors, streamlining workflows, and optimizing inventory management, leading to cost savings and increased productivity.	**Initial investment:** Implementing advanced supply chain management and inventory control systems requires significant upfront investment in technology infrastructure, software platforms, and staff training, which can be costly for healthcare organizations with limited resources.
Real-time visibility: Advanced tracking and monitoring technologies provide real-time visibility into inventory levels, stock movements, and supply chain performance, enabling better decision-making, forecasting, and demand planning to prevent stockouts and minimize excess inventory.	**Complexity and integration challenges:** Integrating disparate systems, data sources, and stakeholders across the supply chain can be complex, requiring interoperability standards and collaboration among vendors, suppliers, and healthcare providers to ensure seamless data exchange and communication.
Improved patient safety: Accurate inventory control and management reduce the risk of medication errors, expired products, and stock shortages, ensuring timely availability of critical supplies and medications for patient care, thus enhancing patient safety and quality of care.	**Data security risks:** Increased connectivity and data exchange between supply chain systems and external vendors may pose cybersecurity risks, such as data breaches, unauthorized access, and theft of sensitive information, necessitating robust security measures and data protection protocols.

(*continued*)

Table 8-2. (*continued*)

Advantages	Disadvantages
Cost reduction: Optimization of inventory levels, procurement processes, and supply chain logistics leads to cost savings through reduced carrying costs, inventory holding costs, and wastage, as well as negotiated pricing and volume discounts with suppliers.	**Staff training requirements:** Healthcare staff require training to operate and utilize advanced supply chain management and inventory control systems effectively, necessitating investment in education, onboarding, and ongoing support to ensure adoption and proficiency.
Demand forecasting and planning: AI-driven analytics and predictive algorithms analyze historical data and market trends to forecast demand, anticipate supply chain disruptions, and optimize inventory levels, enabling proactive planning and resource allocation to meet patient needs effectively.	**Vendor reliability and compliance:** Dependency on external vendors and suppliers for timely delivery, product quality, and regulatory compliance may introduce risks of supply chain disruptions, delays, or noncompliance issues, requiring vendor management strategies and contingency plans to mitigate risks.
Regulatory compliance: Advanced supply chain management systems ensure compliance with regulatory requirements, such as traceability, serialization, and documentation standards, for pharmaceuticals, medical devices, and healthcare products, reducing the risk of noncompliance penalties and regulatory violations.	**Ethical and sustainability concerns:** Global supply chains raise ethical dilemmas regarding sourcing practices, labor conditions, environmental impact, and sustainability, necessitating transparency, accountability, and responsible sourcing practices to address stakeholder concerns and meet ethical standards.

(*continued*)

Table 8-2. (*continued*)

Advantages	Disadvantages
Scalability and adaptability: Modern supply chain technologies are scalable and adaptable to accommodate changes in demand, market dynamics, and business requirements, allowing healthcare organizations to scale operations, expand facilities, or enter new markets with minimal disruption to supply chain operations.	**Dependency on technology:** Overreliance on technology and automation in supply chain management may lead to potential disruptions in case of system failures, technical glitches, or network outages, requiring backup plans and contingency measures to ensure business continuity.

IoT-enabled sensors and AI-driven analytics improve supply chain visibility, enhance inventory management accuracy, and reduce waste, ensuring healthcare facilities maintain adequate supplies and minimize costs. Understanding these capabilities leads to a discussion on how AI and IoT optimize resource allocation, enabling healthcare providers to allocate staff, equipment, and facilities more effectively to meet patient needs.

Optimizing Resource Allocation Using AI and IoT

Optimizing resource allocation is crucial for healthcare facilities to ensure efficient utilization of resources, enhance patient care delivery, and maximize operational effectiveness. By leveraging AI and IoT, healthcare organizations can improve decision-making processes, allocate resources more effectively, and streamline operations across various departments.

Here's how AI and IoT technologies can optimize resource allocation in healthcare settings:

- **Demand prediction and capacity planning:** AI algorithms analyze historical patient data, appointment schedules, and other relevant factors to predict future demand for healthcare services across different departments and facilities. IoT sensors installed in waiting areas, patient rooms, and treatment areas monitor patient flow, occupancy rates, and resource utilization in real time. By combining AI-driven demand forecasting with IoT-enabled occupancy monitoring, healthcare organizations can optimize resource allocation, adjust staffing levels, and ensure adequate capacity to meet patient needs efficiently.

- **Dynamic staff scheduling and task assignment:** AI-powered workforce management systems optimize staff scheduling and task assignment based on patient demand, staff availability, and skill sets. IoT devices track staff movements, workloads, and task completion statuses in real-time, providing visibility into staff productivity and performance. AI algorithms analyze this data to generate optimized schedules, assign tasks dynamically, and allocate resources effectively to match patient demand with staffing levels, reducing wait times, and improving patient satisfaction.

- **Asset tracking and management:** IoT-connected RFID tags, GPS trackers, and asset management systems enable real-time tracking and management of medical equipment, supplies, and facilities. AI algorithms analyze asset utilization patterns, maintenance histories, and inventory levels to optimize asset allocation, minimize idle equipment, and prevent equipment shortages. By integrating AI-driven asset tracking with IoT-enabled maintenance monitoring, healthcare organizations can improve equipment availability, reduce downtime, and extend asset lifespan through proactive maintenance practices.

- **Patient flow optimization:** AI algorithms analyze patient admission rates, discharge processes, and treatment workflows to identify bottlenecks and inefficiencies in patient flow. IoT sensors installed in patient waiting areas, exam rooms, and diagnostic facilities monitor patient movements, wait times, and service delivery metrics in real time. AI-driven patient flow optimization models recommend process improvements, layout changes, and resource reallocation strategies to streamline patient flow, reduce congestion, and enhance throughput across healthcare facilities.

- **Emergency resource allocation:** During emergency situations or surge events, AI and IoT technologies play a critical role in managing resources, triaging patients, and allocating personnel effectively. AI-driven decision support systems analyze real-time data on patient acuity, bed availability, and resource utilization to prioritize patient care and allocate resources based on clinical urgency. IoT sensors provide situational awareness, environmental monitoring, and location tracking capabilities to support emergency response efforts and ensure timely access to critical resources and personnel.

- **Supply chain optimization:** AI algorithms optimize supply chain logistics, inventory management, and procurement processes to ensure timely access to essential supplies, medications, and medical equipment. IoT-enabled supply chain visibility tools track inventory levels, delivery statuses, and supplier performance metrics in real time. AI-driven supply chain optimization models forecast demand, optimize inventory levels, and streamline procurement workflows to minimize stockouts, reduce lead times, and optimize resource utilization across the supply chain.

Figure 8-3 illustrates a distributed task offloading system where users submit tasks to an intelligent agent. The agent assigns tasks to physical servers based on resources optimized through a mapping table and resource optimizer. Completed tasks are returned to the users, who provide quality of experience (QoE) feedback, influencing future task allocation and rewards for the system.

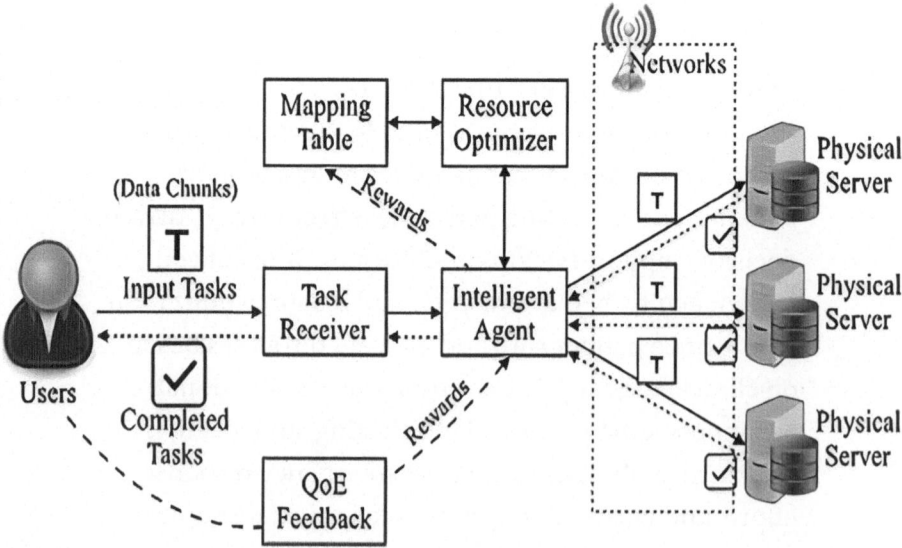

Figure 8-3. *Optimizing resource allocation using AI and IoT*

By leveraging AI and IoT technologies to optimize resource allocation, healthcare organizations can enhance operational efficiency, improve patient care quality, and achieve cost savings. By integrating AI-driven analytics with IoT-enabled monitoring and management systems, healthcare facilities can make data-driven decisions, optimize resource utilization, and adapt quickly to changing patient needs and operational demands, ultimately improving overall performance and patient outcomes in healthcare delivery.

Table 8-3 outlines the benefits and challenges associated with implementing AI and IoT technologies for resource allocation in healthcare settings.

Table 8-3. *Advantages and Disadvantages of AI and IoT for Resource Allocation in Healthcare*

Advantages	Disadvantages
Improved efficiency: AI and IoT technologies enable real-time monitoring and analysis of resource utilization, allowing for dynamic allocation of staff, equipment, and facilities to match demand, leading to increased operational efficiency and productivity.	**Initial investment:** Implementing AI and IoT solutions for resource allocation requires significant upfront investment in technology infrastructure, software development, and staff training, which can be costly for healthcare organizations with limited resources.
Enhanced patient care: Optimized resource allocation ensures timely access to care, reduces wait times, and minimizes bottlenecks in service delivery, resulting in improved patient outcomes, satisfaction, and overall quality of care.	**Data security risks:** Increased connectivity and data exchange between IoT devices and AI systems may introduce vulnerabilities, increasing the risk of cyberattacks, data breaches, and unauthorized access to sensitive patient information, necessitating robust security measures and data protection protocols.

(continued)

Table 8-3. (*continued*)

Advantages	Disadvantages
Predictive analytics: AI-driven predictive analytics analyze historical data, patient flow patterns, and resource utilization trends to forecast future demand and capacity requirements, enabling proactive planning and allocation of resources to meet anticipated needs effectively.	**Complexity and integration challenges:** Integrating diverse AI and IoT systems with existing hospital infrastructure and EHR systems can be complex, requiring interoperability standards and collaboration among vendors, suppliers, and healthcare providers to ensure seamless data exchange and communication.
Cost savings: Optimization of resource allocation minimizes inefficiencies, reduces unnecessary overtime, and eliminates overstaffing, resulting in cost savings through better utilization of human and capital resources, as well as reduced reliance on temporary staffing agencies and overtime pay.	**Staff training requirements:** Healthcare staff require training to operate and interpret data from AI and IoT systems effectively, necessitating investment in education, onboarding, and ongoing support to ensure adoption and proficiency.
Real-time decision-making: AI algorithms analyze data streams from IoT devices to provide actionable insights and recommendations for resource allocation decisions in real time, enabling healthcare leaders to make informed decisions quickly and adapt to changing circumstances.	**Ethical and privacy concerns:** Use of AI and IoT technologies raises ethical dilemmas regarding patient consent, data ownership, algorithm bias, and the responsible use of predictive analytics, requiring careful consideration and ethical frameworks to protect patient rights and privacy.

(*continued*)

Table 8-3. (*continued*)

Advantages	Disadvantages
Scalability and adaptability: AI and IoT solutions are scalable and adaptable to accommodate changes in demand, patient acuity, and operational requirements, allowing healthcare organizations to scale resources up or down as needed without significant disruptions to service delivery.	**Dependency on technology:** Hospitals may become overly reliant on AI and IoT systems for resource allocation decisions, leading to potential disruptions in case of system failures, technical glitches, or network outages, necessitating backup plans and contingency measures to ensure continuity of operations.
Continuous improvement: AI algorithms learn from data over time, enabling continuous optimization of resource allocation strategies based on real-world feedback and outcomes, driving continuous improvement in hospital operations, patient care, and organizational performance.	**Regulatory compliance challenges:** Healthcare organizations must navigate complex regulatory requirements and compliance standards related to data privacy, patient safety, medical device regulations, and healthcare laws when implementing AI and IoT solutions, ensuring adherence to legal and ethical guidelines.

In a large urban hospital, optimizing resource allocation using AI and IoT technologies has revolutionized the way healthcare services are delivered, leading to improved efficiency, patient care, and cost-effectiveness.

One prominent example is the implementation of a real-time patient flow management system powered by AI and IoT. The hospital integrated IoT sensors throughout its facilities to track patient movement, bed occupancy, and equipment utilization in real time. These sensors collected data on patient arrivals, departures, and treatment durations, feeding information into AI algorithms that analyzed historical trends and current demand patterns.

Using predictive analytics, the AI system forecasted patient flow and bed occupancy levels for different units and departments, enabling hospital administrators to proactively allocate resources based on anticipated demand. For example, during peak admission hours, the system automatically alerted staff to prepare additional beds, assign appropriate staffing levels, and prioritize patient admissions based on acuity and urgency.

Furthermore, the AI system optimized operating room schedules by analyzing surgical caseloads, surgeon availability, and equipment utilization to minimize downtime between procedures and maximize operating room efficiency. By dynamically adjusting surgical schedules and resource allocations in real time, the hospital reduced wait times for surgeries, optimized staff utilization, and increased surgical throughput.

In addition to improving patient care and operational efficiency, the AI-powered resource allocation system resulted in significant cost savings for the hospital. By optimizing staffing levels, reducing unnecessary overtime, and minimizing idle time for equipment and facilities, the hospital lowered operating costs while maintaining high-quality care standards. Moreover, the predictive analytics capabilities of the AI system enabled proactive maintenance of medical equipment, preventing costly breakdowns and unplanned downtime.

Overall, the implementation of AI and IoT technologies for resource allocation optimization transformed the hospital's operations, allowing for more efficient use of resources, better patient outcomes, and increased cost-effectiveness. By leveraging real-time data analytics and predictive modeling, the hospital achieved higher levels of efficiency, responsiveness, and adaptability in delivering healthcare services to its community.

Summary

This chapter examined how AI and IoT technologies streamline and enhance various aspects of hospital operations. It explored the role of AI and IoT in optimizing supply chain management and inventory control through data analytics and automation, thereby improving efficiency and reducing operational costs. The chapter also discussed the use of AI and IoT in optimizing resource allocation, ensuring that healthcare facilities can allocate personnel, equipment, and resources more effectively to meet patient needs.

In Chapter 9, we will delve into the critical ethical and legal issues surrounding the implementation of AI and IoT in healthcare. Chapter 9 will explore the ethical implications of using these technologies, including concerns about patient privacy, data security, and the potential impact on human dignity. We will also discuss the existing legal frameworks governing AI and IoT in healthcare and strategies for ensuring ethical practices amidst technological advancements.

CHAPTER 9

Ethical and Legal Considerations in Healthcare 4.0

In Chapter 8, we explored the integration of artificial intelligence (AI) and the Internet of Things (IoT) in healthcare operations management, focusing on improving hospital operations, supply chain management, and resource allocation. This chapter addresses the ethical and legal considerations in Healthcare 4.0, crucial for the responsible and fair implementation of these advanced technologies.

Ethical Issues Surrounding AI and IoT in Healthcare

The integration AI and IoT in healthcare introduces various ethical considerations that must be addressed to ensure responsible and equitable deployment of these technologies. Here are some of the key ethical issues surrounding AI and IoT in healthcare:

- **Privacy and data security:** AI and IoT systems in healthcare collect and analyze vast amounts of sensitive patient data, raising concerns about privacy breaches and unauthorized access. Ensuring robust data security measures, such as encryption, access controls, and anonymization, is essential to protect patient privacy and prevent data misuse or exploitation by third parties.

- **Informed consent and autonomy:** Patients must have the right to understand how their data will be collected, used, and shared by AI and IoT systems in healthcare. Obtaining informed consent from patients for data collection and processing is crucial to respect their autonomy and rights to privacy. Transparent communication about the purpose, risks, and benefits of AI and IoT applications is essential to foster trust and empower patients to make informed decisions about their healthcare.

- **Bias and fairness:** AI algorithms used in healthcare may exhibit bias or discrimination, leading to disparities in diagnosis, treatment, or access to care among different patient populations. Bias can arise from biased training data, algorithmic design choices, or systemic inequalities in healthcare delivery. Addressing bias in AI systems requires transparency, accountability, and diversity in dataset collection, algorithm development, and validation processes to ensure fairness and equity in healthcare outcomes.

- **Transparency and accountability:** Healthcare AI and IoT systems must be transparent about their decision-making processes, algorithms, and data sources to enable scrutiny, accountability, and oversight by regulatory authorities, healthcare providers, and patients. Transparent AI systems allow for better understanding of how decisions are made, facilitate error detection and correction, and enable stakeholders to assess the reliability and validity of AI-generated recommendations or predictions.

- **Quality and safety:** Ensuring the accuracy, reliability, and safety of AI and IoT applications in healthcare is critical to prevent harm to patients and maintain trust in these technologies. Rigorous testing, validation, and monitoring of AI algorithms and IoT devices are necessary to assess their performance, identify potential errors or biases, and mitigate risks before deployment in clinical settings. Continuous evaluation and refinement of AI and IoT systems based on real-world feedback and outcomes are essential to improve their quality and safety over time.

- **Professional responsibilities:** Healthcare professionals have ethical obligations to uphold patient welfare, integrity, and professional standards when using AI and IoT technologies in clinical practice. They must ensure that AI-driven recommendations or decisions align with clinical guidelines, best practices, and ethical principles, and take responsibility for verifying and validating AI-generated insights before making clinical decisions. Healthcare providers should also maintain competence in AI and IoT technologies through ongoing education and training to fulfill their ethical duties to patients effectively.

- **Equity and access:** AI and IoT interventions should prioritize equitable access to healthcare services and address healthcare disparities among underserved or marginalized communities. Ensuring accessibility, affordability, and cultural sensitivity in AI and IoT solutions is essential to promote health equity and reduce disparities in healthcare outcomes. Healthcare organizations and policymakers must consider the social determinants of health and address systemic barriers to access and adoption of AI and IoT technologies to ensure equitable healthcare delivery for all patients.

- **Human oversight and intervention:** While AI and IoT technologies can enhance healthcare delivery and decision-making, they should not replace human judgment, empathy, and ethical reasoning in clinical practice. Human oversight and intervention are necessary to interpret AI-generated insights, consider patient preferences and values, and make morally and ethically sound decisions in complex healthcare scenarios. Healthcare professionals must maintain ethical vigilance and intervene when AI recommendations conflict with clinical judgment or patient needs, ensuring that patient-centered care remains the priority.

Addressing these ethical issues requires interdisciplinary collaboration among healthcare professionals, technology developers, policymakers, ethicists, and patient advocates to develop guidelines, regulations, and ethical frameworks that promote responsible and ethical use of AI and IoT in healthcare. By integrating ethical considerations into the design, implementation, and governance of AI and IoT systems, healthcare organizations can harness the transformative potential of these technologies while safeguarding patient rights, privacy, and well-being in the digital age.

The integration of AI and IoT in healthcare raises ethical concerns regarding patient privacy, data security, algorithm biases, and the ethical use of patient data for decision-making. Exploring these ethical issues sets the stage for examining the legal frameworks and regulations that govern the implementation of AI and IoT technologies in healthcare.

Legal Frameworks for AI and IoT Implementation

Legal frameworks for the implementation of AI and IoT encompass a wide range of laws, regulations, standards, and guidelines that govern the development, deployment, and use of AI and IoT technologies in various sectors, including healthcare, transportation, finance, and manufacturing. Here are some of the key legal considerations and frameworks relevant to AI and IoT implementation:

- **Data protection and privacy laws:** Data protection and privacy laws regulate the collection, use, storage, and sharing of personal data by AI and IoT systems. Examples include the General Data Protection Regulation (GDPR) in the European Union, the Health Insurance Portability and Accountability Act (HIPAA) and California Consumer Privacy Act (CCPA) in the United States, and the Personal Information Protection and Electronic Documents Act (PIPEDA) in Canada. These laws impose requirements for obtaining consent, providing notice, implementing data security measures, and ensuring transparency and accountability in data processing activities.

- **Healthcare regulations:** Healthcare regulations govern the use of AI and IoT technologies in medical devices, electronic health records (EHRs), telemedicine, and patient care. Regulatory agencies such as the US Food and Drug Administration (FDA), the European Medicines Agency (EMA), and the Therapeutic Goods Administration (TGA) in Australia oversee the approval, clearance, and regulation of AI-driven medical devices and digital health solutions. Compliance with regulatory requirements, including safety, efficacy, and quality standards, is essential for AI and IoT applications in healthcare.

- **Consumer protection laws:** Consumer protection laws aim to safeguard consumers from deceptive, unfair, or fraudulent practices related to AI and IoT products and services. These laws may include requirements for product labeling, warranties, advertising practices, and dispute resolution mechanisms. Regulatory agencies such as the Federal Trade Commission (FTC) in the United States enforce consumer protection laws and investigate complaints related to AI and IoT products that violate consumer rights or harm consumers' interests.

- **Intellectual property rights:** Intellectual property laws protect the rights of AI and IoT developers, manufacturers, and users by granting patents, copyrights, trademarks, and trade secrets for innovative technologies, algorithms, software, and hardware components. Intellectual property rights enable creators to monetize their inventions, prevent unauthorized use or reproduction, and enforce legal protections against infringement or misappropriation of intellectual property assets.

- **Cybersecurity and data breach notification laws:** Cybersecurity laws and regulations establish requirements for safeguarding AI and IoT systems against cyber threats, vulnerabilities, and attacks. These laws may mandate measures such as encryption, access controls, vulnerability assessments, and incident response planning to protect against data breaches, unauthorized access, and malicious activities. Data breach notification laws require organizations to notify affected individuals and regulatory authorities promptly in the event of a data breach involving personal or sensitive information.

- **Ethical guidelines and principles:** Ethical guidelines and principles provide ethical frameworks for the responsible and ethical development, deployment, and use of AI and IoT technologies. Organizations such as the Institute of Electrical and Electronics Engineers (IEEE), the Association for Computing Machinery (ACM), and the European Commission's High-Level Expert Group on AI (AI HLEG) have published ethical guidelines and principles for AI and IoT stakeholders to promote transparency, fairness, accountability, and human-centered values in technology design and implementation.

- **International standards and best practices:** International standards bodies develop technical standards, specifications, and best practices for AI and IoT technologies to promote interoperability, compatibility, and quality assurance. Organizations such as the International Organization for Standardization (ISO), the International

Electrotechnical Commission (IEC), and the Institute of Electrical and Electronics Engineers Standards Association (IEEE-SA) develop standards related to AI and IoT security, interoperability, privacy, and performance to support global harmonization and facilitate technology adoption across borders.

- **Liability and risk management:** Liability laws establish legal accountability and responsibility for harms or damages caused by AI and IoT technologies. These laws may address issues such as product liability, negligence, torts, and contractual obligations related to AI and IoT systems. Risk management practices, including risk assessment, mitigation, and insurance coverage, help organizations identify and address potential legal risks associated with AI and IoT implementation, such as system failures, data breaches, privacy violations, or regulatory noncompliance.

By complying with relevant legal frameworks, organizations can navigate the complex regulatory landscape and mitigate legal risks associated with AI and IoT implementation. Collaboration between policymakers, industry stakeholders, legal experts, and technology developers is essential to develop and adapt legal frameworks that promote innovation, protect public interests, and ensure ethical and responsible use of AI and IoT technologies in the digital age.

Legal frameworks such as HIPAA, GDPR, and FDA regulations play a crucial role in ensuring the responsible deployment of AI and IoT technologies in healthcare, balancing innovation with patient protection. Understanding these legal considerations leads to a discussion on strategies and practices that healthcare organizations can adopt to ensure ethical practices in the use of AI and IoT technologies.

Ensuring Ethical Practices in Healthcare 4.0

Ensuring ethical practices in Healthcare 4.0, characterized by the integration of digital technologies such as AI and IoT into healthcare delivery, is essential to protect patient rights, privacy, and well-being while promoting innovation and improving healthcare outcomes.

Here are several key strategies for ensuring ethical practices in Healthcare 4.0:

- **Adherence to ethical guidelines and principles:** Healthcare organizations should adhere to established ethical guidelines and principles developed by professional associations, regulatory bodies, and international organizations. These guidelines emphasize values such as patient autonomy, beneficence, nonmaleficence, justice, transparency, and accountability in healthcare delivery. By following ethical guidelines, organizations can ensure that their practices align with ethical norms and standards, promoting trust and confidence among patients and stakeholders.

- **Informed consent and patient autonomy:** In Healthcare 4.0, patients should have the right to make informed decisions about their healthcare, including the use of AI and IoT technologies. Healthcare providers should obtain informed consent from patients before implementing remote monitoring, data analytics, or other digital health interventions. Informed consent involves providing patients with relevant information about the purpose, risks, benefits, and alternatives of AI and IoT technologies, enabling them to make autonomous decisions based on their preferences and values.

- **Privacy and data protection:** Protecting patient privacy and confidentiality is paramount in Healthcare 4.0, where sensitive health data is collected, processed, and shared using digital technologies. Healthcare organizations must implement robust data protection measures, including encryption, access controls, data minimization, and anonymization techniques, to safeguard patient information from unauthorized access, breaches, or misuse. Compliance with data protection laws and regulations, such as HIPAA and GDPR, is essential to ensure patient privacy rights are respected and upheld.

- **Transparency and accountability:** Healthcare organizations should be transparent about their use of AI and IoT technologies, including how patient data is collected, stored, analyzed, and shared. Transparency builds trust and confidence among patients and stakeholders by providing visibility into healthcare processes, decision-making algorithms, and data governance practices. Organizations should also establish mechanisms for accountability, such as oversight committees, audit trails, and grievance mechanisms, to ensure that ethical standards are upheld and address concerns or complaints from patients or stakeholders.

- **Fairness and equity:** Healthcare 4.0 should strive to promote fairness and equity in access to healthcare services, regardless of patients' socioeconomic status, geographic location, or demographic characteristics. AI and IoT technologies should be deployed in a manner that addresses healthcare disparities, improves access to care for underserved populations, and reduces biases in healthcare delivery. Organizations should consider the potential impact of AI algorithms on healthcare outcomes, including the risk of algorithmic bias, discrimination, or disparities, and take steps to mitigate these risks through algorithmic transparency, fairness testing, and bias mitigation techniques.

- **Continuous monitoring and evaluation:** Healthcare organizations should continuously monitor and evaluate the ethical implications of AI and IoT technologies in healthcare delivery. This includes assessing the impact of digital health interventions on patient outcomes, patient satisfaction, provider workload, and healthcare costs. Organizations should engage in ethical reflection, stakeholder engagement, and interdisciplinary collaboration to identify and address ethical challenges as they arise, ensuring that ethical considerations are integrated into decision-making processes and organizational policies.

- **Professional education and training:** Healthcare professionals, including physicians, nurses, and allied health professionals, should receive education and training on ethical principles, digital health literacy, and responsible use of AI and IoT technologies in healthcare practice. Professional organizations, academic institutions, and continuing education programs can provide training on ethical decision-making, patient communication, and technology adoption best practices to prepare healthcare professionals for the ethical challenges of Healthcare 4.0.

Figure 9-1 depicts a layered system architecture illustrating the interaction between different users, hardware, software components, and data storage systems. At the top, various user roles such as Data Manager, Statistician, and Researcher are depicted, connected to machines, clients, and peripheral devices, representing the interface through which users interact with the system. The middle layer features the "Analytical Domain," controlled by a domain controller, which connects to an application server via a network connection. This layer also includes different application versions, highlighting specific software tools like data extraction and manipulation software. The bottom layer focuses on data management, showing how operations data and anonymized replicated operations data are processed through a database server and then stored in a data storage device and data warehouse. The diagram's arrows and connections indicate the flow of data and interactions between these components, illustrating a complex but organized system architecture.

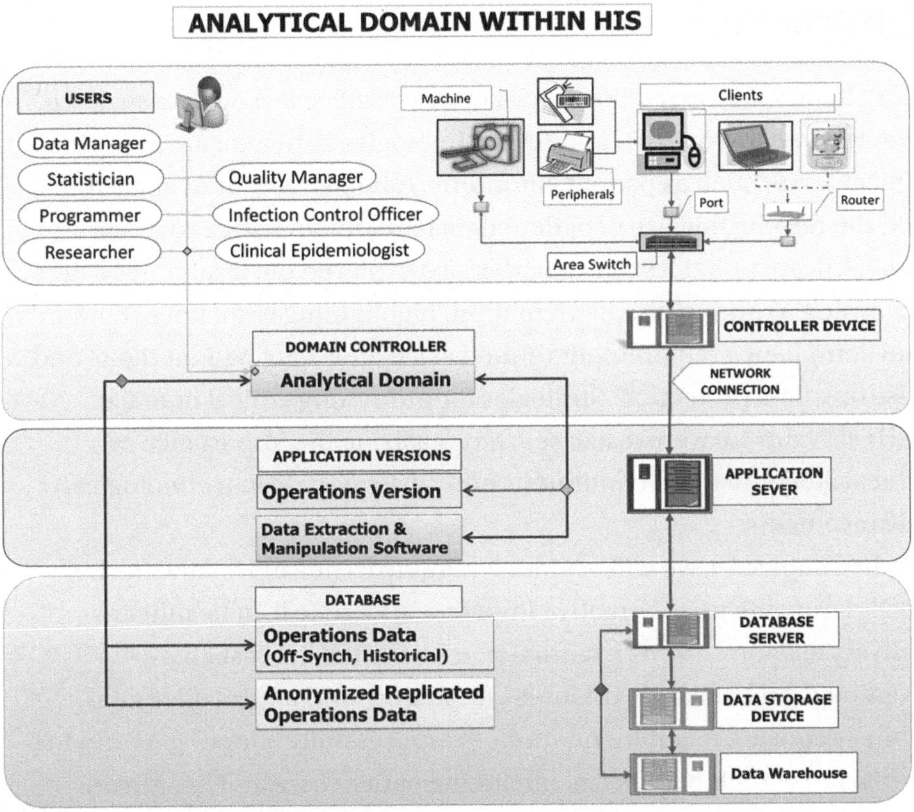

ANALYTICAL DOMAIN WITHIN HIS

Figure 9-1. *Ensuring ethical practices in Healthcare 4.0*

By adopting these strategies, healthcare organizations can promote ethical practices in Healthcare 4.0, uphold patient rights and dignity, and harness the transformative potential of AI and IoT technologies to improve healthcare delivery and patient outcomes. Ethical considerations should be integral to the design, implementation, and evaluation of AI and IoT solutions in healthcare, ensuring that innovation is guided by principles of beneficence, justice, and respect for human rights.

Summary

This chapter addressed the crucial ethical and legal aspects associated with the integration of AI and IoT technologies in healthcare. It examined ethical issues such as patient autonomy, transparency in AI algorithms, and the responsible use of patient data to maintain trust and integrity in healthcare practices. The chapter also explored the legal frameworks governing AI and IoT implementation, highlighting regulatory standards and compliance requirements aimed at safeguarding patient rights and ensuring data protection. Strategies for promoting ethical practices in Healthcare 4.0 were discussed, emphasizing the importance of ethical guidelines and continuous ethical awareness in technological advancements.

In Chapter 10, we will explore emerging trends in Healthcare 4.0, considering the transformative impact of AI and IoT on healthcare delivery. Chapter 10 will examine potential challenges such as technological barriers, workforce adaptation, and ethical dilemmas, while proposing recommendations for successfully adopting AI and IoT to maximize their benefits in enhancing patient care and healthcare efficiency.

CHAPTER 10

Future Perspectives and Challenges

In Chapter 9, we explored the ethical and legal considerations surrounding the implementation of artificial intelligence (AI) and the Internet of Things (IoT) in Healthcare 4.0, emphasizing the need for responsible practices. This chapter shifts focus to future perspectives and challenges in healthcare, highlighting emerging trends, addressing potential obstacles, and offering recommendations for the successful adoption of AI and IoT technologies.

Emerging Trends in Healthcare 4.0

Big data analytics allows healthcare providers to analyze vast amounts of patient data to identify trends, predict outcomes, and improve decision-making. This data-driven approach enhances personalized care, optimizes resource allocation, and supports proactive healthcare management. Cloud computing, on the other hand, provides a flexible and scalable infrastructure for storing and processing healthcare data, facilitating real-time access to patient information across different systems and locations. Together, big data analytics and cloud computing enable seamless data exchange, improve collaboration, and support innovations in patient care, making healthcare more efficient, accessible, and patient-centric. These technologies play a critical role in advancing Healthcare 4.0, empowering providers to offer better, more personalized care.

© Dr. Alok Kumar Srivastav, Dr. Priyanka Das 2024
Dr. A. K. Srivastav and Dr. P. Das, *Emerging Technologies in Healthcare 4.0*,
https://doi.org/10.1007/979-8-8688-1014-5_10

Healthcare 4.0, driven by the integration of digital technologies such as AI, IoT, big data analytics, and cloud computing, is transforming the healthcare landscape in profound ways. Several emerging trends are shaping the evolution of Healthcare 4.0 and influencing the future of healthcare delivery. Here are some of the key emerging trends:

- **Telemedicine and virtual care:** Telemedicine and virtual care have experienced unprecedented growth, driven by the COVID-19 pandemic and the need for remote healthcare delivery. Telehealth solutions, including video consultations, remote monitoring, and digital health platforms, enable patients to access healthcare services remotely, improving access, convenience, and continuity of care.

- **Remote patient monitoring (RPM):** RPM solutions are becoming increasingly sophisticated, leveraging wearable devices, sensors, and AI-powered analytics to monitor patients' vital signs, symptoms, and adherence to treatment plans remotely. RPM enables proactive management of chronic conditions, early detection of health issues, and personalized interventions, leading to improved patient outcomes and reduced healthcare costs.

- **AI-driven diagnostics and imaging:** AI-powered diagnostic tools and imaging solutions are revolutionizing medical diagnostics by enabling faster, more accurate analysis of medical images, pathology slides, and diagnostic tests. AI algorithms can detect subtle abnormalities, identify patterns, and assist radiologists and pathologists in diagnosing diseases such as cancer, cardiovascular disorders, and neurological conditions.

- **Precision medicine and personalized treatment:**
  Precision medicine approaches, which involve tailoring
  medical treatments and interventions to individual
  patients based on their genetic makeup, lifestyle
  factors, and environmental influences, are gaining
  traction in Healthcare 4.0. Advances in genomics,
  biomarker discovery, and AI-driven analytics enable
  personalized treatment plans, targeted therapies, and
  predictive risk assessments for better health outcomes.

- **Population health management:** Population health
  management strategies leverage AI and big data
  analytics to analyze large datasets, identify population
  health trends, and target interventions to improve
  health outcomes and reduce healthcare disparities.
  Population health initiatives focus on preventive care,
  chronic disease management, and social determinants
  of health to promote wellness and reduce healthcare
  costs at the community level.

- **Blockchain technology for health data exchange:**
  Blockchain technology is being explored for secure
  health data exchange, interoperability, and patient-
  centered health records management. Blockchain
  enables tamper-proof, decentralized data storage,
  authentication, and consent management, enhancing
  data security, privacy, and interoperability in
  healthcare ecosystems.

- **Edge computing for real-time analytics:** Edge
  computing architectures are being used to perform
  real-time data analytics and AI inference at the network
  edge, closer to the data source. Edge computing

reduces latency, bandwidth requirements, and reliance on centralized cloud infrastructure, making it suitable for time-sensitive applications such as remote patient monitoring, predictive analytics, and autonomous medical devices.

- **Augmented reality (AR) and virtual reality (VR) in healthcare:** AR and VR technologies are being adopted for medical education, surgical training, patient education, and therapeutic interventions. AR and VR simulations enable immersive, interactive learning experiences, realistic surgical simulations, and virtual rehabilitation programs, enhancing clinical skills, patient engagement, and treatment outcomes.

- **Healthcare cybersecurity and data privacy:** With the increasing digitization of healthcare data and the proliferation of connected medical devices, cybersecurity and data privacy are top priorities in Healthcare 4.0. Healthcare organizations are investing in cybersecurity measures, encryption technologies, and compliance frameworks to protect patient data from cyber threats, breaches, and privacy violations.

- **Regulatory frameworks and policy initiatives:** Regulatory agencies and policymakers are developing frameworks and guidelines to govern the ethical, legal, and social implications of AI and IoT in healthcare. Regulatory frameworks address issues such as data privacy, algorithmic transparency, medical device regulation, and reimbursement models for digital health technologies, shaping the regulatory landscape for Healthcare 4.0.

These emerging trends in Healthcare 4.0 hold the promise of revolutionizing healthcare delivery, improving patient outcomes, and advancing population health. As digital technologies continue to evolve and mature, healthcare stakeholders must adapt to these trends, embrace innovation, and collaborate to realize the full potential of Healthcare 4.0 in addressing global health challenges. Exploring these emerging trends sets the stage for identifying potential challenges and discussing innovative solutions to navigate the evolving landscape of Healthcare 4.0.

Potential Challenges and Solutions

While Healthcare 4.0 offers transformative benefits, it also presents several challenges that must be addressed to maximize its potential. Here are some potential challenges and solutions:

- **Data privacy and security concerns:**

  - **Challenge:** The increased digitization and sharing of healthcare data raise concerns about data privacy, security breaches, and unauthorized access.

  - **Solution:** Implement robust cybersecurity measures, encryption protocols, access controls, and compliance frameworks to protect patient data. Conduct regular security audits, training programs, and risk assessments to mitigate security risks and ensure regulatory compliance.

- **Interoperability and data integration:**

  - **Challenge:** Healthcare systems often use disparate technologies and data formats, hindering interoperability and seamless data exchange between different platforms and stakeholders.

- **Solution:** Adopt standardized data exchange protocols, interoperability standards, and application programming interfaces (APIs) to enable seamless integration of healthcare systems, electronic health records (EHRs), and medical devices. Invest in health information exchanges (HIEs) and interoperability platforms to facilitate data sharing and care coordination across healthcare ecosystems.

- **Ethical and regulatory compliance:**

  - **Challenge:** Ethical dilemmas, regulatory uncertainties, and legal barriers may impede the responsible deployment of AI and IoT technologies in healthcare.

  - **Solution:** Develop ethical guidelines, governance frameworks, and regulatory policies to address ethical concerns, ensure transparency, and uphold patient rights in AI and IoT implementations. Collaborate with regulatory agencies, professional associations, and ethicists to establish best practices, standards, and guidelines for ethical AI and IoT use in healthcare.

- **Workforce training and skills gap:**

  - **Challenge:** Healthcare professionals may lack the necessary training, skills, and expertise to effectively leverage AI and IoT technologies in clinical practice.

- **Solution:** Provide comprehensive training programs, continuing education courses, and certification pathways to empower healthcare professionals with the knowledge and skills required for AI and IoT adoption. Foster interdisciplinary collaboration, mentorship programs, and knowledge-sharing initiatives to bridge the skills gap and promote innovation in healthcare delivery.

- **Health inequities and digital divide:**

  - **Challenge:** Socioeconomic disparities, digital literacy gaps, and unequal access to technology may exacerbate health inequities and widen the digital divide.

  - **Solution:** Implement equity-centered design principles, inclusive technology solutions, and community engagement strategies to ensure that AI and IoT innovations benefit all populations, including underserved communities and marginalized groups. Invest in infrastructure, broadband connectivity, and digital literacy programs to bridge the digital divide and promote health equity for all.

- **Algorithm bias and fairness:**

  - **Challenge:** AI algorithms may exhibit bias, discrimination, or inaccuracies, leading to disparities in healthcare outcomes and perpetuating existing biases in decision-making.

- **Solution:** Employ fairness-aware AI techniques, bias mitigation strategies, and algorithmic transparency measures to detect, mitigate, and prevent bias in AI models. Conduct thorough validation and testing of AI algorithms using diverse datasets and stakeholder feedback to ensure fairness, equity, and transparency in healthcare AI applications.

- **Regulatory compliance and risk management:**

  - **Challenge:** Healthcare organizations face complex regulatory requirements, compliance obligations, and liability risks associated with AI and IoT implementations.

  - **Solution:** Establish risk management frameworks, compliance programs, and internal controls to assess, manage, and mitigate legal and regulatory risks in AI and IoT deployments. Collaborate with legal advisors, regulatory experts, and compliance officers to navigate regulatory requirements, obtain necessary approvals, and ensure regulatory compliance throughout the AI and IoT life cycle.

By addressing these challenges proactively and implementing effective solutions, healthcare stakeholders can overcome barriers to Healthcare 4.0 adoption, unlock its transformative potential, and drive positive outcomes for patients, providers, and society as a whole.

Despite the promises of Healthcare 4.0, challenges include data privacy concerns, interoperability issues, workforce readiness, and regulatory complexities, requiring proactive solutions to ensure successful implementation. Addressing these challenges leads to recommendations for healthcare stakeholders to adopt AI and IoT technologies effectively, enhancing patient care delivery and operational efficiency.

Recommendations for Successful Adoption of AI and IoT in Healthcare

Successful adoption of AI and IoT in healthcare requires careful planning, strategic implementation, and stakeholder engagement. Here are some recommendations for achieving successful adoption:

- **Develop a clear strategy and vision:** Define clear goals, objectives, and a strategic vision for AI and IoT adoption in healthcare. Align technology initiatives with organizational priorities, clinical needs, and patient outcomes to drive value and innovation.

- **Engage stakeholders:** Involve key stakeholders, including healthcare professionals, patients, administrators, IT experts, and policymakers, in the decision-making process. Foster interdisciplinary collaboration, communication, and consensus-building to ensure buy-in and support for AI and IoT initiatives.

- **Assess readiness and capacity:** Conduct a comprehensive assessment of organizational readiness, technical capabilities, infrastructure requirements, and resource availability for AI and IoT adoption. Identify gaps, challenges, and opportunities to inform planning and implementation efforts.

- **Prioritize use cases and pilots:** Prioritize AI and IoT use cases based on clinical impact, feasibility, scalability, and return on investment (ROI). Start with pilot projects or small-scale deployments to test technology solutions, evaluate effectiveness, and refine implementation strategies before scaling up.

- **Ensure data governance and quality:** Establish robust data governance frameworks, data management policies, and data quality standards to ensure the integrity, security, and reliability of healthcare data used in AI and IoT applications. Implement data validation, cleansing, and normalization processes to improve data quality and usability.

- **Leverage interoperability standards:** Adopt interoperability standards, data exchange protocols, and integration architectures to enable seamless interoperability and data sharing between different healthcare systems, devices, and platforms. Facilitate data interoperability to support care coordination, analytics, and decision-making across the healthcare ecosystem.

- **Invest in infrastructure and security:** Invest in scalable infrastructure, cloud computing resources, and cybersecurity measures to support AI and IoT deployments securely. Ensure robust network connectivity, data encryption, access controls, and threat detection mechanisms to protect sensitive patient data and mitigate cybersecurity risks.

- **Promote education and training:** Provide comprehensive education, training, and support programs for healthcare professionals, IT staff, and end users to build awareness, knowledge, and proficiency in AI and IoT technologies. Offer hands-on training, workshops, and certification programs to empower users with the skills needed to leverage technology effectively.

- **Monitor and evaluate performance:** Establish key performance indicators (KPIs), metrics, and benchmarks to monitor the performance, impact, and ROI of AI and IoT initiatives. Conduct regular evaluations, assessments, and feedback mechanisms to measure progress, identify areas for improvement, and optimize technology deployments over time.

- **Adapt to regulatory changes:** Stay abreast of evolving regulatory requirements, compliance standards, and legal frameworks governing AI and IoT in healthcare. Ensure compliance with data privacy regulations, ethical guidelines, and industry best practices to mitigate legal and regulatory risks associated with technology adoption.

- **Foster innovation and collaboration:** Foster a culture of innovation, experimentation, and continuous improvement to drive innovation in AI and IoT applications. Encourage collaboration with industry partners, research institutions, startups, and technology vendors to explore new ideas, pilot emerging technologies, and co-create solutions that address evolving healthcare challenges.

By following these recommendations and best practices, healthcare organizations can successfully navigate the complexities of AI and IoT adoption, unlock the full potential of these technologies, and drive positive outcomes for patients, providers, and healthcare systems.

Summary

This chapter provided insights into the evolving landscape of Healthcare 4.0, highlighting emerging trends driven by advancements in AI and IoT technologies. It explored how these innovations are reshaping healthcare delivery through enhanced diagnostics, personalized medicine, and remote patient monitoring. The chapter identified potential challenges such as technological integration complexities, data security risks, and ethical considerations that accompany the adoption of AI and IoT in healthcare.

Moreover, the chapter offered practical solutions to mitigate these challenges, emphasizing the importance of robust cybersecurity measures, regulatory compliance, and ongoing ethical frameworks. It provided recommendations for successful adoption strategies, advocating for collaborative partnerships between healthcare providers, technology developers, and regulatory bodies to leverage AI and IoT effectively while prioritizing patient safety and healthcare quality.

Bibliography

Agarwal, R., & Gao, G. (2019). *Digital Health Innovation: A Toolkit to Navigate from Concept to Commercialization.* Springer.

Agrawal, P., & Joshi, A. (2020). "Healthcare 4.0: A Review of Frontiers in Digital Health." *Digital Communications and Networks, 6*(1), 1–13.

Al-Taweel, A., Nauman, A., & Khan, S. U. (2019). "Security and Privacy in Internet of Medical Things (IoMT): A Review." *IEEE Access, 7,* 142147–142169.

Amisha, Malik P., Pathania, M., & Rathaur, V. K. (2019). "Overview of Artificial Intelligence in Medicine." *Journal of Family Medicine and Primary Care, 8*(7), 2328–2331.

Bahga, A., & Madisetti, V. (2019). *Internet of Things: A Hands-On Approach.* VPT.

Bensefia, A., & Erritali, M. (2020). "Privacy and Security Issues in Healthcare Systems: A Review." In *2020 8th International Conference on Wireless and Modern Computing (ICWMC),* 1–7.

Bhattacharya, S., & Joshi, A. (2020). "Healthcare 4.0: A Review." *Information Systems Management, 37*(1), 2–17.

Bui, A. L., Haddad, D. E., Lu, R., & Dung, L. V. (2019). "IoT and AI for Healthcare: A Systematic Literature Review." *IEEE Access, 7*, 17649–17665.

Calvillo, J., & Roman, I. (2020). *Machine Learning and Big Data Analytics for Healthcare: Building Smart Health Systems.* Elsevier.

Chen, M., Hao, Y., Hwang, K., & Wang, L. (2020). "Artificial Intelligence in Healthcare: A Comprehensive Review and Bibliometric Analysis." *Journal of Healthcare Engineering, 2020*, 54513.

Chen, M., Hao, Y., Hwang, K., & Wang, L. (2020). "Internet of Things (IoT) in Healthcare: A Comprehensive Review." *Journal of Healthcare Engineering, 2020*, 1429752.

Chen, Y., & Wicks, A. (2019). "Security and Privacy Challenges in Healthcare: A Review." In *2019 IEEE International Conference on Electro Information Technology (EIT)*, 357–361.

Cho, H., Yoo, S., & Oh, J. (2019). "IoT-Enabled Smart Hospital Resource Management." In *2019 International Conference on Information and Communication Technology Convergence (ICTC)* (pp. 1353–1356). IEEE.

Choi, H., Choi, J., & Kang, H. (2019). "Security and Privacy of Healthcare Data: A Review of Security Techniques and Challenges." *Journal of Information Processing Systems, 15*(3), 682–701.

Custers, B., Calders, T., Schermer, B., & Zarsky, T. (2019). "Artificial Intelligence and Data Protection: The Role of Privacy and Data Protection Law in an AI-Driven World." *AI & Society, 34*(4), 787–796.

Davenport, T. H., & Kalakota, R. (2019). "The Potential for Artificial Intelligence in Healthcare." *Future Healthcare Journal, 6*(2), 94–98.

Deng, Z., Wang, H., Zhang, L., & Liu, S. (2019). "Data Security and Privacy Protection Issues in Cloud-Assisted Healthcare Systems: A Survey." *IEEE Access, 7*, 102713–102729.

Diaz, M., & Ruiz, P. (2020). "Artificial Intelligence and Internet of Things for Smarter Hospitals." In *Handbook of Research on Digital Transformation of Supply Chain Management* (pp. 242–263). IGI Global.

Du, J., Tang, Y., Zhang, Y., & Du, X. (2019). "Data Security and Privacy in Cloud-Assisted Healthcare Systems: A Review." *Journal of Medical Systems, 43*(5), 1–9.

El-Hajj, M., Assi, C., Safa, H., & Chehab, A. (2020). "A Survey on Data Security and Privacy in Smart Healthcare Systems." *Future Generation Computer Systems, 102*, 661–678.

European Commission. (2019). "Shaping Europe's Digital Future: Commission Presents Strategies for Data and Artificial Intelligence."

Evans, D., Lea, N., & Parrish, J. (2019). "Real-Time Predictive Analytics for Hospital Bed Management and COVID-19 Capacity Planning Using IoT and AI." In *2020 International Conference on Computing, Networking and Communications (ICNC)* (pp. 1–5). IEEE.

Floridi, L. (2019). *The Logic of Information: A Theory of Philosophy as Conceptual Design.* Oxford University Press.

Garg, S., & Shukla, A. (2020). "Data Security and Privacy in Healthcare Systems: A Review." In *2020 7th International Conference on Computing for Sustainable Global Development (INDIACom)*, 412–415.

Habib, R. H., Khan, M. Z., & Muhammad, G. (2019). "Data Security and Privacy Challenges in Healthcare Systems: A Review." In *2019 5th International Conference on Computing, Mathematics and Engineering Technologies (iCoMET)*, 1–6.

Haider, R., Ghafoor, H., & Asadullah, S. (2020). "A Comprehensive Review of Data Security and Privacy in Smart Healthcare Systems." *IEEE Access, 8,* 37279–37298.

Haluza, D., & Jungwirth, D. (2019). "ICT and the Future of Healthcare: Aspects of Patient Empowerment and Medical Decision Making." *International Journal of Environmental Research and Public Health, 16*(19), 379.

Han, Q., & Niu, J. (2020). "Data Security and Privacy in Healthcare Systems: A Review." In *2020 IEEE International Conference on Bioinformatics and Biomedicine (BIBM)*, 1237–1244.

Hasan, M. M., Islam, M. S., & Al Maruf, M. A. (2019). "Data Security and Privacy Issues in Healthcare Systems: A Review." In *2019 2nd International Conference on Electrical, Computer and Communication Engineering (ECCE)*, 1–4.

Hwang, W. J., Lee, E., & Moon, K. (2019). "Implementation of Healthcare 4.0: A Scoping Review of Research and Practice." *Healthcare Informatics Research, 25*(1), 3–13.

Iqbal, S. T., Latif, R., & Nawaz, R. (2019). "Artificial Intelligence in Healthcare: Current Status and Future Directions." *Journal of Pharmaceutical Sciences and Research, 11*(3), 891–894.

Iyer, A., & Alzahrani, S. (2019). "A Survey on Data Security and Privacy in Healthcare Systems." In *2019 IEEE Jordan International Joint Conference on Electrical Engineering and Information Technology (JEEIT)*, 1–6.

Javed, A. A., Imran, M., & Khan, S. U. (2020). "Data Security and Privacy in Healthcare Systems: A Review." In *2020 3rd International Conference on Advances in Computational Tools for Engineering Applications (ACTEA)*, 1–6.

Javed, S., Rind, A. W., & Javaid, N. (2020). "A Review of Data Security and Privacy in Healthcare Systems." In *2020 4th International Conference on Computing, Mathematics and Engineering Technologies (iCoMET)*, 1–6.

Karim, R., Masud, M., Rashid, M. M., Al Mamun, M., & Chakraborty, C. (2020). "Internet of Things (IoT) in Healthcare: A Review." In *2020 IEEE Region 10 Symposium (TENSYMP)*, 93–98.

Khan, R. A., & Ijaz, M. F. (2019). "Data Security and Privacy in Healthcare Systems: A Review." In *2019 16th Learning and Technology Conference (L&T)*, 1–4.

Khawaja, M. A., Khan, M. A., & Alruwaili, A. (2020). "Data Security and Privacy in Healthcare Systems: A Review." In *2020 7th International Conference on Computing for Sustainable Global Development (INDIACom)*, 412–415.

Khondakar, H., Rana, O., & Hasan, R. (2020). "Data Security and Privacy in Healthcare Systems: A Review." In *2020 3rd International Conference on Advances in Computational Tools for Engineering Applications (ACTEA)*, 1–6.

Khraisat, A. S., Jansen, S., & Ababneh, A. (2020). "Internet of Things (IoT) and Artificial Intelligence (AI) in Healthcare." In *Healthcare Information Systems and Informatics* (pp. 103–120). Springer, Cham.

Kulkarni, R., & Patil, A. (2019). "A Comprehensive Review on Data Security and Privacy in Healthcare Systems." In *2019 International Conference on Intelligent Systems and Information Management (ICISIM)*, 1–4.

Kumar, A., & Mishra, V. (2020). "Data Security and Privacy in Healthcare Systems: A Review." In *2020 5th International Conference on Computing, Communication and Security (ICCCS)*, 1–6.

Kumar, P., Lee, J., & Sohn, S. Y. (2019). "Internet of Things (IoT) in Healthcare: Applications, Benefits, and Challenges." *Advances in Intelligent Systems and Computing, 1033*, 402–409.

Kumar, S., & Kumar, S. (2020). "Data Security and Privacy in Healthcare Systems: A Review." In *2020 4th International Conference on Computer Applications & Information Security (ICCAIS)*, 1–5.

Lavrač, N., Bohanec, M., Pur, A., & Černelč, P. (2019). "Artificial Intelligence in Healthcare: An Expert System for Heart Disease Diagnosis." *Computer Methods and Programs in Biomedicine, 180*, 104992.

Lee, J. J., & Park, J. H. (2019). "Telemedicine in Korea: Improvement of National Health Care Systems Through the Utilization of Telemedicine." *Healthcare Informatics Research, 25*(4), 245–246.

Li, X., & Wang, Z. (2019). "The Internet of Things in Healthcare: An Overview." *Journal of Industrial Information Integration, 15*, 71–78.

Limaye, P., Shaban-Nejad, A., Michalowski, M., & Buckeridge, D. L. (2019). "Public Health Surveillance and Artificial Intelligence: A Narrative Review." *Journal of Medical Internet Research, 21*(7), e11606.

Meher, S., & Satapathy, S. C. (2019). "Internet of Things (IoT) and Artificial Intelligence (AI) in Health Care Sector: A Review." In *Recent Trends in Communication, Computing, and Electronics* (pp. 235–246). Springer, Singapore.

Mehta, N., Pandit, A. (2019). "Concurrence of Artificial Intelligence and Healthcare: A Systematic Review." *Artificial Intelligence in Medicine, 101*, 101738.

Mishra, V., & Kumar, A. (2020). "Data Security and Privacy in Healthcare Systems: A Review." In *2020 4th International Conference on Computing, Communication and Security (ICCCS)*, 1–6.

Mohammed, A., Serrano, M., & Quintero, A. (2020). "Artificial Intelligence in Healthcare: A Comprehensive Review of its Architecture, Deployment, Applications and Future Trends." In *Internet of Things and Big Data Analytics toward Next-Generation Intelligence* (pp. 173–204). Springer, Cham.

Mohammed, N. A., & Sahoo, M. N. (2020). "Data Security and Privacy in Healthcare Systems: A Review." In *2020 IEEE International Conference on Computational Intelligence and Knowledge Economy (ICCIKE)*, 1–5.

Momin, M., & Gadhiya, P. (2019). "Data Security and Privacy in Healthcare Systems: A Review." In *2019 2nd International Conference on Communication System, Data Science & Computing (ICSDC)*, 198–202.

Muruganantham, R., & Prabakaran, B. (2020). "A Survey of Internet of Things and Artificial Intelligence Applications in Health Care." In *Recent Trends in Image Processing and Pattern Recognition* (pp. 119–130). Springer, Singapore.

Naik, S. P., & Shukla, A. (2019). "Data Security and Privacy in Healthcare Systems: A Review." In *2019 International Conference on Artificial Intelligence and Signal Processing (AISP)*, 1–5.

Nasajpour, M., Pouriyeh, S., Parizi, R. M., Doraiswamy, H., & Tafti, A. P. (2020). "Overview of Artificial Intelligence in Medicine." *Journal of Medical Imaging and Health Informatics*, 10(4), 1019–1028.

Nasiakou, V., & Konstantaras, A. (2020). "A Novel Multi-Agent Based Artificial Intelligence Approach for IoT in Health Care." In *European Conference on Mobile Robots* (pp. 205–210). Springer, Cham.

Ortega, S., & Guerra, E. (2019). "Integration of IoT and AI Techniques in Healthcare to Improve Quality of Life." In *2019 IEEE 34th International Conference on Microelectronics (MIEL)* (pp. 377–380). IEEE.

Park, E., Kim, H., & Steinhoff, A. (2021). "Health-Related Internet Use by Children and Adolescents: Systematic Review." *Journal of Medical Internet Research, 23*(1), e22590.

Patel, A., Tiwari, A., & Dixit, A. (2019). "IoT and AI-Enabled Hospital Room Automation System: An Efficient Resource Management." In *2019 IEEE Region 10 Symposium (TENSYMP)* (pp. 1261–1264). IEEE.

Qiu, D., Yu, K., He, H., Chen, K., & Du, Y. (2020). "Predicting Patient Length of Stay in Hospital and Impact Analysis Using Machine Learning Models." *Frontiers in Public Health, 8*, 371.

Rajkomar, A., Dean, J., Kohane, I. (2019). "Machine Learning in Medicine." *New England Journal of Medicine, 380*(14), 1347–1358.

Rao, A., & Dangi, K. (2019). "A Review of Data Security and Privacy in Healthcare Systems." In *2019 IEEE 10th Annual Information Technology, Electronics and Mobile Communication Conference (IEMCON)*, 0019–0022.

Rhoads, S. J., Green, A. L., & Ingram, J. M. (2020). "A Systematic Review of Predictive Models for Cesarean Section in Low-Risk Pregnancies." *Journal of Obstetric, Gynecologic & Neonatal Nursing, 49*(1), 12–21.

Rothstein, M. A. (2019). "Ethics of Digital Health Research." *Nature Medicine, 25*(1), 37–42.

Srivastav, A.K., Das, P., Srivastava, A.K. (2024). Introduction to Biotechnology and IoT Integration. In: Biotech and IoT. Apress, Berkeley, CA. https://doi.org/10.1007/979-8-8688-0527-1_1

Srivastav, A.K., Das, P., Srivastava, A.K. (2024). Historical Development and Convergence. In: Biotech and IoT. Apress, Berkeley, CA. https://doi.org/10.1007/979-8-8688-0527-1_2

Srivastav, A.K., Das, P., Srivastava, A.K. (2024). Smart Laboratories and IoT Transformation. In: Biotech and IoT. Apress, Berkeley, CA. https://doi.org/10.1007/979-8-8688-0527-1_3

Srivastav, A.K., Das, P., Srivastava, A.K. (2024). Healthcare Revolution. In: Biotech and IoT. Apress, Berkeley, CA. https://doi.org/10.1007/979-8-8688-0527-1_4

Srivastav, A.K., Das, P., Srivastava, A.K. (2024). Connected Biomedical Devices and Digital Integration. In: Biotech and IoT. Apress, Berkeley, CA. https://doi.org/10.1007/979-8-8688-0527-1_5

Srivastav, A.K., Das, P., Srivastava, A.K. (2024). Data Management, Security, and Ethical Considerations. In: Biotech and IoT. Apress, Berkeley, CA. https://doi.org/10.1007/979-8-8688-0527-1_6

Srivastav, A.K., Das, P., Srivastava, A.K. (2024). Precision Agriculture and Environmental Monitoring. In: Biotech and IoT. Apress, Berkeley, CA. https://doi.org/10.1007/979-8-8688-0527-1_7

Srivastav, A.K., Das, P., Srivastava, A.K. (2024). Biometric Security Systems and Wearable Devices. In: Biotech and IoT. Apress, Berkeley, CA. https://doi.org/10.1007/979-8-8688-0527-1_8

Srivastav, A.K., Das, P., Srivastava, A.K. (2024). Bioinformatics and Cloud Analytics. In: Biotech and IoT. Apress, Berkeley, CA. https://doi.org/10.1007/979-8-8688-0527-1_9

Srivastav, A.K., Das, P., Srivastava, A.K. (2024). Biotech and IoT. Apress, Berkeley, CA. https://doi.org/10.1007/979-8-8688-0527-1

Srivastav, A.K., Das, P., Srivastava, A.K. (2024). Future Trends, Innovations, and Global Collaboration. In: Biotech and IoT. Apress, Berkeley, CA. https://doi.org/10.1007/979-8-8688-0527-1_10

Siddiqui, A., & Khan, M. M. (2019). "Data Security and Privacy in Healthcare Systems: A Review." In *2019 6th International Conference on Computing for Sustainable Global Development (INDIACom)*, 607–610.

Singh, D., & Bansal, V. (2019). "Internet of Things in Healthcare: A Review." In *2019 2nd International Conference on Inventive Research in Computing Applications (ICIRCA)*, 1091–1095.

Singh, J., & Reddy, C. K. (2019). "Artificial Intelligence in Healthcare: A Review." *Annals of the Romanian Society for Cell Biology*, 1052–1060.

Ting, D. S. W., Pasquale, L. R., Peng, L., Campbell, J. P., Lee, A. Y., Raman, R., ... & Wong, T. Y. (2019). "Artificial Intelligence and Deep Learning in Ophthalmology." *British Journal of Ophthalmology*, *103*(2), 167–175.

Topol, E. J. (2019). "High-Performance Medicine: The Convergence of Human and Artificial Intelligence." *Nature Medicine, 25*(1), 44–56.

Wang, S., & Wang, H. (2019). "The Application of the Internet of Things in Healthcare: A Bibliometric Analysis." *International Journal of Environmental Research and Public Health, 16*(13), 2378.

Wicks, P., Stamford, J., & Grootenhuis, M. A. (2019). "Digital Technology for Health Sector Governance in Low and Middle Income Countries: A Scoping Review." *Journal of Global Health, 9*(2), 020429.

Yamamoto, S., Hoshi, K., & Ohe, K. (2019). "A Quantitative Study of the Relationship Between Digital Health Literacy and Quality of Life Among Users of a Mobile App for Cardiac Rehabilitation: Cross-Sectional Survey." *Journal of Medical Internet Research, 21*(10), e14404.

Yang, C. H., Yang, C. C., & Huang, Y. C. (2019). "Integration of Digital Health Technologies in Health Systems: Scoping Review of Literature." *JMIR Medical Informatics, 7*(4), e12712.

Yoon, J., Kim, Y., & Lee, K. (2019). "A Comprehensive Review on the Internet of Things (IoT) in Healthcare: Applications, Challenges, and Future Prospects." *IEEE Access, 7*, 118190–118214.

Zhang, Y., Guo, Z., Xu, G., Ren, S., & Li, X. (2019). "The Internet of Things in Healthcare: A Survey." In *2019 IEEE International Conference on Industrial Engineering and Engineering Management (IEEM)*, 1385–1389.

Zhu, Q., & Wang, X. (2019). "A Review on the Internet of Things in Healthcare." In *2019 IEEE International Conference on Energy Internet and Energy System Integration (EI2)*, 1–6.

Zhu, Y., Lu, C., Lai, F., & Li, D. (2019). "Research on the Application of the Internet of Things in Healthcare." In *2019 International Conference on Big Data Engineering and Technology (BDET)*, 91–94.

Zou, L., & Hu, X. (2019). "The Application of the Internet of Things in Healthcare." In *2019 International Conference on Machine Learning, Big Data and Business Intelligence (MLBDBI)*, 184–187.

Index

A

Accountability, 294–295, 302
Accuracy and reliability, RPM
  challenges, 224–227
  limitations, 228–232
  strategies, 231–233
ACM, *see* Association for
    Computing
    Machinery (ACM)
Activities of daily living (ADLs),
    210–212
ADLs, *see* Activities of daily
    living (ADLs)
Advanced Message Queuing
    Protocol (AMQP), 84, 90
Agility, 75, 124
AI, *see* Artificial intelligence (AI)
AI-based diagnostic tools
  dermatology, 257
  diagnostic decision support
      systems, 258
  genomic analysis tools, 258
  histopathology, 258
  imaging solutions, 308
  medical imaging, 256
  ophthalmology, 257

remote diagnostic tools, 259
Amalgamation, 183
American Recovery and
    Reinvestment Act
    (ARRA), 139
AMQP, *see* Advanced Message
    Queuing Protocol (AMQP)
ANNs, *see* Artificial neural
    networks (ANNs)
APIs, *see* Application programming
    interfaces (APIs)
Application programming
    interfaces (APIs), 40, 65,
    88–90, 97, 127, 312
AR, *see* Augmented reality (AR)
ARRA, *see* American Recovery and
    Reinvestment Act (ARRA)
Artificial intelligence (AI), 1, 13, 61,
    131, 269
  advantages and
      disadvantages, 127
  applications, 43–50
  approaches, 30
  challenges and
      considerations, 191–199
  challenges and
      opportunities, 51–58